THE
HUNTING
HORSE

ELLIOT GOLDENBERG

THE HUNTING HORSE

*The Truth Behind the
Jonathan Pollard Spy Case*

FOREWORD BY
ALAN DERSHOWITZ

Prometheus Books

59 John Glenn Drive
Amherst, New York 14228-2197

Published 2000 by Prometheus Books

Inquiries should be addressed to
Prometheus Books
59 John Glenn Drive
Amherst, New York 14228–2197
VOICE: 716–691–0133, ext. 207
FAX: 716–564–2711
WWW.PROMETHEUSBOOKS.COM

04 03 02 01 00   5 4 3 2 1

Library of Congress Cataloging-in-Publication Data

Goldenberg, Elliot, 1946–
    The hunting horse : the truth behind the Jonathan Pollard spy case / Elliot
Goldenberg ; foreword by Alan Dershowitz.
        p. cm.
    Includes bibliographical references and index.
    ISBN 1–57392–854–2 (alk. paper)
    1. Pollard, Jonathan Jay, 1954– 2. Spies—Israel—Biography. 3. Spies—United
States—Biography. 4. Espionage, Israeli—United States—History—20th century.
I. Title.

UB271.I82 G65 2000
327.125694073'092—dc21   00–041484
                                                                          CIP

Printed in the United States of America on acid-free paper

This book is dedicated to my parents,
Abe and Pearl Goldenberg,
who always tried to do their best.

CONTENTS

The obscure we see eventually.
The completely apparent takes a little longer

—Edward R. Murrow

ACKNOWLEDGMENTS

M any people have helped to make this book a reality. First, I'd like to thank the staff at Prometheus Books, especially editor-in-chief Steven L. Mitchell, who believed in this project; the delightful Chris Kramer; publisher Paul Kurtz; permissions editor Michele Lombardo; and senior editor Mary A. Read, who did a wonderful job of editing my manuscript. They have all been a pleasure to work with and have made our relationship an easy and smooth one.

Unlike too much of the publishing industry today, Prometheus is willing to take a chance on books other houses would consider too controversial. We would be far better off in this country if there were more houses like Prometheus, and more decision-makers like Steven Mitchell.

I'd also like to thank my longtime associates, Suzanne Migdall and William Northrop. Suzanne put a lot on the line, financially and otherwise, to help secure a motion picture deal based on this book. She believed in the Pollard story from the onset, and knew how to "walk the walk" and "talk the talk" with the dozens of film industry executives she pitched the project to over a period of eight years. Will, my "deep throat," is a warrior, in the best sense. His incredible life—he's the kind of person the Steven Seagals and Chuck Norrises of the world make movies about—speaks volumes.

Our attorney Ronald D. Kurtz, of the Los Angeles law firm of Kinsella, Boesch, Fujikawa & Towle, was with us when we went into battle against a major Hollywood studio. During that time, Dale F. Kinsella's support never wavered while Ron proved to be a brilliant legal tactician. To Suzanne, Will, and me, he was literally manna from heaven.

My personal attorney, Allan Midgall, has also been an invaluable source of legal expertise.

Another legal eagle deserves my personal thanks: the prolific and extraordinary Alan Dershowitz, of Harvard Law School. Professor Dershowitz has been a voice of reason over the years, keeping this case in the public consciousness. For again agreeing to write my foreword, as he did for my first book, *The Spy Who Knew Too Much*, the State of Israel owes Alan a debt of gratitude, as do I. It is a debt I'll probably never be able to repay. Alan's assistant, Manny Lim, has been most helpful as well.

I'd be remiss if I didn't thank the Wolper organization at Warner Brothers, including the late Janet Borrows for her grit, guts, and vision; Kevin Nicklaus; David Wolper; and Mark Wolper.

Jonathan Pollard's sister, Carol; mother, Mollie; and father, Dr. Morris Pollard, have been there for me literally from the first day I became involved in this case. The family has gone through a collective nightmare. Their integrity and support for all my efforts has always been greatly appreciated.

As a journalist over the years I picked up tips from Arnie Leshin, Bob Sandler, Andy Polin, John Levitt, Alan Kravitz, Steve Sands, and many others. Dr. Gary Rubin, Rhonda Seriani, Rochelle Friedman, Michael Sterne, Zoraida Garcia, Rondi Schechter, Lauren Shaw, and the rest of the staff at the Jewish Federation of Broward County have been extremely supportive. I also cannot forget Rabbi Bruce Warshal, to whom I owe a special thanks.

I'd like to thank my many friends, including Wendy Rosenow, for laughing at my jokes, and my sister, Barbara, for usually putting up with me.

Last, but not least, are those I've met along the way who have been in some way inspirational. They are too numerous to name, but include Daniel D. Cantor, a philanthropist among philanthropists; Florence Ross, a human dynamo who proves you're never too old to leave your mark; and best-selling author Dr. Wayne W. Dyer, my former graduate school advisor, who once told me, as he has told thousands of others, that "you don't want to die knowing you've left your art inside you."

A PERSONAL NOTE

Much of what you will read in this book that's attributed to Jonathan Pollard comes from letters he sent me over the years from his prison cell. Since Pollard was basically censured from speaking to the press—with the exception of two interviews allowed by Naval Intelligence: one with Wolf Blitzer, the other with Mike Wallace—this was the only way Pollard could tell his side of the story.

It's important to stress that nothing in those letters Pollard sent me falls under the heading of "classified information," although some of their contents might prove to be highly embarrassing to certain individuals in our defense establishment, as well as a number of those who served in the Reagan and Bush administrations.

Naval Intelligence censors ostensibly saw these letters from Pollard before they ever reached my hands. Frankly, no one seemed too concerned prior to the publication of my first book on the Pollard case, *The Spy Who Knew Too Much*, in 1993.

The Hunting Horse, while including much of the same information, also takes the reader into previously uncharted waters, and explores what Pollard knew (and uncovered) about the symbiotic (and disastrous) relationship existing between the United States and Iraq in the years leading up to the Gulf War.

Throughout this book, Pollard, and others, make many claims. Due to the nature of those claims—which include descriptions of covert operations and allegations about people and events not easily verified—in certain cases the reader must place his or her own value judgment on what these people say.

All I can do is guarantee the authenticity of my sources. You must be the judge of their veracity.

—Elliot Goldenberg
May 2000

FOREWORD

ALAN DERSHOWITZ

As a loyal American, I am deeply ashamed of the way my government has handled the Jonathan Pollard case. To begin with, our government has broken the plea bargain it made with Pollard. Pollard pleaded guilty, thereby giving up his constitutional right to a trial at which he might well have been acquitted, in exchange for a promise by our government that it would not seek life imprisonment. Then, in one of the sneakiest moves I have ever observed in nearly forty years of law practice, the government arranged for the secretary of defense, Caspar Weinberger, to submit an affidavit which, in effect, demanded life imprisonment. Moreover, the affidavit was, in my professional opinion, false. This should not be surprising, since it was written by an anti-Israeli zealot who was later accused of giving false testimony and had to plead for a presidential pardon. The judge, an African American, was then spoken to illegally, on an ex parte basis, by United States government officials who pandered to his ethnicity by falsely reporting to him that Pollard had provided crucial information helpful to the apartheid regime in South Africa. In an attempt to justify Pollard's sentence of life imprisonment, Joseph DiGenova—the U.S. attorney who promised Pollard he would not seek life imprisonment—has invoked the old canard of dual loyalty by Jews who support Israel. He has argued that a Jew who spies for Israel should receive a higher sentence than a non-Jew who spied for the former Soviet Union, since few people supported the Soviet Union but many Jews support Israel. This sort of soft-core anti-Semitism has resulted in the double standard being applied to Jews and non-Jews who work for American intelligence agencies. Finally, in a desperate attempt to prevent Pollard from being released after serving fifteen years, United States intelligence officials illegally leaked classified intelligence information to Seymour Hersh, who published it uncritically in the *New Yorker* magazine.

Hersh provided detailed descriptions of American intelligence operations. These include what Hersh referred to as our "exotic capability" to take "off-axis photographs" from special satellites that can reach "areas that were seemingly far out of range." He described how American officials trained in Hebrew used sophisticated equipment to intercept "Israeli military, commercial, and diplomatic communications." He explained how the Navy's Sixth Fleet Ocean Surveillance Information Facility (FOSIF) in Rota, Spain, produced daily reports on all Middle East activity based on data "supplied both by intelligence agents throughout the Middle East and by most advanced technical means of intercepting Soviet military communications." Hersh revealed that FOSIF shared space with another larger NSA (National Security Agency) intercept station, "occupied by more than seven hundred linguists and cryptographers, which was responsible for monitoring and decoding military and diplomatic communications all across North Africa." Hersh described the Defense Intelligence Agency's Community On-Line Intelligence System (DIAL COINS), which "contained all the intelligence reports filed by Air Force, Army, Navy, and Marine attachés in Israel and elsewhere in the Middle East." And he described "what is perhaps the most important day-to-day information in signals intelligence: the National SIGINT Requirements List, which is essentially a compendium of the tasks, and the priority of those tasks, given to various NSA collection units around the world."

Perhaps Hersh's most explicit revelation came in his description of the RASIN, a ten-volume reference manual of radio-signals notations that the

NSA uses to compile the parameters of every known communication signal. Hersh reports that the RASIN, which is "classified 'top-secret Umbra,' " was listed in the "still secret declaration to the court before Pollard's sentencing hearing." Hersh reported—as per an unnamed Justice Department official—that "the RASIN was the ninth item on the . . . damage-assessment list." Hersh asked Pollard's trial lawyer to respond to these classified allegations, but he could not lawfully do so, "citing national security." Hersh's governmental sources felt no such constraint. Pollard's current lawyers have been denied the very information leaked to Hersh, on the ground that it remains classified. Indeed one of the arguments made for retaining Pollard in prison is that he would disclose some of the very information that Hersh has now published. That is the lawless Catch-22 in which Pollard finds himself.

Hersh has acknowledged that he had long tried unsuccessfully to obtain this secret information from members of the intelligence community but had always been rebuffed. But now that President Clinton is considering keeping the promise the government made to Pollard in its plea bargain—that it would not seek life imprisonment—some members of the intelligence community have decided to break the law in order to keep him in prison.

Let there be no mistake about the fact that any present or former government official with security clearance who discloses classified information without authorization is guilty of a serious crime, even if the disclosure is to the press. Another former Navy analyst, Samuel Morrison, was sentenced to two years in 1985 for leaking to the British magazine *Jane's Defence Weekly* U.S. intelligence pictures of a Soviet aircraft carrier under construction. The court of appeals ruled that such press leaks were covered by the statute. Hersh has a First Amendment right to publish leaked classified materials, but his intelligence sources have no right to leak it.

In his article, Hersh quotes intelligence sources as speculating that some of the materials Pollard gave to Israel may have been bartered by Israel to the Soviet Union. This is false, as the late Israeli prime minister

Yitzhak Rabin confirmed. But the classified information leaked to Hersh has certainly gotten to our enemies. If this material poses no danger to our national security, it should be declassified so that Pollard's lawyers can respond to the exaggerated charges now being made against Pollard. If it does pose a continuing danger, then those who improperly leaked it should be prosecuted.

After reading the *New Yorker* article, I wrote the Justice Department requesting a criminal investigation of who leaked the classified material to Hersh. This is part of what I wrote:

> The equal application of the law demands that everyone who improperly discloses classified national security information must be prosecuted. Pollard is a victim of selective disclosures. All Americans are the victims of the unfairness of allowing those with security clearance to pick and choose what they will withhold and disclose. It is impossible for me to assess whether any of the disclosures provided by Hersh may pose any danger to our nation's security, but I am certain that if Pollard had disclosed the identical material, it would be claimed that he endangered our security.

I have received no response.

The bottom line is that our government has behaved despicably in regard to the Pollard case. Regardless of what government officials may believe about Pollard's actions, the ends do not justify the kinds of means used in this case. Justice demands fairness and equal protection for Jonathan Pollard, and fairness and equal protection mandate Pollard's immediate release. I hope this book helps to persuade readers of the injustices of our government's action toward Jonathan Pollard.

PROLOGUE

I want to be known as the president who, working with our allies and the Soviets and others, led to the elimination of all chemical and biological weapons from the face of the earth.

—President George Bush, October 21, 1988

One of the great cover-ups in American history began late in the summer of 1982. Its roots took hold in the pristine corridors of the Pentagon, only a few months following William Casey's secret trip to Baghdad during which the elderly CIA (Central Intelligence Agency) director tried to get Iraq removed from the State Department's list of nations supporting terrorism.

With a stroke of his pen, Ronald Reagan, the affable president who was then riding a crest of popularity, signed a national security directive that, according to sources in the intelligence community, began an eight-year secret relationship with Saddam Hussein. Not surprisingly, it was feared that, somewhere along the line, the truth of that relationship would eventually be leaked. For the "good of the country," the Reagan administration (and, later, future administrations) would go to great lengths to prevent this from happening. Not only was congressional oversight on a number of related matters curtailed when both Reagan and Bush held the world's highest office, but intelligence sharing with Israel, America's stated ally, was sharply cut back.

The deep cover-up had to be maintained at any and all cost. As for the serpentine path leading back to the steps of the White House, it had to remain forever hidden, blurred and obscured.

When I placed a phone call to the chambers of U.S. District Court Judge Shelby Highsmith on Friday, February 24, 1995, I stirred up a veritable hornet's nest in what, at the time, was arguably America's most important trial. Indeed, while the far more publicized "Trial of the Century" was taking place in Judge Lance Ito's courtroom, the O. J. Simpson circus paled in historical comparison to what was transpiring, at the same time, three thousand miles away in Miami.

The defendants appearing that day before the judge were Edward A. Johnson and Ronald W. Griffin, both of whom were accused of conspiring to illegally ship 130 tons of zirconium to South America in the 1980s, which was then used in the making of Iraqi cluster bombs. In truth, this so-called conspiracy was but the tip of the iceberg commonly known as "Iraqgate"— a scandal that likely led to the Oval Office occupied by presidents Reagan and Bush. As for the defendants, they may have been little more than inconsequential pawns in a complex spider's web that included names like Defense Secretary Caspar Weinberger and Attorney General Edwin Meese.

Aside from Johnson and Griffin, who both worked for the Swissco Management Group (the Miami company controlled by alleged Chilean bombmaker Carlos Carduen), two other key players in this unfolding drama were Assistant U.S. Attorney Eduardo Palmer, who was prosecuting the case, and Miami defense attorney Gerald Houlihan, who represented Johnson. From what I knew about *U.S.* v. *Carlos Carduen et al*, I agreed with what Houlihan said in his opening statement when he argued that the U.S. government actually sanctioned the defendants' activities and that they were, in fact, part and parcel of an overall policy to support Iraq in its eight-year war against Iran.

It was Houlihan whom I was trying to reach when I called the judge's chambers. In retrospect I should have instead called Houlihan's office because, although Houlihan got the message that I called, so did the prosecution—since the judge told both sides about my phone call during a sidebar. Houlihan would later tell me that the lawyers literally raced to a telephone to find out what my call was about, since I had left a message stating that I was the author of *The Spy Who Knew Too Much* and that I knew of a potential witness who might aid the defense.

A member of the defense team (her first name was Gail; I forget her last name) reached me first. After she introduced herself I told her that the main subject of my book, Jonathan Pollard, knew a great deal about the illegal U.S. arming of Iraq, was charged with passing U.S. military secrets to Israel, and—after plea bargaining in good faith—was nevertheless sentenced to life in prison. Pollard, I suggested, could possibly help Mr. Houlihan's client's case. Perhaps, I said, someone from the defense team could take Pollard's deposition from prison. Better still, perhaps Pollard could testify in person. (Of course, by testifying, Pollard would indirectly get a chance to argue his own case, something the U.S. government had been careful to never let him do before.)

Not twenty seconds after Gail hung up, I received another call, this time from a fellow who said he was with the Commerce Department. I told him I wasn't going to tell him who my "source" was, and that I had nothing else to say. The prosecution, though, was not about to let me slide.

Later that evening I received a call from the assistant U.S. attorney himself. He had a number of other people with him (I believe they were also attorneys) and he told me he was taping our conversation.

21

"All we ask is that you give us a level playing field so that we know what we're dealing with and we're not at a disadvantage," Palmer said in a friendly tone.

"I can't give you my source's name," I replied.

"Why not?" he asked.

"Because I don't trust the government as regards this case," I said.

"You mean you trust the defense more than the government of the United States?" Palmer asked incredulously.

I answered Palmer by telling him some of what I knew had already been written in the media about Iraqgate, adding that I had serious concerns about my "source's" well-being if the government discovered his identity.

"I can assure you we will do everything in our power to ensure this person's personal safety," Palmer said. "But we do want an opportunity to meet with this person, or at least speak to him on the phone."

As a journalist I'd like to think I've developed a "sixth sense" about how to get people to reveal what, deep down, they want to tell me anyway. Palmer was gamely trying to use the same ploy, but the affable prosecutor had one serious problem: Under no circumstance was I going to give him the name of my source unless I was questioned under oath after being subpoenaed to appear in court. So I felt I was in complete control of our conversation (one of my intelligence sources later told me it was Palmer who was in control, not me, and that I just should have hung up on him) when one of Palmer's associates asked: "Mr. Goldenberg, what is *The Spy Who Knew Too Much* about?"

Suddenly, I felt a large lump in my throat. If I said my book was about Pollard, surely they would have put two and two together. If my answer was evasive and someone had already informed them (or they subsequently found out) that my book was about the Pollard case, here, too, they could have logically concluded that Pollard was my "source."

As the old saying goes, "When in doubt, punt." I told Palmer I wasn't answering any more questions, that I was already late for an appointment, but agreed that, if I had anything further to say, I would call George Nowicki, of U.S. Customs, after the weekend. Instead, I called my own attorney and left a message for Houlihan at his office (which in retrospect is probably what I should have done in the first place). As for the prosecution team, I figured they could prosecute their own case without my help.

To my knowledge, Houlihan never did contact Pollard. I don't know if it would have made any difference, but Houlihan's defendant was convicted.

And Jonathan Pollard still hadn't had his day in court.

ENIGMA
IN A
RIDDLE

From May of 1984 until November of 1985, the Israelis had an agent-in-place—a mole—operating deep inside American intelligence. This agent, Jonathan Pollard, was run by a specialized unit known by the acronym LAKAM. He was one of Israel's most prolific spies, but his true identity was restricted to a very few. To the rest of Israeli intelligence, who knew of his probable existence only through his voluminous work product, he was respectfully given the name "The Hunting Horse."[1]

The day Jonathan Jay Pollard plunged headfirst into the espionage profession he entered the spy novelist's realm of Tom Clancy and John Le Carré. Part blinded by ideology, part consumed by what he believed to be the truth, the difference is that Pollard became a very real inhabitant of a mostly unseen world in which covert operators lurk, secret agendas flourish, and its most dangerous predators play their deadly games for keeps. It is a world where fact and fiction easily coexist; a world the reluctant "black" operative quickly had to master. (As a "white" operative Pollard officially worked for the office of Naval Intelligence; as a "black" operative, he also worked as a spy for Israel.)

No doubt, Pollard proved to be a fast learner. Still, while researching my book on his case, I was never able to fully comprehend why the United States government went after the young Jewish spy with such a vengeance. As the author of *The Spy Who Knew Too Much: The Government Plot to Silence Jonathan Pollard*, I obviously knew what the government had alleged about the brilliant double agent—a former civilian Naval Intelligence analyst who, in 1987, received a life sentence in prison for passing on classified U.S. secrets to the State of Israel. And I knew that former Defense Secretary Caspar Weinberger, Pollard's ultimate boss at Naval Intelligence, had once castigated him as "doing substantial and irrevocable damage to this nation." In Weinberger's universe, Pollard was more of a traitor than John Walker,* or, even, Benedict Arnold.

Yet, as I dug deeper into this strangest of cases, I became increasingly convinced that there must also have been some kind of hidden agenda firmly in place here: first, to deal with what Jonathan Pollard had stumbled upon, and, second, to ensure this man remained sequestered behind bars until the day he died. So I continued asking many hard questions, some of which touched on an American foreign policy that had seemingly gone awry in regard to our longtime friendly relationship with Israel—once considered to be not only an extremely strong alliance, but a mutually advantageous one to both nations. From Pollard's unique vantage point, at least, more and more it appeared that the country of his birth was, for some reason, selling out his ancestral homeland. In a position to do something about this, he did. For his efforts, he paid an exceedingly high price.

I understood all of that. Attempting to follow the trail Pollard blazed,

---

*A retired U.S. Navy chief warrant officer, John Walker operated as a full-time agent for the USSR and masterminded, organized, and recruited his own spy ring.

while trying to think like he thought and feel what he must have felt, I came to believe that Pollard was a principled person who compromised American secrets, not for financial reward, as many have suggested, but to help ensure the survival of the Jewish state. What I never fully understood, though, was not *if* Israel was being betrayed by certain very powerful people in the United States government, since I felt that was obvious. What I could never quite figure out was *why?*

I heard the theories, of course. The most convincing, to me, was what I call the "Fear of Fundamentalist Muslim Revolutions" scenario. It went something like this: Saudi Arabia, because of its oil, had suddenly become far more important to American national interests than Israel. In the past, Israel was at least useful as a buffer and an intelligence outpost, protecting us against Soviet expansionism in the region. But as the Soviet Union weakened (and eventually collapsed), whatever the Saudis wanted from us, they usually got, regardless of how the pro-Israel lobby in Washington felt. At the same time, the Saudi leaders (as the wealthy patrons of a repressive society) not only feared having a democratic Western country (or as they called it, a "Zionist entity") in their midst; they lived in constant fear of a fundamentalist Muslim takeover orchestrated by Iran—a fear shared by the United States which certainly did not want its oil supplies endangered.

So I asked people in the intelligence community if some dangerous mix of terrorism and Muslim fundamentalism could not only threaten the stability of the Middle East region, but was the main reason—along, of course, with the fall of the Soviet Union—for, what I believed, was the apparent swing in U.S. policy away from Israel. The answer I got was always the same. Yes, they would say, if the United States was pulling away from Israel, then this was one of the reasons. But, no, some would also add, it was not the whole reason.

Like the fictional Lt. Columbo—who always knew where he wanted to go but wasn't sure about what he was looking for when he got there—I was baffled. Searching for answers that I knew existed—while trying to solve a puzzle in which the pieces were meticulously hidden—would be the purpose, I decided, of writing this book.

27

On March 26, 1994, only three days after President Bill Clinton (nearly parroting former Defense Secretary Weinberger) officially turned down Jonathan Pollard's request for clemency—citing the "grave nature of his offense and the considerable damage his actions have caused our nation"—I received a thick parcel of mail from Pollard himself, in care of Butner Prison in North Carolina. Like all the rest of Pollard's mail to me, this, too, had a Washington, D.C., postmark on the envelope because, contrary to what another former defense secretary, Les Aspin, had alleged in an earlier "confidential" memo to Clinton (that was subsequently leaked by the White House to the media), all of Pollard's outgoing mail had to pass through the gauntlet of intelligence community censors.

Aspin had stated in his well-publicized December 27, 1993, memo to the president that Pollard tried to "slip classified information" into fourteen of his letters sent from behind bars, although, according to Michael R. Gordon in the December 28, 1993, New York Times, "officials would not say what was in the letters, to whom they were addressed, or why Mr. Pollard would put classified information in correspondences that he knew would be monitored." While an unnamed Pentagon official tersely described the incarcerated spy as "a walking library," Pollard's attorney, Theodore Olson, quickly responded to Aspin's charges, stating that neither he nor Pollard had ever been told that any of Pollard's prison letters violated national security. Noted Gordon in the New York Times: "[Olson] said he did not know anything about the classified information cited by Mr. Aspin, and he suggested the information might have been nothing more than passing references Mr. Pollard used in defending himself against the government's charge that he damaged American security."

Olson, a Washington insider; a partner in the powerful law firm of Gibson, Dunn and Crutcher; and former president Ronald Reagan's personal attorney, called the Pentagon's "one-sided charges, to which we have not had an opportunity to respond, extremely unfair." He added: "If the Pentagon uses accusations to hurt [Pollard], they have an obligation to allow him to confront his accusers. This is a violation of his fundamental constitutional rights which is what they continue to do with Mr. Pollard."

The mail I received from Jonathan Pollard on March 26, 1994, was not the first time I had been contacted by my prolific "pen pal." As the author of *The Spy Who Knew Too Much*, I was no doubt high on the list of those with whom he wished to correspond. Since my book detailed what I believed to be an extensive government cover-up to keep the truth about what he learned secret, I had always felt it was in the public interest that whatever was in Pollard's letters should be brought out into the open. After all, the fact that those letters had to be cleared by Navy Intelligence would seem to be prima facie evidence that they in no way violated U.S. national security, as Mr. Aspin claimed, and should therefore have been made part of the public record.

Actually, I have received literally hundreds of pieces of mail over the years from Pollard. But what he sent me this time was different. It included an op-ed piece by Douglas M. Bloomfield, a Washington-based columnist, with the headline: "Inman out of the picture, but troubling questions remain." Unlike Pollard's usual letters to me in which he would either plead his own case or chronicle a growing number of influential citizens and organizations calling for his release from prison, this time he added his own notes to the words of another writer.

What Bloomfield revealed was nothing earth-shattering to anyone who had read the front pages of their local newspapers. He noted that following Israel's bombing of Saddam Hussein's Osirak nuclear reactor, in June of 1981, Adm. Bobby Ray Inman, then deputy director of the CIA, used his authority to slap a 250-mile limit on intelligence sharing with Israel, in essence insisting that Iraq, Iran, and Libya were "nonthreats" to Israeli security. Wrote Bloomfield: "As Saddam and his Scud missiles later demonstrated, that was not only a very bad judgment call, but a very dangerous one as well."

Presidential *candidate* Bill Clinton would have agreed. On the eve of the Florida Democratic presidential primary in March 1992, the future president appeared at a synagogue in Delray Beach, Florida, and, speaking to a crowd of more than five hundred people, proclaimed, "If Israel hadn't bombed that Iraqi nuclear reactor, Iraq would probably have the bomb today."[2]

It was nearly two years later, on January 18, 1994, that Inman, President Clinton's nominee to replace Les Aspin as secretary of defense, announced he had had a change of heart and would not take the prestigious job the president was offering him. During a rambling (some say bizarre) news conference, Inman went so far as to charge *New York Times* columnist William Safire—who weeks earlier had written a column highly critical of Inman—of plotting against him with the help of Sen. Bob Dole (R-Kan.). In his column, Safire noted, among other things, that Inman's "animus [against Israel] also later contributed to the excessive sentencing of Jonathan Pollard . . . ."

During that same news conference, Inman disclosed previously secret details of military aid the United States gave Israel during the early 1980s, as well as a U.S. effort to nevertheless limit the sharing of satellite-based information with Jerusalem. Inman also admitted that while deputy director of the CIA it was he who made the decision to bar Israel from receiving certain satellite pictures after the Israelis had used these U.S.-originated photos to help them bomb the Osirak facility. (Contrarily, a well-connected Israeli intelligence source of mine told me that Israel had in fact *never* been allowed "overheads.") Inman said he then ordered that Israel would not be given satellite photos of countries more than 250 miles from its borders. He recalled that this provoked Safire—who somehow learned about the order—to go to then CIA director William Casey and ask that Inman's order be rescinded. Inman said that when Casey agreed to rescind the order, he (Inman) then went over Casey's head and got Defense Secretary Weinberger to make sure the order stood.[3]

Pollard, meanwhile, has long insisted that he only began spying for the Israelis because of what appeared to be a sudden logjam of intelligence information from the United States to Israel, beginning in 1982, a year after Weinberger began his watch as secretary of defense. In addition, Pollard has said that the first major piece of intelligence information he gave to Israel had to do with satellite photographs that he passed on to his initial Israeli handler, Col. Avi Sella—the same Col. Sella who, only a few years earlier, had led the Israeli bombing raid on Osirak.

In the op-ed piece Pollard sent me, Bloomfield noted that the Inman incident raised many questions that would linger beyond Inman's abrupt withdrawal from public life. "What was the impact on Israeli security and early warning capabilities of Inman's restrictions on intelligence sharing?" Bloomfield asked.

"Major," Pollard wrote, right next to the question.

"Was [Inman] eroding Israel's qualitative edge at a time when his president, Ronald Reagan, was pledging to protect it?" Bloomfield continued. "Did [Inman] have his own agenda?"

"Yes and yes," Pollard wrote.

(As to his second "yes," Pollard may have been a bit off the mark. As one of my intelligence sources told me in a telephone interview: "This was policy—secret and political, but a *policy*. Bobby Inman, in spite of being, in my opinion, a rabid anti-Semite, was still a soldier. He followed policy; he did not set it. It was, in all fairness, Pollard who set his own policy— and he was neither elected nor appointed to set policy.")

Bloomfield also insinuated that Inman was a bit of an anti-Semite.

"What consequences," Bloomfield asked, "did Inman's Jewish fixation have on the CIA and National Security Agency, which he headed, and how much residue remains?"

Scribbled Pollard: "Just look at the well-orchestrated disinformation effort to prevent my release."

Pollard then noted that these and other points Bloomfield underlined were "key questions which lie at the heart of my operation."

"Why has it taken so long for them to be raised?" Pollard wrote. "And now that they all have, will people finally be able to appreciate the nature of the threat I saw to Israel's security?"

Insisted Pollard, it was the shortsighted policies of Bobby Ray Inman, among others, that had helped turn him into an Israeli spy. At the very least, it seemed probable that Pollard still held a key to an invisible door that, when opened, would have revealed a room filled with secrets that were supposed to remain hidden from both public view and congressional scrutiny.

At whatever the cost, I knew this was a room that I, too, would now try to enter.

NOTES

1. William Northrop, a former Israeli intelligence operative, said the name "Hunting Horse" referred to someone who was a gatherer of unusually large amounts of intelligence data. The name was given Pollard by AMAN (Israeli Military Intelligence) officers in 1984. Said Northrop, "Hunting Horse" is a transliteration from the Hebrew, and loosely means he would "hunt" up information on request and that he was a "horse" for his handlers; an exceptional agent on whose back his handlers ride up the promotional ladder.

2. Clinton was referring to the Osirak reactor located at Al Tawaitha.

3. In *Veil: The Secret Wars of the CIA 1981–1987*, author Bob Woodward writes that after the destruction of Iraq's nuclear reactor by Israeli pilots using U.S. supplied warplanes, Inman checked and found that, under the intelligence-sharing agreement set up with Casey's approval, Israel had almost "unlimited access" to U.S. satellite photography and had used it in planning its raid. (A well-placed Israeli intelligence source of mine disputes this point, however. "Israel had absolutely no access to U.S. 'overhead' prior to Pollard turning it over," my source told me.) Nevertheless, Woodward notes: "Inman didn't see how the United States could maintain any balanced policy if Israel was permitted to drop bombs all over the Middle East using American intelligence." According to Woodward, Casey went along with Inman's new restriction on satellite data for Israel but was nevertheless "pleased that the Israelis had disposed of the problem, and he admired their audacity." Woodward adds that when the White House imposed sanctions on Israel for the bombing raid—withholding delivery of several F-16s—"Casey felt it might be a necessary diplomatic and political gesture, but privately called it 'bullshit.' "

CHAPTER 2

A
HEAVY
SNOW

Jonathan Pollard has always insisted he became a spy because the United States, for some reason, had been unwilling to share certain military secrets with the State of Israel. It was logical to assume that this refusal to share information with the Israelis was based on one of two scenarios. The first was that the U.S. intelligence community was simply afraid that TOP SECRET or TOP SECRET CODEWORD (Above Top Secret) documents might somehow fall into the wrong hands. In the intelligence-gathering community this relates to what is commonly known as "security," the protection of which is always vital. A second scenario was far more sinister: that the blackballing of Israel's intelligence services was a deliberate attempt to weaken *Israel's* security.

Pollard was well aware that the feeling in certain circles of U.S. intelligence that Israel couldn't be trusted with American secrets was not a recent development. This could perhaps be traced all the way back to the late 1940s, when "anti-Zionist" members of the U.S. State Department and the British Foreign Office tried to prevent the creation of an independent Jewish state, arguing that such an entity would quickly become a beachhead for Soviet infiltration in the Middle East.

Later on, anti-Zionist elements within the Eisenhower administration made unsubstantiated charges that Israeli intelligence had, in fact, been so completely infiltrated by Communist agents that any sensitive information shared with the Mossad—Israel's version of the CIA—would automatically be compromised. It was also alleged that given the close relationship existing at the time between Israel and France—whose intelligence service was known to be penetrated by the Soviets—the Russians would have had yet another way of obtaining whatever American secrets were released to the Israelis.

This defamatory campaign proved to be extremely difficult for the Israelis to counter. Even the Mossad's numerous attempts to demonstrate its reliability were viewed rather skeptically by Washington as tacit admissions of guilt.

The Israelis, who were in a no-win situation, took the drastic measure of implementing guidelines that would allay some of the American fears. They even went to the extreme of permitting James Jesus Angelton—then the CIA's chief of counterintelligence—to periodically review Israel's internal security procedures. After years of careful observation, Angelton came to the conclusion that the Israeli intelligence services (Mossad, AMAN, and Shin Bet)[1] were far from the sieves they previously had been made out to be.

Nevertheless, the CIA has apparently always had some serious fears revolving around Israel's intelligence services and their relationships with Soviet spies. This is based mostly on the premise that the Jewish state was founded by Eastern European Socialists, and that the Labor Party (Socialists) were in power in Israel from 1948 to 1977. Angelton, however, believed in the Israelis and fostered closer cooperation between the intelligence communities. To everyone's benefit, he set up certain procedures to be used by Israeli intelligence that resulted in no known penetrations by the Soviets (at least after the discovery of AMAN's Lt. Col. Israel Beer—a former training and operations head for Israel's David Ben-

34

Gurion–led Haganah faction, and a close associate of Ben-Gurion's, who was arrested by the Israelis as a double agent). One of the procedures required that no agents were to be recruited from the ranks of emigrants to Israel from the Eastern bloc.

Angelton soon concluded that Israel's intelligence services were, if anything, light-years ahead of their western European counterparts when it came to the ability to thwart Communist penetration. It was this glowing assessment by Angelton, perhaps more than anything else, that finally dissipated the clouds of suspicion that had hung for years over the Israeli intelligence establishment.

"A heavy snow fell on Washington today and it came from Austin," wrote Leon Wieseltier in the February 7, 1994, *New Republic*. Wieseltier was sarcastically referring to Texan Bobby Inman's decision, only days earlier, to withdraw his nomination as President Clinton's new secretary of defense. To Wieseltier, Inman appeared to reflect the image of a man with something he was anxious to conceal.

William Safire, the main journalistic thorn in Inman's apparently thin hide, said his first run-in with Inman came after he actually praised him in a 1980 column. "As America's chief eavesdropper, [Inman] had overheard a suspicious call by President Carter's brother, Billy, to the Libyan embassy, and properly brought the wiretap to the attorney general for criminal investigation," Safire recalled in his soon-to-be infamous commentary that appeared in the December 27, 1993, *New York Times*. "But praise from me brought [Inman] glares from the White House, and Inman—recorders whirring—called me to denounce the 'irreparable harm you have done by revealing our sources and methods.' "

Spy Jonathan Pollard was himself often castigated by Inman's friend Secretary Weinberger, and U.S. attorney for the District of Columbia,

Joseph diGenova, for revealing America's "sources and methods" when Pollard moonlighted for Israel. Revealing our sources and methods—thereby allowing for the possibility that other countries might know how we're spying on them—sounds like a most serious offense until one realizes how often, and at times erroneously, this charged terminology is used.

So what Inman told him stuck in Safire's craw. "It's hard to believe that the Libyans did not know that all embassy phone lines were routinely tapped," Safire said in his column, "but I respectfully asked [Inman] if he would entertain one question."

Icily, Safire noted, Inman said he "never talked to the press, but what was it I wanted to know?"

"I asked him," Safire replied, "how a grown man could go through life calling himself 'Bobby.' He slammed down the phone."

Safire wrote in his column—picked up in hundreds of newspapers across the country—that, as time went on, Inman was convinced that he (Safire) joined CIA Director William Casey in a conspiracy to block Inman's advancement. Said Safire: "This was because I reported that Inman, in a not-for-attribution session at CIA headquarters, had planted a false story with a group of newsmen that Israel was the source of rumors that a Libyan 'hit team' was on its way to the U.S." According to Safire, in December 1981 Inman charged that Israel was trying to provoke an attack on Libyan strongman Col. Muammar Qaddafi.[2]

"[Inman] was displeased at having his cover blown and his anti-Israel bias shown," Safire continued, adding that Inman claimed he (Safire) actually got erroneous information from a pro-Israel source "who was smarting over Inman's insistence that Israel not get any satellite photos."

Safire called Inman's explanation untrue. "An earwitness, who was in the room, reconfirms that Inman planted that false story on that day in December 1981," Safire wrote.

Safire also lashed out at Inman's relationship, after he quit the CIA, with James Guerin, the head of International Signal and Control, a company that, according to Safire, manufactured cluster bombs for the Pentagon. Described by Safire as "a conman" as well as "a longtime Inman

36

intelligence source," Guerin eventually served time in a Florida prison after being convicted of illegally transferring military technology to Iraq and South Africa.

Before Guerin was sentenced, Inman, who sat on the proxy board of Guerin's company, wrote the following letter (dated April 27, 1992) to Judge Louis Bechtle of Philadelphia asking for leniency in Guerin's case: "During the period 1974–1982, I served successively as the Director of Naval Intelligence, Vice Director of the Defense Intelligence Agency, Director of the National Security Agency, and finally as Deputy Director of Central Intelligence. During the period from 1975–1978, I came to know and worked with Mr. James Guerin on classified U.S. government activities that related to the potential proliferation of nuclear weapons capability. While many U.S. business executives have provided assistance to the U.S. government in this vein over the past forty-five years, which has substantially augmented efforts by our own intelligence gathering agencies, the mid to late 1970s was not the best of times for such cooperation . . . . Mr. Guerin displayed patriotism toward our country and a willingness to provide useful information even though it would have risked unfavorable publicity for his company." The letter was signed "B. R. Inman, Admiral, U.S. Navy (Ret)."

Alan Friedman's book *Spider's Web: The Secret History of How the White House Illegally Armed Iraq*—in which the full text of Inman's letter to the sentencing judge in the Guerin case can also be found—would appear to give readers a unique bird's-eye view of the complex world of covert operations. Although stopping short of alleging any criminal wrongdoing by former President George Bush—the commander-in-chief at a time when many unexplained dealings with Iraq were taking place—Friedman continually claims in his book that Bush, nonetheless, personally attempted to thwart any congressional investigations of the secret U.S. arming and financing of Iraq before the Gulf War. In addition, Friedman maintains that the Reagan administration also hid from Congress the truth about improper arms shipments to Iraq, and that this was in violation of laws requiring intelligence oversight committees be informed of such covert operations.

"Senior Reagan administration officials skirted arms export control legislation by using non-government operatives to ship the arms— including cluster bombs—between 1982 and 1985," a Reuters News Service report said. One of those apparently caught in this particular *"Spider's Web"* was Bobby Inman's close friend James Guerin.

In an article appearing in the *New York Times* on January 26, 1992, Seymour Hersh, a Pulitzer Prize–winning journalist and author of *The Samson Option* and *The Target Is Destroyed*, noted that, according to former intelligence and State Department officials, the Reagan administration had secretly decided to provide highly classified information to Iraq, ten years earlier, in the spring of 1982. Hersh did not elaborate. He also maintained that the United States permitted the sale of American-made arms to Iraq, at around the same time, as part of a successful effort to help Iraqi leader Saddam Hussein avert imminent defeat in Iraq's war with Iran. Wrote Hersh: "The American decision to lend crucial help to Baghdad so early in the 1980–88 Iraq-Iran War came after American intelligence agencies warned that Iraq was on the verge of being overrun by Iran, whose army was bolstered the year before by covert shipments of American-made weapons."

An anonymous State Department official would later explain the rationale, saying it was to counterbalance the effects of what would later become known as "Iran-Contra." The idea was "not to hitch the U.S. wagon to Saddam Hussein," he insisted. Rather, it was to avoid having either Iran or Iraq win a clear-cut victory and, in so doing, become too powerful in the region.[3]

During the time many of these dealings with Iraq were supposedly taking place, the deputy director of the CIA was ex-director George Bush's good friend, Robert Gates. During October 1991, Gates was questioned at length by the Senate Intelligence Committee about the secret relationship the United States had with Iraq even after that country's war with Iran had ended. Gates, who was then President Bush's personal choice to be the new head of the CIA, was grilled by a number of committee members including Sen. Bill Bradley (D-N.J.). Bradley, not one to skirt a sensitive issue, asked Gates whether U.S. intelligence sharing with Iraq, as well as the continued sale of weapons to Saddam Hussein—right up until Iraq's invasion of Kuwait—could in some way have been construed as a covert action that both the House and Senate Intelligence committees were obviously entitled to know more about.

Gates appeared unfazed by the question. He replied that he saw no problem with the pre–Gulf War relationship that existed between the United States and Iraq. Bradley pressed further, but committee chairman David Boren (D-Okla.) intervened and warned Bradley against disclosing classified information.

Yet Gates never denied that this relationship with Iraq existed.

Indeed, prior to the Gulf War, Iraq had also received valuable aid in its bloody conflict with Iran through the Bank of Credit and Commerce International (BCCI). On August 4, 1991, two months prior to Gates's appearance before the House and Senate Intelligence committees, U.S. Attorney General Richard Thornburgh stressed that new federal indictments would be handed down for money-laundering and bank regulatory violations in the so-called BCCI scandal. However, the *Los Angeles Times* quoted Thornburgh as saying that while he expected indictments in the scandal to be forthcoming, he saw no signs of an extensive CIA involvement with the bank, which had been shut down a month earlier after bank officials were found not only to be engaging in fraud, but were allegedly also laundering drug money while aiding the Palestinian terrorist Abu Nidal. The bank had reportedly handled millions of dollars in illegal arms transactions for Abu Nidal in an effort, the *Los Angeles Times* quoted a high-ranking bank official as having said, "to persuade its wealthy Mideast backers that the bank was staunchly pro-Arab."

Nonetheless, while the CIA officially admitted no wrongdoing in its relationship with the controversial bank, the *Los Angeles Times* also reported that CIA officials acknowledged that the agency did maintain some BCCI bank accounts—and transferred funds through the bank—while continuing to use the bank as a source of intelligence gathering.

So the question still needed to be asked: If the U.S. intelligence community's relationship with Iraq during its war with Iran could be explained, if not condoned, what was the rationale for the undeniable secret U.S. relationship with Iraq that existed even after that country's war with Iran had ended? After all, the direct and indirect U.S. backing of Saddam Hussein's regime continued right up until the dawn of the Gulf War when President Bush was forced to deal with the monster he had no doubt helped create. And although the policy of aiding Saddam Hussein may, to some, have been in the best interests of the United States, it nevertheless seemed a bit strange, especially in light of Saddam's bent toward militarism.

Regardless, key policymakers in the Bush administration apparently felt Saddam could be trusted. It was widely reported that only nine months before Iraq's invasion of Kuwait, President Bush signed a TOP SECRET national security directive ordering closer ties to Baghdad and opening the way for $1 billion in new aid to Iraq. That $1 billion commitment—which was in the form of loan guarantees for the purchase of U.S. farm commodities—enabled Saddam to buy needed foodstuffs on credit while using his then scarce reserves of hard currency on yet another massive arms buildup. International banks were said to be alarmed that Iraq, while falling behind in the payment of its debts, was continuing to pour money into arms purchases even though the war with Iran had ended. Getting a loan from its new friends in Washington was obviously critical for Saddam Hussein's regime.

As late as the spring of 1990, senior Bush aides overrode concern among other government officials and insisted that Iraq also be allowed to buy "dual-use" technology—advanced equipment that could be used for both civilian and military purposes. "The Iraqis were given continued access to such equipment," the *Los Angeles Times* reported, "despite emerging evidence that they were working on nuclear arms and other weapons of mass destruction."

According to a source who spoke to investigative reporter Joel Bainerman (who wrote the book *The Crimes of a President: New Revelations on Conspiracy and Cover-up in the Reagan and Bush Administrations*), more than $1.5 billion worth of dual-use products having both civilian and military uses, including helicopters, computers, and electronic equipment, were actually sold to Iraq between 1985 and 1990. That source added that from January 1985 to August 1990 more than 770 license applications for exports of U.S. products to Iraq were approved. Charged Bainerman's source: "These sales were made behind the backs of Congress and with the full knowledge and even active support of the Reagan and Bush administrations."

In an article appearing in the *New York Times* on July 29, 1990—just days before Iraq's invasion of Kuwait on August 2—Gary Milhollin, director of the Wisconsin Project on Nuclear Arms Control, and his assistant, David Dantzic, claimed that Saddam Hussein, in addition to "rattling his saber against Kuwait," was also looking to build nuclear weapons. "U.S. technology could contribute to this awful enterprise if senior officials in the Commerce and State Departments have their way," Milhollin and Dantzic wrote. According to Milhollin and Dantzic, those Commerce and State Department officials were supporting giant IBM in that company's attempts to put a "supercomputer" into the hands of a Brazilian team that was helping Iraq build long-range missiles that could conceivably carry nuclear warheads.

As it turned out, though, Iraq was more interested in something far simpler to produce.

On October 15, 1988, nearly two years before Iraq's invasion of Kuwait, Robert Gates had delivered a speech to the Association of Former Intelligence Officers. "The most immediate threat to world peace and to the security of the United States and its allies may well come from the proliferation of chemical and biological warfare capabilities in the Third World," Gates said. "Chemical weapons have become the poor man's atomic bomb. Essentially, the technology needed to produce chemical weapons is not significantly more complicated than that required to produce fertilizers—or soft drinks."

Saddam Hussein had indeed found his perfect weapon. Perhaps more important to Saddam, however; his American patrons did not appear overly anxious to stop him from using it.

NOTES

    1. The Mossad is the equivalent of the CIA; Shin Bet is the equivalent of the FBI; AMAN is Israeli military intelligence.

    2. In *Veil*, author Bob Woodward notes that "much of this information [about Libyan hit squads] was traced to a shadowy figure with ties to Iranian and Israeli intelligence services—Manucher Ghorbanifar, a wealthy Iranian arms salesman who had been a secret CIA source." Woodward said Ghorbanifar saw the initial hit-squad reports as "an opportunity to make trouble for the Libyans, and he single-handedly kept the issue alive for several months. Soon the CIA officially and secretly declared Ghorbanifar a 'fabricator.' "

    3. An Arab country (Iraq) invaded a non-Arab country (Iran). Israel supported Iran; the Arab states supported Iraq. The United States tried to play both sides.

CHAPTER 3

AUSCHWITZ
IN THE
SAND

W hen host Ted Koppel began his *Nightline* telecast of July 2, 1991—part of a joint ABC/Financial Times investigation that dealt with the subject of "Saddam's Chemical Connection"—he began by reminding his audience that when "[Muammar] Qaddafi built his chemical weapons plant in Libya, the U.S. administration was outraged. But the man who helped Qaddafi build it constructed a new chemical plant in Boca Raton, Florida. The FBI knew about it; the CIA knew about it. But no one moved to stop it."[1]

Considering Saddam Hussein's numerous threats to "burn Israel to the ground"—threats not taken lightly by the Israelis—there is some dark irony in the fact that the city of Boca Raton is part of Florida's South Palm Beach County, which may have a higher percentage of Jews living in it than any other county in the United States. And the man who was linked to this Boca Raton plant was the man most responsible for the construction of the chemical weapons facility at Rabta in Libya—Dr. Ihsan Bar bouti—a person, Koppel said, who at various times in his life had been a professor of architecture, a businessman, and a consultant to the Iraqi Ministry of Defense.

William Northrop, a former Israeli intelligence operative whom I spoke to often while writing my first book on the Pollard case—and got to know much better later on—has been identified by the United States government as "an Israeli agent who is known to travel on eleven different passports." Northrop has continually denied being an Israeli agent. During the Iran-Contra affair, Northrop even denied that he was an Israeli citizen. In 1991 Congress subpoenaed Northrop, but Israel forbade his testifying citing "security" reasons.

Northrop, who seemed to know a great deal about Barbouti, explained to me that Barbouti's efforts in the United States on behalf of Iraq were actually quite specialized. "He would locate a business with a particular critical technology," Northrop said. "He would buy in as a partner, divert the technology, and force his American partner out. This left a group of very unhappy former partners throughout the United States."

Back in 1969, the slippery Barbouti had, for some reason, even gone to the trouble of faking his own death. The reasons why are unclear, although some have maintained that he was a double agent who was also working for the CIA. (One of my sources says Barbouti simply "got in trouble" with the Baath Party—Saddam Hussein's political party and the ruling political party of Iraq.) What is clear, however, is that before the outbreak of the Gulf War Barbouti was working for the government of Iraq, was putting together a chemical weapons plant in the United States, and was doing his dirty work virtually out in the open.

On *Nightline*, Koppel acknowledged that while comparing the chemistry needed to produce soft drinks to that of concocting chemical weapons (as Robert Gates had implied) may have seemed like "a bit of a stretch," it really wasn't. "Even as Robert Gates was talking to the former intelligence officers," Koppel said, referring to Gates's October 15, 1988, speech, "a Baton Rouge chemical engineering firm was finalizing design plans and equipment specifications for a plant that would produce natural cherry flavoring from apricot

pits. The inventor of this process, Louis Champon, had been trying unsuccessfully, for some time, to find a partner to put up the necessary money.
Most potential investors weren't interested, perhaps put off by the fact that
extracting bitter almond oil—that's what gives you the natural cherry
flavor—from fruit pits also creates a nasty by-product: cyanide."

But Ihsan Barbouti, Koppel insisted, was anything but disturbed.

Champon said that Barbouti—who would become his business
partner in the spring of 1988—never showed any interest in almond oil,
but seemed to be very interested in the by-product, ferrocyanide. "It's not
a harmful product," Champon stressed, "but in the wrong hands you can
extract out the pure cyanide and it's extremely deadly." By July of 1988,
Barbouti and Champon had rented a large building in Boca Raton, for
$21,000 a month, that was part of an industrial park near Interstate 95.
While Champon maintained his only interest was in producing soft drinks,
Barbouti obviously had something far different in mind.

The chemical plant in Rabta, Libya—which former CIA director William
Webster called the "largest plant that I know of for chemical warfare"—
was getting most of its equipment and chemicals from two companies in
Germany: Imhausen Cheme and Ihsan Barbouti Incorporated (IBI). Barbouti was acting in his capacity as an "official agent of Libya," while IBI was
the "project manager" for the Rabta plant. The Reagan administration was
so concerned about the German connection to Libya that it held a high-
level briefing in Washington for German Chancellor Helmut Kohl and one
of his foreign ministers. Former U.S. Ambassador to Bonn, Rick Burt, told
Nightline that the chancellor and his foreign minister were briefed on the
Libyan facility and information U.S. intelligence had about assistance the
Libyans had received from Germany and other European countries.

Stated Koppel: "As those briefings were underway, as the secretary of
state, the director of the CIA, and the president's national security advisor
were trying to convince the German government to move against the
companies that were building Rabta, the owner of one of those companies was here, in the United States."

Barbouti had, in fact, just given his final approval for the design of the Boca Raton plant. "It would be a pilot project," said Koppel, "to see how effectively cyanide could be extracted from fruit pits, which are, after all, abundant in the Middle East."

Yet the attention of the U.S. government, the *Nightline* report went on to emphasize, was not focused on Barbouti's activities in Boca Raton. Nor was it seemingly interested in what Barbouti was doing in Texas, where he was trying to acquire an anticorrosive coating process for piping that could be used in nuclear or chemical weapons projects. There was also little White House interest, it appeared, in Barbouti's activities in Oklahoma, where he was trying to buy the formulas for advanced rocket fuel additives. However, the U.S. government was apparently very interested in the connection between Germany and Libya.

"When the Germans refused to shut down the flow of chemicals to the plant at Rabta, the State Department leaked some highly classified material to the media," Koppel said. "In a bitterly angry column, William Safire, of the *New York Times*, described the Rabta plant, and its German suppliers, as 'Auschwitz in the sand.' "

Peter Kawaja was the man Barbouti hired to set up a $1 million security system for his new plant in Boca Raton. Allegedly a specialist in the field, Kawaja told *Nightline* he was hired in early 1989 to provide armed guards and an elaborate electronics system to keep unwanted people out of this factory that was allegedly going to produce cherry-flavoring chemicals. Among the items Kawaja was told to install included a hydrogen cyanide detection system. Another of his duties was to bring a coterie of armed guards to Barbouti's other properties in Texas and Oklahoma. Kawaja also provided bodyguards for Barbouti's partner, Champon, and Barbouti's son, Haidar, who was then perhaps in his early twenties. Kawaja—who said he tried to warn agencies of the U.S. government about what was going on—was described by Koppel as a whistle-blower. Kawaja considered that an appropriate description.

"I saw a company and a man who built a plant in a foreign country that we were going to bomb, chemical weapons produced in my country, the United States, and what was wrong was it was being done almost literally in the open," Kawaja told millions of *Nightline* viewers. "It just seemed too easy for [Barbouti] or IBI to operate, if not prior to 1988, in 1989, when the plant at Rabta became common knowledge and IBI's role was exposed."

Kawaja stressed that even after 1989, however, IBI continued to wire-service millions of dollars to and from Europe and the Middle East. "IBI operated boldly," Kawaja said, "and Barbouti felt no threat in operating in the United States."

Koppel drew a similar conclusion: "The U.S. government knew who Dr. Barbouti was. To use the government's own description, he was a 'linchpin of the Libyan chemical warfare plant at Rabta.' Is it conceivable that U.S. government agencies could have been unaware of Dr. Barbouti's activities in this country? After all, Dr. Barbouti did not exactly maintain a low profile. He ran a network of companies and investments through which he channeled more than $100 million into real estate, shopping centers, and oil-drilling rigs. But his particular passion was companies, particularly chemical companies with duel-use technologies that had military as well as civilian applications—like the natural cherry-flavoring plant in Boca Raton."

Kawaja claimed that in the spring of 1989 he called the CIA and told them about Barbouti's Boca Raton plant. "I basically outlined that the plant was being constructed by Dr. Barbouti, the same IBI builder of the chemical weapons plant at Rabta," Kawaja said. "I also identified myself to them." Kawaja apparently did not want to reveal on the air what any possible relationship he had with the CIA may have been (if in fact one existed at all) but said: "[The call] was not an anonymous phone call or the first time, possibly, that I had contacted the CIA." Since the CIA charter prohibits it from legally operating in the United States, Kawaja said he was told to contact the FBI (Federal Bureau of Investigation).

If Kawaja was telling the truth, it appears that he was getting a classic runaround. He said he subsequently had a lengthy conversation with one FBI agent, in particular, who seemed extremely knowledgeable about chemical and biological weapons, and who asked him some very intricate questions dealing with the subject. But at the end of their conversation, the agent said that since the plant was a food-processing plant, Kawaja would have to call the Food and Drug Administration.

The *Nightline* reporter interviewing him then asked Kawaja what he said to the FBI agent after being told to go to the FDA.

"My mouth fell open," Kawaja recalled. "I'm not sure what I said, exactly. But I was literally in shock."

Like Peter Kawaja, Art Valantz, a senior vice president of IBI in Houston, also contacted the FBI. Valantz and Barbouti had a falling out in July of 1989 and Valantz told *Nightline* that he took a file of incriminating documents he had accumulated while running Barbouti's Texas operation. "I went to the FBI," Valantz said. "I had bank account numbers and names. If he had wire-transferred money to me—at IBI Industries in Houston, or money had been wired from IBI Houston—I kept a record of all those transactions. When I realized what I thought was a bad situation for myself and that I had been set up, I went to the FBI and said, 'Look, if something happens to me, this is why.' At that point, the FBI guy looked at me and he said, 'These are bad people. We know they're bad people.' And I said, 'Well, what do you propose I do?' And he said, 'Do you know how to shoot a gun?' I said, 'Yes, I do.' And he said, 'It's a misdemeanor. Carry one.' That was the end of the conversation."

According to Valantz, U.S. Customs later contacted him and asked if he would be interested in talking to them. Valantz said he would. Recalled Valantz: "I told [U.S. Customs] what I had given the FBI and that this was very important information." Valantz claimed that when U.S. Customs contacted the FBI, however, the information he gave them "had gotten lost."

Other items that could be traced to Barbouti were getting lost as well. During November 1989, approximately 210 gallons of hydrogen cyanide, a by-product of the extraction process, disappeared from Barbouti's Boca Raton plant. Said Champon: "To the best of my knowledge, I knew that we were missing approximately seven empty drums from our plant, and I believe that approximately 2,000 pounds had been taken out of the plant." The subsequent investigation by *Nightline*—whose sources included two arms dealers and shippers whose contract employment with the CIA was confirmed by sources within the Bush administration—revealed that the hydrogen cyanide, in seven thirty-gallon barrels, was trucked from Boca Raton to Houston. From Houston, the barrels traveled by sea to the port of Baltimore. (I would later find out, through my own sources, that the hydrogen cyanide went directly from Boca Raton to Baltimore.) In Baltimore, the barrels were loaded into a twenty-foot container and marked as the personal property of an Iraqi diplomat. The container transited Europe en route to the Jordanian port of Aqaba. From Aqaba, it was trucked overland to Iraq.

Insists former Israeli intelligence operative William Northrop, that particular shipment of hydrogen cyanide to Iraq was actually used in a trial manufacture of a poison gas. The man in charge of the shipment, Northrop told me in an interview, was an Iraqi intelligence officer stationed at the Iraqi embassy in Washington. Northrop adds there is now additional evidence showing that, in June of 1990, there was yet a second shipment of hydrogen cyanide from Barbouti to Iraq.

Yet before either Kawaja or Valantz officially informed the CIA, the FBI, and U.S. Customs about what Ihsan Barbouti was up to, the CIA had an informant, by the name of Moshe Tal, who was already watching Barbouti's every move.

In March of 1988, Koppel said, there was "a chilling convergence of events" involving Barbouti and Iraq. As the war between Iraq and Iran was winding down, Saddam Hussein's forces had used chemical weapons against their own people in the Kurdish village of Halabja, causing international outrage. Koppel reported that a few months later, in August of 1988, Moshe Tal, whom Koppel described as another business associate of Barbouti's, told a CIA contact of his about Barbouti's plant in Boca Raton. Tal also told his CIA contact that Barbouti was trying to buy hydrogen-cyanide detection units. According to Koppel, Tal ran a company based in Oklahoma City that had developed several fuel-enhancing formulas that could be used in jet aircraft and rockets. Perhaps most important to Barbouti—and the reason why he arranged to do business with Tal—was that those formulas were also made up of ingredients that could be used in chemical and biological weapons. Barbouti, Koppel said, was particularly interested in the fact that Tal's company had licenses to export these chemicals.

Adds Northrop, who maintained an office, for a while, in Oklahoma City: "Tal's company was authorized to export a wide range of 'sensitive' chemicals. In short, it was a prime candidate for a Barbouti takeover."

Northrop says that Tal may have harbored deep-seated suspicions of Barbouti early on, but these were allayed by Barbouti's legal counsel whom Northrop says was an Iraqi-born Israeli by the name of Arie Ezra David. Northrop says, at first, Tal believed the lawyer's assurances that Barbouti would never do anything to harm Israel, but later Tal changed his mind.

One year prior to Tal's first meeting with his CIA contact, Barbouti, in August of 1987, arranged a meeting in Zurich in which he introduced Tal to a German identified only as "Peter." *Nightline* reported that "Peter" was actually Jurgen Hippennstiel-Imhausen, the other chemical manufacturer responsible for the Libyan chemical weapons plant at Rabta.

"Dr. Barbouti gave me a list of chemicals that he wanted me to solicit and get—basically a shipload of those chemicals—to ship to Rotterdam or to the European facility," Tal told *Nightline*. "Peter went over the chemical list with me and told me, specifically, which chemicals he would like to have in larger quantities and the urgency and the need of those chemicals."

When Tal had the list of chemicals analyzed by experts, he was told it was a virtual shopping list for chemical and biological weapons production. Tal then contacted Israeli intelligence to find out more about his new associate, Barbouti.

"They asked me to get some detailed information about [Barbouti] such as passport numbers, date of birth, and things of that nature," Tal recalled. "It took them several months but about mid-March, or a little bit after mid-March of 1988, they confirmed that he was the chief contractor for the Rabta chemical weapons plant."

In June of 1988, Tal made contact with Sen. Dennis DeConcini (D-Ariz.), at the time a member of the Senate Intelligence Committee. DeConcini passed the information along to William Webster, then director of the CIA. On June 15, 1988, at Webster's direction, John Helgerson of the CIA wrote to DeConcini: "We would like one of our officers to meet with Tal to determine whether he can provide any fresh insights into the activities and contacts of Dr. Barbouti."

According to Tal, the CIA became interested in anything they could find out about Barbouti. "They wanted to know what he liked to eat, how he walked, what he liked to do, where he was staying," Tal said. For months, Tal and his CIA handler maintained almost daily telephone contact. In time, Tal wanted to break off his relationship with Barbouti, but the CIA asked him to keep it going.

A few months after Saddam Hussein used chemical weapons against the Kurds at Halabja, Tal—in August of 1988—informed his CIA contact that Barbouti was ready to set up his new plant in Boca Raton, Florida, and stressed he knew Barbouti was trying to buy hydrogen cyanide detection units. "I gave [the CIA] basically all the information," Tal said. "They seemed like they were very excited about it, but they—I don't know if you ever dealt with the CIA—you know, they are well-trained, and they hear but they don't talk."

A *Nightline* interviewer then asked Tal: "So we're talking about how in August of 1988 you supplied this information [to the CIA]. Yet the plant, subsequent to that, was designed, built, constructed, operated, and, in fact, never shut down. How do you explain this?"

Answered Tal: "It seems that Barbouti, or some of his people, had a lot of pull in Washington."

Koppel revealed that Tal was also told by Barbouti that he (Barbouti) was supplying Iraq with weapons. "Tal insists he passed that information on to the CIA," Koppel said. "They didn't seem to care."

Tal agreed. "When I approached the CIA or when I met with the CIA,"

Tal said, "it seems that Iraq was not a concern to them. They didn't want to concentrate on that. They were more interested in Libya." But by 1989, the cherry-flavoring plant in Boca Raton was not only producing a special cyanide that could be used in the development of battlefield-grade poison gas; it was shipping samples of the cyanide to Iraq.

Koppel looked puzzled. He wondered aloud why it was necessary for Ihsan Barbouti to go to the trouble of shipping samples of cyanide. "Why not just send the formula?" Koppel asked another *Nightline* guest, Alan Friedman, author of *Spider's Web*. Friedman explained that the shipped samples sent by Barbouti were needed so the Iraqis could prove to themselves that the process taking place in the Boca Raton factory did, indeed, work.

"What [the Iraqis] were trying to do," Friedman said, "was get from Boca Raton enough quantities, not military significant, but just enough to show that this could be produced as an extract and could be used in a larger scale plant in Iraq."

Friedman was then asked what he thought was the primary reason why the U.S. government gave Barbouti so much room to operate in the United States.

"Well," Friedman answered, "that's the question we've been looking at and we've been told by Dr. Barbouti's own lawyer that at the time of the Rabta affair, Barbouti was in contact with the CIA. The lawyer didn't elaborate why. We've also been told by some of the federal investigators that they surmise that by being in London all those years, Dr. Barbouti may have been in a relationship with the British secret services. And Moshe Tal, one of our sources, told us that Dr. Barbouti told him directly that he had a deal with western intelligence to supply information on Iraq and Libya in exchange for being taken care of by the Brits."

In the United States, Friedman surmised, it was becoming clear that Barbouti also operated without apparent worry. "What we're finding," Friedman said, "is there was a great deal of latitude for Iraqi intelligence people, Iraqi procurement agents, to operate throughout the U.S. They bought companies, they made investments, and they were really not touched. Indeed, what we're looking at now is how the Iraqis may have penetrated a major U.S. corporation. So clearly, we're finding a pattern here of lots of information that the U.S. government had, and lots of Iraqi activity which was not prosecuted."

Is it possible that what Barbouti was attempting to achieve was just considered unimportant by U.S. intelligence agencies? In *The Crimes of a President*, author Joel Bainerman notes the opinion of former CIA agent Victor Marchetti, who reveals an attitude in the CIA that chemical weapons were not very practical and were difficult to control. "They were known to backfire if the winds change," Bainerman writes. "There was also the notion that chemical weapons weren't really that much of a danger, and, since the U.S. and the Soviets were moving away from them, any nations still interested in them were amateurs."

Nonetheless, Saddam Hussein managed to use chemical weapons successfully against the Kurds, during his war with Iran (at the Majnoon swamps), and would have no doubt used them against Israel if he had gotten the chance. And when Barbouti's business associates in the United States brought attention to his activities in this country, the fact remains that apparently nothing was done to stop him.

A tombstone in the English county of Surrey is now said to denote the final resting place of the mysterious Dr. Barbouti. Considering Barbouti's past history, Lloyd's of London was naturally reluctant to pay off on the "dead man's" life insurance claim. As for Barbouti himself, he was obviously unavailable for comment on the events that swirled around him like some gathering of old ghosts. Like onetime Teamster boss Jimmy Hoffa, this alleged terrorist "Renaissance man" was also no longer talking to the press.

NOTE

1. Taken from the transcript of *Nightline*, July 2, 1991.

DREYFUS REVISITED

After Captain Alfred Dreyfus was sentenced to life on Devil's Island for allegedly furnishing secret French documents to the German attaché in Paris in 1894 he never ceased protesting his innocence. During his court martial, the fact that Dreyfus was a Jew no doubt weighed heavily on the minds of the judges. The controversial case flared up again, in 1896, when Captain Georges Picquart discovered evidence pointing to Major Ferdinand Walsin Esterhazy as the real traitor. While Picquart was silenced by the French authorities, Dreyfus's family pressed for a new trial.

The Dreyfus case would become a major issue, and Dreyfus a cause célèbre. France was literally divided between Dreyfus supporters (among them socialists and anticlericalists) and his detractors (royalists, militarists, and many Catholics). A well-known French writer, Émile Zola, wrote an article ("J'accuse") in 1898 in which he charged the French authorities of framing Dreyfus. For his efforts, Zola was thrown in jail. The Austrian Jew Theodor Herzl was another journalist who covered the Dreyfus case.

He would eventually write an eighty-eight-page pamphlet *Der Juden Statt* (The Jewish State) based on his analysis of that case, which became the manifesto of the new movement Zionism.

In 1899, a second court martial again found Dreyfus guilty. It wasn't until 1906—twelve years after he was unjustly accused of treason—that Dreyfus's name was finally cleared. He went on to have a distinguished career in the French military.

Although himself buried for five long years in a maximum security prison—hopefully, his enemies wished, out of sight and out of mind—Jonathan Pollard's name once again surfaced in the media when, in 1992, his friend Rabbi Avi Weiss got under the skin of then Republican presidential candidate Pat Buchanan. Weiss, Pollard's rabbi and confidant, had visited Pollard many times at Marion Prison, but this time was attending a Buchanan rally on February 2 in West Manchester, New Hampshire. Thirty seconds into Buchanan's speech, the activist rabbi (along with three others in the audience) rose up from the crowd wearing symbolic death-camp uniforms and holding signs that read: "Don't Vote for an Anti-Semite," and "Pat Equals Duke Without the Sheet." (The name "Duke" referred to David Duke, the former Grand Dragon of the Ku Klux Klan who had entered the political arena in Louisiana, and was a man whose membership in the party of Lincoln had to be embarrassing to even Buchanan.)

Recalled Weiss in a press release from AMCHA (a Jewish, nonviolent, direct-action group headed by Weiss), Buchanan did not protest as the signs were torn down and a member of the audience cried out, "We should have finished the Jews in the camps." But Weiss was not finished dogging Buchanan. On March 2, 1992, during a Buchanan rally just before the Georgia primary, Weiss's group (this time bolstered by a dozen rabbis as well as two dozen Holocaust survivors) was in the audience while Buchanan spoke. "I hollered 'Anti-Semitism makes America last,' " Weiss said. Buchanan spotted Weiss in the audience and shot back: "This rally is of Americans, for Americans, and for the good old U.S.A., my friends."

Buchanan's response to Weiss created a furor. On ABC's *Nightline*, televised March 11, 1992, interviewer Chris Wallace questioned fellow journalist Buchanan—who was often a guest on the show—about the incident. He then asked Buchanan to respond to charges made by Jews (as well as non-Jews) that he was an "anti-Semite and a fascist." Buchanan turned red. "Let me talk about one of those people," he snapped. "His name is Rabbi Weiss and he is one of the defenders, as I understand it, of Jonathan Pollard, who is a traitor and spy who stole our secrets and gave them to the Israeli government, and, according to Seymour Hersh, the Israeli government then gave them to the Soviet Union."

In actuality, Pollard was never accused of treason, and Seymour Hersh's assumptions (in his book *The Samson Option*) may well have been based on some erroneous information, but Pollard's name was once again front-page news, and, for that, Pollard's supporters had the feisty Pat Buchanan to thank as much as anyone else.[1]

By 1992, the man former U.S. Secretary of Defense Caspar Weinberger once described as "the worst spy in American history" had already spent nearly half a decade in solitary confinement in an underground prison cell with temperatures, in the summertime, that reached well over one hundred degrees. Once a day, the guards would allow him out of his cramped cell for an hour of recreation. For Jonathan Pollard—a bright, articulate, and well-educated former U.S. Navy Intelligence analyst who committed the crime of passing military information over to an American ally, and whom some were calling America's Dreyfus—every day, like the one before, was just another day in hell, a hell, that many would nonetheless argue, was clearly one of his own making.

Pollard was accused, specifically, of supplying the Israelis with more than one thousand classified documents which he sourced from several classified libraries. Balding and slightly overweight, and with what he claimed to be a zealot's love for Israel, he so enraged his superiors in Naval Intelligence and the Pentagon that he was punished in a way that no one spying for an ally had ever been punished before. His supporters continued to ask: Was it in fact what Pollard *did* that the government found so abhorrent? Or was it the country that he did it *for*?

"I wish I had a better command of the English language so that I could convey precisely what it was like to live in an environment of total bedlam," Pollard wrote about his old prison cell at the Springfield Medical Center for Federal Prisoners, in Springfield, Missouri. Pollard stayed at the Springfield prison for nearly eleven months before being transferred to the federal penitentiary in Marion, Illinois—often called the toughest maximum security prison in America.

A letter from Pollard graphically described his first stop at Springfield.

"The inhuman screams of the patients around me sounded like something straight out of Dante's *Inferno*," he wrote. "And then there were the attempted suicides. Witnessing a man cut his own throat from ear to ear was something I could have done without. In fact, I saw this happen so many times that I actually developed the ability to distinguish between the ones who were serious about killing themselves and those who were merely bent on a little self-mutilation."

Carol Pollard described the Springfield prison, where her brother had previously been held, as little more than a psychiatric ward for the criminally insane. "Federal Director of Prisons Michael Quinlan stated, in a letter to Rep. Lee Hamilton (D-Ind.), that Jay was not in Springfield for treatment," Carol Pollard said. "And Jay would probably still be in Springfield if Hamilton hadn't protested Jay's treatment to the Justice Department." Quinlan later wrote Hamilton that Pollard was the only sane inmate of a federal prison to receive such treatment.

Pollard would eventually be transferred to the K-Unit at the Marion Penitentiary, where he would be held, for the most part, in solitary confinement. Pollard described Marion as the "Bates Motel" of the federal prison system. "The KGB officers who operate Lefortovo Prison in Moscow could definitely learn a few things from the staff at this facility," Pollard wrote. David Ward, a University of Minnesota professor who contributed to an article about America's prisons for *Newsweek* magazine, said of the prisoners in Marion Penitentiary's K-Unit: "They are there for symbolic reasons—to show what the federal government can do if it really gets angry."

The government was obviously very angry at Pollard, who was immediately incarcerated after being charged with passing U.S. military secrets over to the State of Israel. He admitted his guilt in this matter. Specifically, he pleaded guilty to one count of conspiracy to violate a federal statute that prohibits a person from communicating to a foreign government information relating to the national defense—either with intent (or reason to believe) that the information will be used to the injury of the United States or to the advantage of a foreign nation. But Pollard was never charged with intent to injure the United States. Explained New York attorney David Kirshenbaum, a longtime Pollard supporter, Pollard was charged with "having intent and reason to believe that the information would be used to the advantage of Israel."

Arrested on November 21, 1985, Pollard was sentenced fifteen months later, on March 4, 1987, to life imprisonment. The sentencing judge added a recommendation that Pollard never be paroled. "What was it about the Pollard affair," Kirshenbaum asked in a letter that was sent to various media, "that resulted in a sentence that was not only grossly deviant from sentences meted out to other individuals who passed classified information to American allies, but even more harsh than the punishments imposed on Americans who spied for America's adversaries, causing massive damage, including the compromising of American operatives in Communist countries and the resulting deaths of Americans?"

Pat Buchanan's nemesis, Rabbi Avi Weiss, voiced similar concerns. "What Pollard did was illegal," Weiss admitted. "But whereas Pollard was indicted for the illegal transfer of classified material, he was not charged with the more serious crimes of causing harm to U.S. agents, damaging American security, or treason."

Emphasizing in an op-ed that Pollard had in fact entered into a plea bar gaining agreement with the government, Weiss added: "Persons who have committed offenses comparable to Jonathan Pollard's—spying for an ally in time of peace—and then have pled guilty and cooperated with the government, have been given a median sentence of four to five years and have served, on the average, between three and four years. Why is this case the exception?"

Alan Dershowitz—the noted Harvard Law School professor and author of *Chutzpah* and *Reversal of Fortune*—had similar concerns. "The issue in Pollard's case is not whether what he did was wrong, but whether the punishment he received fits the crime," Dershowitz said. "History provides at least some relative parameters which allow one to conclude, with reasonable confidence, that if comparable information had been provided by a French-American to France or a Swedish-American to Sweden, it is unlikely that the sentence would have been as severe."

Dr. Morris Pollard, Pollard's father and a professor of microbiology at the University of Notre Dame, also took issue with the way the government treated his son: "Caspar Weinberger called my son's case a major catastrophe involving security. But what Weinberger failed to acknowledge was that the grand jury record shows Jay was only indicted on a single count of aiding an ally—Israel. In spite of all that, he was given a life sentence."

"He was never accused or indicted on a treason charge," Carol Pollard concluded, "because my brother did not commit treason."

Explaining why her brother chose to plead guilty to the one-count indictment, Carol Pollard said it was because the government, in return, promised not to seek a life sentence. "The government made my brother promises and broke them all," she insisted. "First, it promised not to seek a life sentence. Yet the entire tenor of its written and oral submissions at sentencing was a request for just such a sentence. It also promised to inform the court of my brother's cooperation and of the considerable value of that cooperation. But the government reneged on that too."

Certainly, the life sentence Pollard received seemed to go way beyond the sentences handed out in other cases involving Americans passing classified military secrets to non-Communist countries.

Thomas Dolce, a former army weapons analyst—who signed an

agreement with prosecutors that preempted more serious criminal charges—pled guilty to one count of communicating information to an agent of a foreign government. From 1979 to 1983, Dolce furnished South Africa with a wide variety of defense-related information. Compared to how it dealt with Pollard, the Justice Department was extremely lenient in Dolce's case. His prosecutors recommended the maximum punishment of ten years imprisonment and a $10,000 fine.

Abdel Helmy got off relatively easy, as well. An Egyptian-American senior jet propulsion engineer, he participated in a scheme to smuggle missile technology to Egypt which was later used to increase the range of Iraq's Scud-B missiles. Helmy was allegedly recruited by Egypt's defense minister, Abdel Halim Abu Ghazala (who, next to President Hosni Mubarak, was the most powerful man in his country). The U.S. government agreed to recommend a maximum imprisonment of four years and nine months in addition to a $358,600 fine. Helmy was then sentenced, in 1989, to a forty-six-month prison term in a minimum security institution. He was given "credit" for his eighteen-month presentence period and served less than four years.

Samuel Morrison—like Pollard, a former U.S. Naval Intelligence analyst—was caught stealing secret Navy documents in 1985 for the British publication *Jane's Defence Weekly*. He was sentenced to two years and released after only eight months.

There was also the case of U.S. Navy Ensign Stephen Baba who was sentenced in 1982 for selling electronic warfare documents to South Africa. Baba served two years in prison and was quietly released.

Sharon Scrange, a former CIA employee convicted in 1986 of spying for Ghana, had the court reduce her sentence from five years to two years in prison.

Other well-publicized espionage cases included those of CIA secretary Virginia Baynes, who pled guilty to a single count of passing national defense information to the Philippine government and received a sentence of three and a half years; William Holder Bell, who provided information on antitank missiles and radar technology to a Polish agent and received an eight-year prison term; and U.S. Army Specialist Albert Sombolay, who spied for Iraq during the Gulf War—and only received a nineteen-year sentence.

But even most American spies who gave U.S. information to the Soviets fared better than Pollard.

Sergeant Clayton Lonetree, a U.S. Marine stationed at the U.S. embassy in Moscow, "consorted and fraternized" with a female Soviet agent and allowed Soviet agents access to the embassy. Lonetree was given a twenty-five-year prison term in 1987 and was made eligible for parole in 1997. The commandant of the Marine Corps, Gen. Alfred M. Gray Jr., recommended, further, that Lonetree's sentence be reduced from twenty-five years to fifteen years.[2]

John A. Walker Jr., a retired U.S. Navy Chief Warrant Officer, operated as a full-time agent for the USSR and masterminded, organized, and recruited his own little spy ring that did extensive cold-war damage to the United States. Beginning while he was in the Navy, and continuing into his retirement, Walker divulged critical U.S. intelligence information to Soviet agents in the United States and worldwide. Like Pollard, he, too, was handed a sentence of life imprisonment. Unlike Pollard, though, there was no recommendation by the court that Walker never be paroled.

Barbara Walker, John Walker's estranged wife, allegedly knew of her husband's spying for the Soviet Union, but, even after their divorce, did not contact the authorities. Barbara Walker—who was never sentenced in this case—revealed her husband's activities only after she became involved in a nasty custody battle over her grandson.

John and Barbara Walker's son, Michael, also spied for the Soviet Union while in the U.S. Navy. While holding a security position on an aircraft carrier, Michael Walker passed military secrets over to his father who, in turn, passed them on to the Soviets. Given a twenty-five-year prison sentence, he was eligible for parole in eight years and four months from the time of his sentencing.

John Walker's brother, Arthur, a retired U.S. Navy lieutenant commander, gave his brother military secrets, as well, while he was in the Navy, and, later, while working as a defense contractor. Given three life terms plus forty years on seven counts of espionage, he nevertheless has full prison privileges.[3]

On May 2, 1991, three attorneys—David Kirshenbaum, Michael Rosenzweig, and Larry Dub—received permission to visit Pollard at the Marion Penitentiary. Said Kirshenbaum in a letter to the media: "The main purpose of our visit was to discuss with Mr. Pollard the ramifications of an amicus (friend of the court) brief being submitted in connection with his upcoming appeal." According to Kirshenbaum, Pollard's visitation rights had been severely restricted. The attorney said he therefore viewed the visit as an opportunity to "provide not only some form of assistance to Pollard, a man desperately in need and deserving of help, but also a chance to meet someone who has been the subject of so much press coverage, yet has been seen by only a handful of people over the past six years."

Kirshenbaum was convinced that the "campaign of disinformation" that was unleashed against Pollard following his arrest—and which "continued unabated and with increasing intensity up until the day of his sentencing"—was a major factor in Pollard's receiving a life sentence. One of the most notorious pieces of such disinformation, Kirshenbaum stressed, was the highly confidential "Weinberger memorandum." Written by the former secretary of defense, the memorandum was delivered to Judge Aubrey Robinson, the presiding judge in the Pollard trial, and stated that he (Weinberger) could "conceive of no greater harm to national security" than that caused by Pollard.[4]

Insisted Kirshenbaum: "That canard has been repeated over and over again by those who oppose a commutation of Pollard's sentence."

But not only had there been disinformation about the nature and circumstances surrounding Pollard's activities on behalf of Israel, Kirshenbaum argued; there had been a great deal of disinformation about Pollard himself.

"Though I had corresponded with Pollard, and had read and written about the case, I, like everyone else, wondered exactly what kind of person I would find on my visit," Kirshenbaum said. "As we walked through the twelve or thirteen iron gates at Marion Prison on the way to our meeting with Pollard, the tension and mysteriousness kept building. Finally, we reached a staircase above the room where our meeting was to take place and I looked inside and saw this person who looked like the picture I had seen of Jonathan Pollard. He got up from his chair and looked up and waved to his new visitors with one of the happiest and friendliest faces I've ever seen."

Kirshenbaum described his meeting with Pollard as "an emotionally charged one" for all who participated, but said perhaps the most emotional moment came when he first saw the expression on Pollard's face. "In that instant," Kirshenbaum said, "all the tension, all the mystery, and all the discomfort dissipated, and I immediately felt a bond with Jonathan."

The meeting between Pollard and the three attorneys took place around a table in a large room and in the presence of a member of the National Security Agency who said he was there to insure that Pollard did not pass on any classified information. Pollard was dressed in prison garb and wore a knitted yarmulke on his head. Kirshenbaum found this surprising. "It requires tremendous inner strength and fortitude to wear a yarmulke in an institution like Marion Prison," Kirshenbaum recalled thinking.

Kirshenbaum said all three lawyers found Pollard to be exceptionally outgoing, friendly, clear-thinking, and communicative. "He had an excellent sense of humor, which you wonder how he retains in a place like Marion," Kirshenbaum said. "His most outstanding feature, however, was his brilliance, which became apparent after only a few minutes of talking to him."

And he appeared nothing like the person portrayed by the Justice Department. In good spirits, he was obviously buoyed by the visit from the attorneys, and—at least to the extent the government would permit it—was looking forward to more visits from lay and religious leaders, both from within and from outside the Jewish community.

But he was also keenly aware of something else—that he still had some very powerful enemies in Washington who would do whatever they could to ensure that he stayed exactly where he was. He knew that Judge Robinson, the man who sentenced him, had heeded Caspar Weinberger's recommendation that he (Pollard) never be paroled. And he knew that the prosecuting attorney in his case, Joseph diGenova, had made a stiff recommendation of his own.

"Jonathan Jay Pollard," the U.S. attorney for the District of Columbia sternly warned, "should never again be allowed to see the light of day."

NOTES

1. Article III, Section 3, of the Constitution uses specific language in its definition of treason: "Treason against the United States," the Constitution states, "shall consist only in levying war against them, or, in adhering to their enemies, giving them aid or comfort."

2. According to an article by Neil A. Lewis in the *New York Times*, National, May 13, 1991.

3. According to *Family of Spies: Inside the Walker Spy Ring*, by Pete Earley, the only member of the Walker spy ring who fared worse than Pollard was Jerry Whitworth who was sentenced to 365 years in prison with no possibility of parole until he reached the age of 107.

4. Pollard never had a trial. However, in letters he sent me he sometimes referred to his closed hearings as a trial.

SUITLAND

The son of Mollie and Dr. Morris Pollard was born in Galveston, a sleepy Texas town near Houston on the Lone Star State's eastern panhandle, and the title of a onetime hit song by country and pop singer Glen Campbell. But Jonathan Pollard's strong ties to Israel began even before his birth. During World War II, one of his uncles, while in charge of the Allied Forces Army Hospital, diverted four thousand pairs of surplus combat boots to the fledgling Israeli army. He could never have known that years later he would have an infamous nephew who, in his own unique way, would try to follow in his footsteps.

Coming into the world on August 7, 1954, the young Pollard soon proved to be precocious. As a youth, he learned, among other things, to speak six languages and play the cello. As sensitive as he was bright, he was also aware, at a very tender age, that he had lost seventy-five members of his family to the ovens of the Holocaust.

His older brother, Harvey, born in 1943, went on to graduate from medical school and, as a physician, would specialize in cancer research at the National Institute of Health in Bethesda, Maryland. His older sister, Carol, born in 1950, became a musician and artist who worked in hospital administration in New Haven, Connecticut. After her brother was imprisoned, both she and her father began traveling across the country to try to raise the "public consciousness" over what they claimed Jonathan really did—and why he did it. Carol, who did far more of this than her elderly father, was partly financed in these endeavors, she says, by her benefactor—a wealthy philanthropist who preferred to remain anonymous. There are rumors that her benefactor may in fact have been the Israeli government.

Dr. Morris Pollard was a world-renowned microbiologist who headed the prestigious Lobund Laboratory on the campus of Notre Dame University in South Bend, Indiana. During the Second World War, Dr. Pollard served in the U.S. Army's Brooke Medical Center Laboratory in Fort Sam Houston, Texas. As a pioneer in immunology whose work helped protect American soldiers against the tropical diseases they were coming down with in the Pacific, he was awarded the Army Commendation Medal as well as a presidential citation.

Dr. Pollard's children grew up in a ranch-style home close to the Notre Dame campus. The Pollard family moved from Galveston to South Bend when Jonathan Pollard was seven. In 1956, when Pollard was eighteen-months-old, his father—who had just been named a McLaughlin Faculty Fellow at Cambridge University—took his entire family to England where they spent the rest of the year. Pollard celebrated his fourth birthday at the International Congress of Microbiology in Stockholm, Sweden, where a chorus of Nobel Prize winners sang "Happy Birthday" to him.

In 1967, when Pollard was an impressionable thirteen-year-old, the Israelis defeated the Arabs in the Six-Day War and Gen. Moshe Dayan became a household name. During the next five years Pollard proceeded to collect over one thousand books on Judaica. In 1968, he would go with his parents to Europe. During that trip, the fourteen-year-old boy would take a tour of the Dachau concentration camp where tens of thousands of Jews were tortured and killed by the Third Reich.

Young Pollard traveled to Israel for the first time during the summer of 1970, the summer before his junior year at Riley High School in South Bend. For the serious-minded high school student, who was painfully aware of what he perceived to be the anti-Semitism in the area in which he was raised, going to Israel was in many ways a dream come true. Back in South Bend during his senior year in high school, Pollard, then seventeen, was chosen as one of the outstanding students in English in the country by the National Council of Teachers of English. He was also named Riley High School's Outstanding Senior Social Studies Student. He made the National Honor Society and was accepted at Stanford University. As the son of a Notre Dame professor he could have had a free ride at Notre Dame, but, as he would later say, he wanted to get as far away from South Bend as he possibly could.

He immediately enrolled as a premed major at Stanford, but later changed his major to political science. It was during the summer between his junior and senior years at Stanford—when he went to Paris to work as an intern at the Atlantic Institute, a private "think tank"—that the fledgling political science major got perhaps his first real taste of the sophisticated world of intelligence gathering.

Wolf Blitzer, in his comprehensive and extremely well written book about the Pollard case, *Territory of Lies*, said Pollard once referred to the Atlantic Institute as a "CIA front," a description to which Blitzer apparently gave little credence. Blitzer wrote that he found "no evidence to support Pollard's claim."

However, in a letter he wrote to me, Pollard put it this way: "If the institute was a CIA front, do you think people would simply tell [Blitzer] it was so? When I worked at the institute I had to have a security clearance which, in and of itself, should have alerted Wolf to the fact that something more than just academic analysis was going on there. The top two floors were off limits to everybody, save the institute's president, two American secretaries, three 'maintenance technicians,' and several armed guards. In 1984, the institute was blown apart by a bomb which had been planted by the French terrorist organization 'Action Directe.' In their subsequent explanation for the incident, the group said that, as the institute was a known front for the CIA, its destruction was an act of 'revolutionary justice.' "

Pollard graduated from Stanford in June of 1976, with a B.A. in political science, and enrolled at the Notre Dame Law school. He quit after only a few months. He subsequently registered at Indiana University where he studied political science for one semester, then matriculated at the Fletcher School of Law and Diplomacy at Tufts University in Boston.

During the summer after his first year at Fletcher, Pollard served an internship at the Naval War College in Newport, Rhode Island. Later, Pollard claims he worked as an unpaid research assistant to Prof. Robert Pfaltzgraff at the Institute for Foreign Policy Analysis in Cambridge, Massachusetts. Pollard says Pfaltzgraff may now be somewhat hesitant to admit this because, according to Pollard, Pfaltzgraff still gets much of his funding from the Department of Defense. In *Territory of Lies*, Blitzer wrote that Pfaltzgraff denied Pollard ever worked there.

"Although Pfaltzgraff continues to publicly deny I ever worked for him, during an FBI interview he admitted that I had, in fact, been his research assistant for one semester," Pollard said.

No matter who is telling the truth here, there is no question that the world of intelligence gathering was becoming increasingly attractive to Jonathan Pollard. Soon after his twenty-fifth birthday he was hired as an Intelligence Research Specialist by the Field Operational Intelligence Office of the U.S. Navy in Suitland, Maryland, a Washington, D.C. suburb. His first job at Naval Intelligence involved tracking Soviet naval and air movements in and over the Norwegian Sea, the North Atlantic, the Baltic Sea, the Caribbean, and the South Atlantic. His second job for the Navy was at NISC—the Navy Intelligence Support Center—where he quickly rose to become the section head in charge of analyzing the technical characteristics of the Soviet fleet as regards helicopter carriers, cruisers, and destroyers.

An old Navy man himself, Pollard's father was not particularly happy about his son's career move. "I felt that unlike with the other armed forces, the

Navy was a bit of an anti-Semitic outfit," Dr. Morris Pollard told me. "After all, I had some insight since I served for two years as a chairman of the Naval Advisory Committee."

In spite of his father's misgivings, Pollard would eventually be reassigned to the merchant ship division of NISC where he would be collecting and analyzing data on Soviet scientific research vessels and other "free world" merchant ships that were either being used as intelligence collectors or arms carriers. For the year that he worked there Pollard was also the section head in charge of Mediterranean/Middle East navies. During the first intelligence exchange with the Israelis that Pollard ever participated in, he was the Navy's representative in charge of major Communist warships. During the next bilateral meeting in which he participated, his area of responsibility was Arab navies.

While working at Naval Intelligence, Jonathan Pollard began sensing what he felt could best be described as a kind of "antagonism toward Israel," and perhaps Jews in general. Part of this was due, in no small part, to Israel's assault on the U.S.S. *Liberty* during the Six-Day War in 1967. The U.S.S. *Liberty* was an American intelligence-gathering ship that allegedly was in international waters north of El-Arish when Israeli warplanes and torpedo boats deliberately attacked it on June 8 of that year, killing more than thirty American sailors. Israel insisted at the time that the attack was a tragic mistake and that the Israeli pilots thought they were firing on an Egyptian ship.

Pollard claims he studied the incident fully, and that when the *Liberty* was attacked it was actually operating well within the war zone. In addition, Pollard said an Egyptian naval transport that looked very similar to the American ship had been spotted by the Israeli air force in the same area on the day preceding the attack. The Israelis knew that the Egyptian ship had aboard several hundred commandos who were planning an assault on a newly occupied Israeli air base. When Israeli jets came out the next day to find this ship, the *Liberty* was the only vessel in the area.

According to some Israeli sources, at least, by refusing to hoist colors and make a dash for international waters, the *Liberty* brought the resulting

71

Israeli air attack upon itself. "Anyone who believes Israel purposely attacked an American ship is uninformed," Pollard said. "Nothing could be further from the truth."

Actually, the Israelis may have indeed shot at the *Liberty* knowing it was an American vessel. And, according to sources in both U.S. and Israeli intelligence, the Israelis may have had little choice. The White House of Lyndon Johnson was tied into the oil interests, and those oil interests did not want to alienate the Arab oil producers by allowing Israel to win a decisive military victory. So the CIA threw the Arabs a bone, those sources insist—that bone being intelligence gathered by the *Liberty*, one of the most sophisticated spy ships of its time.

If Israel allowed the *Liberty* to operate, Israel conceivably could have lost what quickly became known as the Six-Day War. So, as distasteful as it was for Israelis to attack and disable an American ship, the attack may well have been intentional. Note John Loftus and Mark Aarons in *The Secret War Against the Jews*: "In the last quarter of a century, more disinformation has been spread about the *Liberty* incident than any other episode in U.S.-Israeli relations. The fact that both the United States and Israeli governments continued to lie about the incident, a quarter of a century later, is testimony to the sensitivities felt by both about what really happened."

The *Liberty* incident notwithstanding, the Navy, historically, never seemed to have the same close working relationship with the Israelis enjoyed by both the U.S. Air Force and the U.S. Army. Discounting what on the surface appeared to be a warming of relations between the Navy and Israel (especially when John Lehman was secretary of the Navy), Pollard, during the course of his work at Naval Intelligence, therefore became increasingly worried about just how much sophisticated Soviet military equipment was pouring into the Middle East. This equipment, in the hands of Israel's sworn enemies, no doubt had only one eventual purpose, Pollard felt. With that in mind, in 1981 Pollard decided to get more involved. He went to the Washington offices of the American Israel Public Affairs Committee (AIPAC). There he spoke to Tom Dine, AIPAC's executive director.

The Reagan administration, at the time, was trying to push a Saudi AWACS (Airborne Warning and Control System) package through the Congress. Much to Pollard's distress, the administration was totally outmaneuvering AIPAC—or so Pollard felt. Said Pollard: "It was during this debate, that Dine was quoted as saying that with AIPAC's 'power' on Capitol Hill, the AWACS sale was all but dead. Hardly any member of Congress likes to hear that talk, however, particularly when constituents start calling them up and inquiring about PAC contributions."[1]

It was only a few months after he first visited the executive offices of AIPAC that Pollard met a young woman named Anne Henderson. A twenty-one-year-old, green-eyed redhead, Henderson was then working as a secretary at the Chemical Specialties Manufacturers Association while she also took night classes at the University of Maryland. Their relationship quickly blossomed into romance. Pollard and Henderson would soon move in together—they shared a two-bedroom apartment in Washington—and would eventually become engaged.

Although happier in his love life than he was with his career at Naval Intelligence, Pollard nevertheless stayed on the same career track, continued to move up the ladder, and even received a medal from the Secretary of the Navy in addition to three Navy citations for excellence. This was in spite of a major intelligence blunder he literally stumbled upon that temporarily cost him his security clearances—and nearly cost him his job. The story, which Pollard insists is true, sounds like something straight out of the *X-Files*.

Late in 1981, while he was working at the Atlantic Desk in the Navy Ocean Surveillance Information Center, Pollard claims he was asked by the Navy if he could establish a "back channel" (a contact done in secrecy) to Lt. Gen. P. W. van der Westhuizen, then South Africa's chief of military intelligence. The United States had been having a major problem with intelligence collection in the South Atlantic, especially during the last years of the Carter administration when the strains between the United States and the apartheid government of South Africa had virtually reached their breaking point. As a by-product of this poor working relationship, both nations wound up expelling each other's spies, something that proved damaging to both countries' intelligence operations.

To the United States, this was particularly damaging, though, because America was facing a growing intelligence void when it came to the movement of Soviet ships going around the South African Cape. To perhaps serve the interests of each country, therefore, van der Westhuizen had secretly come to the United States with a five-member military delegation. Unfortunately for those who helped arrange that meeting, months later the story was leaked to the press and a number of Reagan administration officials wound up having egg on their collective faces.

Pollard insists he never volunteered to establish this "back channel" to the South Africans. It was no secret, however, that he had nurtured a friendship with a South African military attaché in Washington—a man named DuPlessis—whom he had met during the course of his graduate studies, and who shared with Pollard a common interest in Roman military history.

Recalled Pollard: After one of the Navy's air carrier battle groups had complained about the lack of intelligence support in the South Atlantic, he was called into Captain Thomas Brooks's office. (Brooks was Pollard's immediate supervisor at the time and later became the director of Naval Intelligence.) Pollard claims Brooks then questioned him very closely about his contacts with influential South Africans, particularly DuPlessis. A few days later, Pollard was asked whether or not he would be willing to establish a relationship with DuPlessis's successor in Washington. It was only then—after getting the okay from the director of Naval Intelligence and an operations team from the CIA—that he went to the South African embassy and created a so-called back channel. Meanwhile, Pollard was given very firm ground rules as to what he could discuss and was carefully debriefed after each meeting. "About three months later," Pollard said, "the South Africans asked if I could be assigned to the American embassy in Pretoria as an assistant to the Naval attaché—something I reported to the Navy—when all hell broke loose."[2]

Once the story came out that the U.S. and South African intelligence services were in fact developing closer ties, Pollard said the CIA wanted him to be immediately reassigned for overseas duty. Pollard felt he would be a convenient scapegoat for the whole sordid affair since he did, after all, have a prior relationship with a South African military attaché.

According to Pollard, the Naval Investigative Service (NIS), on the other hand—perhaps looking for a way to embarrass van der Westhuizen after the press leak—decided, instead, to charge Pollard with being a "South African mole" who was attempting to penetrate the U.S. embassy in Pretoria. To prove his "loyalty," Pollard said, the Navy then ordered him to place some incriminating documents on one of the South Africans— something, Pollard insisted, he had to refuse to do on moral grounds.

"Perhaps I'm naive," Pollard said, "but I had given my word to the South Africans that I had the authority to open up a back-channel. So when I said I wouldn't follow through with this 'sting operation'—I was descended upon by the Navy with a vengeance."

Like *The X-Files'* Agent Mulder getting "too close to the truth" and having the "Cigarette-Smoking Man" right on his trail, Pollard claims he was subsequently picked up one night by four agents as he was taking out the garbage from his apartment, taken to a motel room, actually handcuffed to a chair, and interrogated. Furious, the next day Pollard claims he stormed into the office of his commanding officer at NIS—a Captain Hoffman—and told him that if the matter wasn't resolved, he was prepared to take his case to a private attorney and sue the Navy. The following afternoon, Pollard recalled, he was "examined" by a Navy psychiatrist and declared mentally ill and unfit for further duty.

When he again protested to Captain Hoffman, Pollard says he was offered two options: Either he would resign from Naval Intelligence "without prejudice," or he would get fired and have the record indicate that he had been declared psychologically unbalanced. Pollard says he then brought this up with the Naval Intelligence Command inspector general who told Captain Hoffman that unless matters were "equitably resolved," he would have to formally address Pollard's complaints.

With the inspector general now apparently on his side, Pollard's next step was to see a second psychiatrist who, Pollard says, gave him a clean bill of health. According to Pollard, this "absolutely infuriated NIS" which insisted that Pollard again be reexamined, this time by a "Company" (CIA) psychiatrist. Claims Pollard, after the CIA psychiatrist concurred with the second psychiatrist, however, Hoffman had no choice but to give him back his clearance and previous job in the surface ship division. "It was everybody's understanding that the matter was over and that there would be no repercussions, which there weren't," Pollard insists. "My subsequent promotions were all approved. And my additional clearances were granted without any reservations."

But for Pollard, his problems with the Navy were only just beginning. And although he had no way of knowing it back then, this connection between himself and the government of South Africa would, indeed, one day come back to haunt him.

NOTES

1. Pollard insists Dine listened to what he had to say and even offered him a job as an advisor—which Pollard politely turned down. Dine admits meeting with Pollard but denies ever offering him a job. When I spoke to Dine he said it was Pollard, not he, who raised the issue of employment.

2. In an article that appeared in the October 12, 1996, *Jerusalem Post International Edition*, Brooks, the director of Naval Intelligence from 1988–91, is quoted as saying about Pollard: "I thought he was a bit eccentric. I thought he was very bright. For a while, before he had clearance and access to classified information, I sent him to the Library of Congress to read Soviet writings. Later, a senior civilian in my command came to me and said Pollard was saying some bizarre things. My instructions were to watch him. After a while, it

became clear that this man was unbalanced. He was moved out of my place and taken to another command. I never gave it another thought. Then I learned he was working somewhere else in Naval Intelligence and later he was arrested for spying."

CHAPTER 6

THE MAKING OF A SPY

As his security clearances increased, Pollard also found himself becoming increasingly frustrated over instructions he received from the office of Defense Secretary Weinberger. Pollard believed those instructions—which in essence prevented him from giving anything "of real value" to the Israelis—were in clear violation of the 1983 U.S.-Israel bilateral exchange of information agreement which was signed by Weinberger's boss, President Reagan. "In essence, the material I was authorized to give Israel had been so sanitized and distorted," Pollard said, "that, to the Israelis, it was essentially worthless."[1]

Pollard recalled that his supervisors at Naval Intelligence nevertheless kept emphasizing that his department could only pass on enough information to "scare the hell out of the Israelis," but not enough so the Israelis would be able to do anything about what they learned. It was around this time, too, Pollard said, that one of his supervisors leaned over his shoulder and commented about possible fears the Israelis may have had concerning Arab countries arming themselves with biological and chemical weapons. "Jews are too sensitive about gas," Pollard claims his supervisor told him.

In 1984, Pollard, then twenty-nine, went to hear a lecture by Col. Avi Sella, the Israeli air force ace who had helped lead Israel's successful air assault against Syrian warplanes in the 1982 war in Lebanon. Pollard first learned about Sella from a family friend, stockbroker Steven Stern. Stern had previously heard Sella speak in New York when the Israeli war hero gave a lecture in front of a group of Jewish stockbrokers to help stimulate the sale of Israel Bonds. A charismatic man, Sella knew how to keep his American audiences spellbound by weaving tales of dogfights and aerial warfare. Intrigued by Sella, Stern had asked Pollard if he would like to meet with Israel's "top gun."[2]

"When I told Stern about my frustrations over the Defense Department's withholding of vital information from Israel, and as a result was considering resigning and making *aliyah* (going to Israel to live), Stern asked me to delay my resignation from Navy Intelligence until I at least had a chance to meet with Sella," Pollard said. "According to Stern, once I met with Sella 'other options' might be available. I understood what Stern meant, and he knew that I knew what he meant. As my polygraphs later established, I had exactly two conversations with Stern pertaining to Sella before my first meeting with him."

As a near legendary pilot of the crack Israeli air force, Sella had to have what author Tom Wolfe called "the right stuff." Pollard, as a U.S. Navy Intelligence analyst—who was torn between either resigning from his job or finding a way to help the Israelis—no doubt possessed the "right stuff" to entice Sella as well. With that in mind, Sella agreed to meet with Pollard. He would hear what Pollard had to say.

On May 24, 1984, Pollard and Sella met for coffee in the lobby of the Washington Hilton Hotel, only a short walk away from Pollard's Washington apartment. Wolf Blitzer's recounting of Pollard's answering the phone call during which the initial meeting was set up was described as "totally ridiculous" by Pollard.

While Blitzer's book, *Territory of Lies*, was an extraordinary work of journalistic research by a topflight reporter who later rose to be CNN's White House bureau chief—and for the most part was extremely balanced throughout—Pollard nevertheless found fault with much of the book. One such section that particularly irritated Pollard had to do with that first phone call from Sella. And, indeed, Blitzer's description of it did appear to play into the government's stereotype of Pollard as a bumbling "wannabe," who was, at the same time, a dangerous enemy of the state. Blitzer wrote: "'Shalom,' Pollard replied, jumping up from the chair, literally standing at attention as he held the phone. He couldn't believe how excited he became simply hearing Sella's low but pleasant voice." Pollard wrote to me, however, that he never "jumped at attention" when Sella called, and he certainly didn't use the word "shalom" over the telephone. "Since we never discussed this incident," Pollard noted, "how can Wolf claim to know how I reacted when Sella called? I think Wolf is trying to categorize me as a Jewish equivalent of Sergeant Shultz."[3]

Like two topflight boxers sizing each other up in the first round, each man was actually a bit wary of the other when they met that day in the Hilton. "Our conversation was incredibly discreet and circumspect," Pollard recalled. Nevertheless, Pollard felt he could basically trust Sella because he had carefully read the Defense Intelligence Agency's biographical sketch of the Israeli. Still, Pollard insisted, at the beginning of the conversation he made sure to choose his words carefully. Eventually, Pollard said, he got to the point. Laying his cards on the table, he admitted he was willing to hand over to Israel certain classified information he felt Israel was entitled to, but was not getting. He said he also made it clear that there would be no business relationship established, and that he was not looking to get paid for his services. Sella, convinced Pollard was on the level, replied that his government had no interest in "spying" on the United States—but did have some genuine interest in finding out just what the Arabs and Soviets were doing. The distinction between spying against his own country and helping Israel was not lost on Pollard. That distinction, Pollard felt, was an important one.

Pollard suggested an arrangement for setting up future meetings between them. Concerned about using his home phone, Pollard handed Sella a list of pay phones in the area and assigned each of the phones a corresponding Hebrew letter which Pollard had already memorized.

When Sella returned to New York he contacted Yosef Yagur who in turn contacted Rafi Eitan—the head of the Israel Defense Ministry's Office of Scientific Liaison (LAKAM or LAKEM)—in Tel Aviv.[4] Having been given the green light to proceed by Eitan, Sella arranged a second meeting with Pollard. That meeting took place on July 7, 1984, again in the lobby of the Washington Hilton. After meeting in the lobby, both men walked to Sella's car which was parked in the hotel garage. They then drove to a park. After a short drive, they found a space just opposite the park where they could keep an eye on the car while they talked. As Pollard had suspected, the park was virtually deserted, save for a few dogs and sleeping sunbathers. Since there was a large cemetery behind them, they were free to conduct their business in relative safety.

Pollard this time brought with him a brown leather briefcase literally bulging with highly classified documents and satellite photographs. The Israelis obviously did not have the spy satellite technology that American intelligence had. And while the Mossad took second place to no other spy agency in the world regarding the ability of its agents to gather information from within other countries—the exploits of masterspy Eli Cohen, who, disguised as an Arab, managed to rise to the top of the Syrian government before his masquerade was discovered and he was hanged by the Syrians in 1966, have been well documented—spy satellites were not part of Israel's espionage arsenal.[5] So handing Sella an aerial photo of the bombed-out Osirak nuclear reactor in Iraq—taken virtually hours after Sella himself had led the mission to destroy it—no doubt impressed Sella, but, at the same time, had to also cause him a great deal of anxiety. How come, he must have thought, was he not privy to this information before?

Spying, although risky, can be a monetarily rewarding enterprise. Of course, not all spies do it for the money and Pollard has always claimed he became a double agent strictly for ideological reasons; he was not in it to get rich. It was in the Israelis' interests, however, that Pollard begin doing it for the money. This way, they felt, he would feel obligated to continue his activities on their behalf. And as long as he wasn't caught, the Israelis figured, everyone would benefit in the end.

"Money never even entered into my calculations when I first went to the Israelis," Pollard said. "I originally intended to restrict my espionage activities to a few months at most, and then resign from the Navy. All I ever really wanted to do was ensure that the Israelis received the material which had been withheld from them in contravention of the bilateral intelligence-sharing agreement (signed by President Reagan in 1983)."

As Sella began to identify all the other information which had never before been exchanged, however, Pollard began to feel that Sella was describing "a disaster just waiting to happen." Pollard soon found himself being asked to significantly extend the period of time that he would be working in a clandestine capacity for the Israelis, although he admittedly had never envisioned the operation lasting more than a few months.

What the Israelis began proposing, Pollard said, was a full-time job with everything that entails in terms of increased risks. This is how the concept of "a second salary" came into the picture. Pollard said he reluctantly decided to take the money the Israelis were offering. He did this, he claimed, in order to confirm his association with Israeli Intelligence, as well as allay any anxiety he felt at the prospect of exposing himself to the danger of what he was doing. "In a sense, then," Pollard said, "the money was used as a narcotic to overcome my natural inhibitions."

The exchange of money would also compromise the Israelis, just as it was being used by the Israelis to compromise Pollard. As a result, Pollard and the Israelis were no longer merely linked in spirit. The money he would get from the Israelis was not, in and of itself, sufficient to tempt him to become a long-term Israeli spy, however. Rather, it was the list of what Pollard described as the "intelligence deficiencies" that Avi Sella showed him during the course of their second meeting that ultimately proved decisive in moving Pollard away from his original intention.

Pollard stressed that during the second meeting with Sella he also became acutely aware of the exact extent to which Israel was "suffering" from Secretary of Defense Weinberger's undeclared intelligence embargo against the Jewish state. "As I came face to face with the grim reality of what was going on," Pollard recalled, "the money, more than anything else, became a means to an end."

But, regardless of his original motives, Jonathan Pollard was now hooked. For all intent and purposes, he had become a full-fledged spy.

The Navy's Anti-Terrorist Alert Center (ATAC) had been in business for only seven months when Jonathan Pollard began working there in June of 1984. Torn between possibly quitting Naval Intelligence on the one hand, and working his way up the ladder on the other, Pollard felt that, at ATAC, he would perhaps be in a better position to help what he considered to be his "brethren" in Israel.

On July 19, 1984, Pollard took a number of documents out of his files at Naval Intelligence—which included information on new Soviet weaponry in Syria—and brought them to the home of Ilan Ravid, a science counselor who was with the Israeli embassy in Washington. At the meeting at Ravid's home, Pollard was told by Sella that he would have to fly to Paris to meet "the old man" (Eitan). The reasoning behind this was that, in the United States, there was the possibility that both Eitan and Sella could be recognized (and compromised) if they were seen together. Pollard, at the time, was not yet privy to Eitan's identity, but he was admittedly curious. Still, he wasn't particularly intrigued by who "the old man" was. Insisted Pollard: "I had gotten to know a lot of so-called old men in my profession—and they usually turned out to be little more than self-promoting bureaucrats."

The idea of having to fly all the way to Paris to meet with Sella's boss, however, was something that certainly did not sit well with Pollard. He objected to the Paris venue throughout the course of this meeting, due to the fact that he could not afford to make this kind of trip. But when he raised the possibility of meeting Eitan in Canada, Sella told him this was out of the question even though he understood that Pollard could drive to such a meeting and would not have to clear his trip with the NIS security office. Canada, Pollard countered, was inexpensive, close at hand, and safe, given the fact that nobody from his office would know he'd ever been there for a long weekend. Nevertheless, Pollard recalled, none of those arguments made any impression.

The Israelis instead concocted a cover. Pollard had recently become engaged to Anne Henderson, the young woman he had been living with since 1982. So the trip abroad would be an engagement gift from a wealthy (but fictitious) "Uncle Joe Fisher." Wolf Blitzer, in *Territory of Lies*, noted that Pollard liked that idea. Pollard disagreed, saying he thought the idea was "ludicrous." The sudden appearance of a rich uncle who had presumably underwritten his expenses would never wash. Pollard explained to Sella that as part of his background investigation at Naval Intelligence, he had to provide the names of all relatives who were living abroad. Clearly, "Uncle Joe Fisher" was not on that list and this fictitious person's sudden appearance would almost certainly arouse suspicion. Nevertheless, the Israelis refused to budge.

No amount of money was discussed at the July 19 meeting. Since in reality there was no rich uncle, Pollard was told he would instead have to make his own arrangements to get to Paris. Once he was there, the issue of compensation would then be addressed. When he told Sella that he could barely afford to pay for the airline tickets for himself and his fiancée, Pollard was advised to take a loan out from his credit union, which he ultimately did. Then there was the issue of hotel bills which were beyond their means as well. Recalled Pollard: "In response to this problem, Avi told me to put everything on our American Express card."

Pollard was also hit with a second bombshell that day. He was informed by Sella that he would have a new "handler" whom he would be introduced to in Paris when he met the "old man"—and that Sella was being ordered to return to Israel.

Pollard was sorry to see that Sella would be leaving the operation since the two had become friends. And Sella himself was not content to be replaced without a fight. He repeatedly asked Pollard to insist that he be retained as Pollard's handler. "It was evident that Avi liked the prospect of traveling on an expense account," Pollard quipped.

Perhaps most importantly, Sella wanted to stay close to the new information he was being provided, especially since much of it dealt with the Syrian air defense establishment. It was only natural, Pollard surmised, that his friend Sella wanted to see this information as soon as possible rather than wait for it to be filtered first by LAKAM and then by Israeli air force intelligence. After all, one of Sella's responsibilities at the time was to design anti-surface-to-air missile (SAM) tactics which required the most current assessment of an enemy's technical capabilities.

Pollard again went to Ravid's home nine days later—on July 28, 1984—and gave the Israelis more important documents. According to Pollard, there was still no exchange of money.

Two months later, Shimon Peres, of Israel's Labor Party, became Israel's prime minister. In an unusual arrangement, after two years were up his role in the Israeli government would flip-flop with that of Likud Party leader Yitzhak Shamir who would initially serve under Peres as foreign minister.

Around the same time, in early October of 1984, Pollard heard that a daytime position at ATAC (he had served on the night shift) was opening up. He applied for the position—which made him a research specialist for the Caribbean—and got the job.

It was only weeks later that Pollard flew to Paris with his fiancée, Anne Henderson, just as the Israelis had instructed him to do. During a taxi ride to the "safe house" in the center of Paris, Pollard said Sella reminded him over and over again of the same thing. He told him to insist that he remain as Pollard's handler. Pollard recalled that this was also discussed during a meeting he had with Sella in the Tuileries, the day before his scheduled meeting with Eitan. Sella kept stressing that there was no reason why he should be replaced by someone who would not be able to appreciate the full value of the intelligence Pollard was providing on the Syrian air defense network.

"It's so remarkable how uncontrolled this whole operation was," Pollard recalled. "Here was Sella, who was supposed to act as a calming influence upon me, pursuing his own agenda behind Eitan's back. Making things even worse, however, was the advice Avi gave me: 'Never, under any circumstances, trust Rafi,' he said."

Pollard met with Eitan three days after his arrival in Paris. Eitan got into specifics concerning what he needed from Pollard in terms of intelligence gathering. Pollard laid his cards on the table as well. He told Eitan that he would refuse to provide Israel with any kind of intelligence information that could be used against the United States. Under no circumstances would he spy against his own country, he said. Nor would he ever compromise the names of American agents. His objective, he told Eitan, was to help Israel, but not if that meant hurting his own country.

Later, Pollard would insist that, contrary to the "distorted portrait" of himself that has been drawn by many "misinformed" individuals, he was not some "wild-eyed true believer" who operated under the simple premise that any act could be justified as long as it was done on behalf of Israel. Pollard called this a crucial distinction between his case and the case of, say, the Walkers.

A latent danger Pollard faced, not surprisingly, was that of American "moles" operating within Israel's intelligence services. Aware of the danger those moles could pose to his own operation, Pollard maintains that he still refused to find out who they were. In essence, while he was certainly not a well-trained spy, he claimed he tried to operate within a "set of guidelines" which would have him avoid doing any damage to the United States—even if it meant accepting a far greater degree of risk to himself.

During his meeting with Eitan in Paris, Pollard was also told by Sella to go to Mappin and Webb—a jewelry store on the Place Vendome—and to ask for an Algerian-born Jewish salesman who would suggest a "suitable" present for Anne. Although the money eventually spent on the diamond—$7,000—was later seen as "proof" of Pollard's monetary seduction by the Israelis, Pollard said he had no choice but to buy it. "According to Eitan, since my 'Uncle Joe Fisher' was a diamond broker, it would only make sense that he offered such a gift to my fiancée," Pollard said.

Yet it was also obvious to Pollard that, by throwing his money around, he could easily risk drawing unwanted attention to himself, something no spy in his right mind ever wanted to do. Moreover, when he left Paris—as the Israelis instructed him to—and traveled with Anne to Saint-Tropez, Cannes, Monte Carlo, Munich, and Rome, it was as if he was leaving a trail for all to see.

It was a trail, he knew, that could soon be coming to an abrupt end.

Pollard would eventually settle into a kind of routine regarding his work with the Israelis. Approximately three times a week he would visit various intelligence libraries at the Defense Intelligence Agency (DIA) and the Naval Intelligence Support Center (NISC). If he found anything the Israelis had asked him to collect, he would bring those documents back to his office and store them in his safe. Pollard was especially concerned with documents that, when officially presented by the United States to the Israelis, had various paragraphs or pages blacked out. LAKAM wanted those originals and Pollard would try to provide them. At first, Pollard was asked to provide only the censored parts of the documents. On one particular occasion, though, he was asked to bring in the entire document because the Israelis had even discovered some problems with the *officially* transferred data when they tried using it in the field.

Much to their chagrin, the Israelis found that not only were they being denied information they needed, but that some of the legally obtained intelligence had actually been doctored. "At that point," Pollard said, "alarm bells started going off, since no one knew what percentage of all the other information which Israel had received was 'cooked' as well."

Fortunately for Pollard, almost everything was on microfiche. If not, he would have literally had to "haul tons of material" around Washington. And although he had no way of confirming it, he was told by the Israelis that roughly 10 percent of the officially transmitted information was found to be faulty.

During July of 1985 Pollard took another overseas trip, this time to Israel. Staying with Anne in a house outside Tel Aviv, Pollard was told that the home's owner, a man named "Uzi," would replace Yagur (who had in turn replaced Sella) as Pollard's handler.[6] Blitzer maintains in his book that the Israelis, at that time, asked Pollard to step up his activities on their behalf—and immediately upped the ante—something Pollard categorically denies.

According to Pollard, during a meeting he had with Yagur, a day before he was to again meet with a now bedridden Eitan, he explained to Yagur that he was "burning out" and wanted to redirect his activities. Yagur understood where Pollard was going: that he wanted to resign from the Navy since he could no longer manage what had become two stressful jobs at the same time. Pollard's intent was to finish his covert collection efforts at the end of the year. At that point, he would no longer be a double agent.

Pollard maintains that Yagur never pushed him to expand his information-collection activities. "In fact," Pollard said, "he asked me to slow it down, even though he would get screamed at by Eitan for doing so."

Not surprisingly, when Pollard did finally tell Eitan that he wanted to resign from the Navy, Eitan "nearly went through the roof," Pollard said. After all, Pollard was Eitan's "key to the kingdom," and had made Eitan look like a genius to his superiors in Tel Aviv. Either the Israeli leadership didn't know, or didn't want to know, where Eitan's valuable information was coming from. Certainly, they would have been surprised to find out that, rather than running his own well-honed intelligence network, what Eitan had been providing the Israeli government was mainly the work of one well-placed person: Jonathan Pollard.

So it was only when he threatened to stop his spying activities altogether that a desperate Eitan decided to sweeten the pot. The risks, Pollard told Eitan, were becoming just too great. Eitan, knowing he was about to lose Pollard, then brought up the option of a Swiss bank account.

Pollard said he at first objected. "However, Yagur called me aside and suggested that I go along with him since Eitan, who was about to have eye surgery, looked like he was going to have a stroke right then and there if I didn't."

Nevertheless, with the way the account was set up, Pollard was not going to have unimpeded access to it. He was prevented from withdrawing any money without Eitan's authorization. Moreover, it was clearly understood that no funds could be withdrawn until ten years had passed. However, in the event Pollard was captured, Eitan assured him that Anne would have access to the account as a safety net.

Yagur wasn't so sure. He admitted there would probably never be the additional $270,000 in a Swiss bank account that Eitan had promised. And Pollard kept hearing the words in his head that Sella had said, over and over again, about Eitan. "Never trust him," Sella warned.

NOTES

1. By the time of the first intelligence sharing conference, Pollard—who was a Navy representative at these meetings—had already received two Outstanding Performance Awards. Army and Air Force Intelligence, as well as the CIA, also had their own representatives on the American delegation.

2. In *Territory of Lies*, Wolf Blitzer writes that Stern's lawyer, Jonathan L. Rosner, told the *New York Times* that Stern had no idea that the initial Pollard-Sella contact would eventually lead to espionage. Stern testified before the fed-

eral grand jury investigating the case and was never charged with any crime. Pollard believed, however, that Stern was a "talent spotter"—a deep-cover Israeli agent who spots individuals who are suitable for intelligence organizations, either as agents (spies) or as intelligence officers.

3. A harmless, bumbling prison guard in the television series *Hogan's Heroes*, who often proclaimed, "I know nothing, I hear nothing, I say nothing."

4. Rafael "Rafi" Eitan is not the same person as Gen. Rafael Eitan, an Israeli military hero and the subject of a book, *A Soldier's Story*, published by S.P.I. Books. Rafi Eitan was also the Prime Minister's Special Advisor on Terrorism before he was replaced by Amiram Nir in September of 1984.

5. Cohen was executed in Syria on the morning of May 19, 1965, although heads of state, the Vatican, and various statesmen appealed to the Syrian authorities to spare Cohen's life and give him a fair trial. According to Reuters News Service, before the sentence was carried out, the verdict said Cohen was to be sentenced to death "in the name of the Arab people in Syria after being found guilty of entering a military place in disguise and obtaining classified information and passing it to the enemy." The Egyptian-born Cohen, who was forty years old at the time of his death, had come to Syria by way of Beirut in 1962, carrying the passport of a Lebanese emigrant in Argentina and using the name of Kamel Amin Thabat.

6. Yagur was the resident *katsa* for LAKAM in New York. A *katsa* is the equivalent of an American case officer—an intelligence officer who runs agents and agent networks.

THE GOLDEN GOOSE

On August 9, 1985, in a civil ceremony in Venice, Italy, Jonathan Pollard and Anne Henderson were married.

The Israelis provided a passport for Pollard to be used when Pollard made *aliyah*, and "came home" to Israel. Pollard recalled that once he made up his mind to help the Israelis by providing them with American intelligence secrets, his decision to eventually move to Israel had already been made. "The dilemma in my mind was over," Pollard said.

The Israelis gave Pollard both an Israeli passport with the name Dan Cohen written on it, and the numbers of the Swiss bank account opened for him using that same name.[1] But after he signed the signature cards, Pollard realized that the whole process of opening up the account would be an exercise in futility. Pollard had been told by Yagur that Eitan was unlikely to abide by his financial promises. "In reality," Pollard said, "when Yossi [Yagur] opened up my account, Eitan told him not to deposit any funds." At the time Pollard was arrested, four months after the Swiss account was activated, according to Yagur there was still no money on deposit.

During his preliminary hearing after his arrest, Pollard would tell his accusers that he never used the thousands of dollars he admitted had been given to him by the Israelis in order to purchase items such as gold jewelry for his wife.

Actually, it was an important Saudi Arabian contact who had become number one on Pollard's gift list. According to Pollard, he had made a number of contacts with well-connected Saudis during his two-year stay at the Fletcher School of Law and Diplomacy at Tufts University in Boston. He continued to nurture those relationships over the years. His Saudi friends knew that Pollard had begun working for Naval Intelligence. What they didn't know was that their friend was spying for Saudi Arabia's sworn enemy, Israel. "One particular Saudi contact cost me a lot of money," Pollard said. "That money was spent on airline tickets, hotel rooms, dinners (cash, not credit card), and—how shall I put this diplomatically—'companionship.' I also gave him roughly $6,000 worth of jewelry for his daughter, wife, and mistress."

Pollard offered no apologies. He said the monies were "well spent." It was through this same Saudi that the Israelis first learned of President Reagan's secret decision to ship several hundred Stinger missiles to Saudi Arabia in return for their support of the Contras. This man also provided Pollard with documentary proof that Defense Secretary Weinberger was discussing the "Israeli threat" with various Saudi officials, including Prince Sultan, the Saudi minister of defense.[2]

Pollard's Saudi friend alerted him to something else as well—an impending development that was causing a considerable amount of consternation back in Israel.

By October of 1985, the Saudis were seriously considering a request to allow a select group of Syrian pilots to qualify on the F-15. According to Pollard's source, the objective of this arrangement was to permit the Syrian air force to develop a better understanding of Israel's tactics and capabilities. Pollard said that although he was able to obtain enough information via the U.S. Air Force attaché in Riyadh to confirm the story, he was arrested before he could learn what decision the Saudis had made with regard to the Syrian request. According to Pollard, Wolf Blitzer was also aware of this, but failed to mention it in *Territory of Lies*, despite the fact that if the "truth was learned" it no doubt would have jeopardized future sales of sophisticated military hardware to Saudi Arabia.

Yagur, meanwhile, was fully aware of Pollard's decision to resign from the Navy at the end of 1985 and also of Pollard's plans to redirect his efforts toward the Saudis. In fact, the week the Pollards were arrested someone from the Saudi embassy left a message on their answering machine indicating that Anne—who was doing freelance public relations in Washington—should bring a public relations proposal in for the Saudis' consideration.

It was possible that through the public relations efforts of his wife, Pollard could have nurtured an even closer working relationship with the Saudis. Indeed, he figured that the possibility of having access to an office inside the Saudi embassy was a turn of fate almost too good to be true. For Pollard—who would have felt like a fox left unguarded in a hen-house—the Saudis conceivably could have yielded a virtual bonanza in terms of political and military intelligence.

As for his work with the Navy, which was hopefully soon to be behind him, Pollard felt he had already done his "job" of serving both his country of birth and his ancestral homeland. As for any feelings of guilt on his part, they were easily rationalized away. "I was told point-blank by the Israelis," Pollard said, "that the information I provided them would probably enable Israel to win the next Middle East war."

Kurt Lohbeck was a freelance journalist who, according to Pollard, was heavily involved with the Mujahedin "freedom fighters" in Afghanistan—particularly Abdul Haq, the resistance commander responsible for Kabul, Afghanistan's capital. Pollard said that during the course of his activities on behalf of Haq, Lohbeck also met and befriended the guerrilla's principal backer within Pakistani intelligence, a man named Hamza who was Pakistan's military attaché in Washington. "As I understand it," Pollard said, "Hamza was becoming increasingly agitated over the CIA's attempt to redirect some of the U.S. covert assistance to less fundamentalist groups within the Mujahedin."

Pollard charged that Lohbeck, like himself, was heavily involved in supercovert operations except that Lohbeck's operations were being run directly out of the National Security Council in Washington—and were personally being handled by National Security Advisor Robert McFarlane.

In *Territory of Lies*, Pollard's boss at the Anti-Terrorist Alert Center (ATAC), Jerry Agee, is quoted as calling Pollard's allegations "bullshit."

Pollard tells a different story. He said he actually got to know Lohbeck fairly well and even shared with him intelligence that pertained to certain Argentinean antitank missiles and Mistral SAMS—French-made surface-to-air missiles. "I had also given to Lohbeck a few unclassified maps of the Afghan border area which were nevertheless more accurate than the ones he had received from the Defense Intelligence Agency," Pollard stated.[3]

Mary Williams Walsh, Toronto bureau chief for the *Los Angeles Times* when I first spoke to her in 1993, often crossed paths with Lohbeck in Afghanistan, got to know him, and seemed to corroborate Pollard's allegations that Lohbeck was more than just the freelance writer he claimed to be. From 1983 through 1989, Walsh worked at the *Wall Street Journal* where she eventually became the *Journal*'s principal correspondent in south and southeast Asia, covering Pakistan and Afghanistan between

1987 and 1989. "It was in 1987, seven years after the Soviets invaded Afghanistan, that CBS put Kurt Lohbeck on contract as a long-leash reporter, its day-in and day-out eyes and ears on the war," Walsh wrote in a *Wall Street Journal* article that also appeared in the *Columbia Journalism Review* for January/February 1990. "Based in the Pakistani border city of Peshawar, he traveled into Afghanistan with the guerrillas, filming their operations, and filing reports."

But, according to Walsh, Lohbeck was hardly unbiased. "Lohbeck was a partisan of the Mujahedin and one of the guerrilla leaders, Abdul Haq, for whom he served in effect as a publicist," Walsh noted. "Moreover, other reporters claim that he sought by various means to shape their coverage of the war. There is even evidence to suggest that he tried to help put together at least one weapons deal for the Mujahedin."

Walsh noted that when Lohbeck was later asked about his relationship with Pollard, he admitted that while he had known Pollard socially, and had gotten information from him, he had done so "strictly in the spirit of journalistic inquiry."

"I received things from Jon Pollard," Walsh quoted Lohbeck as having said. "My employers were aware of that. Subsequently, the FBI was aware of that. The CIA was aware of that. I violated no laws, period."

During Pollard's closed hearing after his arrest, this Pandora's box involving Kurt Lohbeck was never opened. According to Pollard, there was a very good reason. The prosecution would have been hard-pressed to bring espionage charges against him in this particular case, Pollard said, since the information in question was not really "classified" in the "full sense of the word." However, Pollard added, he also let Assistant U.S. Attorney Charles Leeper know that if Leeper did charge him with passing secrets through Lohbeck to the Pakistanis, "then I was prepared to tell the grand jury everything I knew about a certain letter McFarlane wrote to Hamza." It was McFarlane who, in 1986, purportedly came in secret to Tehran, Iran, to discuss a cessation of Iranian support for terrorists in return for the delivery of spare parts for weapons.

"At around the same time that I was arrested, in November of 1985, the first shipment of Israeli Hawk SAMS had actually just been delivered to Iran," Pollard said. "It's my feeling that when Leeper or [U.S. Attorney for the District of Columbia] Joseph diGenova checked my story out with the National Security Council, someone there told the Justice Department to avoid the issue like the plague. And I think this is what happened, because whenever I mentioned my knowledge of the McFarlane letter to the FBI and intelligence-community interrogators, nobody took any notes. Nobody even suggested that I provide an affidavit for the record, which is rather strange. Not even Barry Culver, the FBI's chief polygrapher, was willing to test me on this subject. It's hard to imagine such a situation where a person who is accused of espionage is essentially turned down in this way by his interrogators."

Jerry Agee nevertheless said that when Pollard came to him at the time, and first told him about Lohbeck and his connection to both the Afghans and McFarlane, he felt Pollard was making up a pack of lies. Agee said he also became annoyed over Pollard's "lack of production." To Pollard, Agee's allegations of poor work habits, after the fact, were an attempt to later portray his underling as a man who virtually ceased working for the United States when he began working, on the side, for Israel.

Contrary to the image presented by Agee, however, Pollard insisted he was working "feverishly" for his boss at the time. An extremely comprehensive East German intelligence report had just been together by Pollard. His area was the Caribbean, and, according to Pollard at least, Agee didn't even know that the East Germans were active in the Caribbean. By the time Pollard was arrested, he had already finished and published the top secret version of the report and had begun to edit it down for dissemination as a secret-level document.

According to Pollard, three other lengthy reports he had published by the time of his eventual apprehension included: appraisals of the Grenadian Communist Party's support network in the United States; the Venezuelan Intelligence Services' Caribbean apparatus; and a report on the intelligence services of the eastern Caribbean including

Trinidad, Barbados, Jamaica and the Dominican Republic. He had also collaborated with a CIA analyst to produce a short assessment of Libyan activities in Martinique.

Pollard admits, however, that he was slow in completing a Domestic Terrorist Threat to Navy Assets report that he had been assigned in September of 1985. He explained that it wasn't until October of 1985, one month before his arrest, that all the research material he needed finally arrived from NIS.

Another report Pollard had been assigned to write dealt with domestic U.S. organizations opposed to U.S. involvement in Central America and possible connections those groups may have had with hostile governments. As far as the Central American paper was concerned, Pollard claimed this was really the responsibility of his assistant, Moira Lazada. "Moira was trying as hard as she could to finish it," Pollard said. "But Agee didn't appreciate the fact that I refused to put the screws to her—no doubt because he considered me 'too soft.' "

Pollard insisted that he was also bothered by the issue of the domestic surveillance assignment itself. He felt there was more to this project than just an academic assessment of organizations that were opposed to U.S. policies in Central America. What he was actually supposed to do, he felt, involved identifying which groups should be targeted for "black bag" operations: break-ins, electronic bugging, and harassment. Making matters worse was that he was expected to take full responsibility for this particular operation if it was compromised. Pollard said he therefore consciously sabotaged the project by refusing to compile a list of groups "which would have been subjected to this kind of treatment." (This operation was in many ways similar to the Counter Intelligence Program—or COINTELPRO—that was run by law-enforcement and intelligence agencies against U.S. citizens who were opposed to the Vietnam War. As one of my intelligence sources told me: "The whole program was as illegal as hell.")

Pollard said he was surprised that Agee was "brazen enough" to reveal to Wolf Blitzer that the domestic-surveillance project Pollard was to oversee even existed (since it is alluded to in Blitzer's *Territory of Lies*). "This clearly indicates," said Pollard, "that Agee stills feels that ATAC can essentially behave as if the Constitution doesn't exist."

By late October of 1985, Agee had became increasingly disturbed over the fact that Pollard was spending what, to him, seemed to be less and less time at the office. Once, when passing the desk of a clerk who was responsible for receiving and logging in classified material, Agee asked the clerk why there were top secret documents on his desk dealing with the most advanced Soviet weaponry which was being supplied to the Arab world. The clerk said the documents had been ordered by Pollard.

Heavily into his spying activities for Israel, Pollard, at the same time, realized he was facing a growing problem of logistics. What he decided to do with all the material he couldn't get rid of was to organize it into a small research library at ATAC which was available to all the analysts. Pollard said a major roadblock he still faced dealt with the kinds of documents that could not be returned to the library without possibly arousing some kind of suspicion. His first option would be to see whether a microfiche copy could be obtained. Unfortunately, much of the material he needed was so new and sensitive that the various intelligence libraries had not yet been able to produce any microfiche copies, which, due to bureaucratic delays, was a rather lengthy process. This was the material that he had to find a way to store in such a manner that it would be as inconspicuous as possible, hence the idea of an office library.

Pollard said he was not at all surprised that Agee later failed to mention this. "After all," Pollard said, "it's rather embarrassing that he was the person who had been thoughtful enough to appoint me the librarian in charge of it in the first place."

One of the repercussions of the *Achille Lauro* incident—the highjacking of an Italian cruise ship that took place in October of 1985, and was in retaliation for the Israeli attack on PLO leader Yasser Arafat's secret headquarters in Tunis—was that the Navy's Anti-Terrorist Alert Center began tightening internal security. Pollard was well aware of this. He also knew that while intensifying his efforts on behalf of Israel, he was running on a fast track which he would soon have to get off. No doubt, he was becoming increasingly disenchanted with U.S. foreign policy and how that policy seemed to be affecting Israel. But more and more he was convinced that he could not continue his spying activities forever, and that the odds were bound to catch up with him. For this reason alone, he said, he would have had no intention of participating in Eitan's ten-year scenario with a Swiss bank account dangling on a $300,000 stick. Still, the prosecution would later emphasize during his hearing (since he never had a trial), that it was the prospect of receiving the money which had figured prominently in Pollard's decision to spy for Israel—even though, in reality, this 'retirement fund' was not even mentioned by the Israelis until sixteen months into the operation. "And in no way," said Pollard, "did I have the burning desire to remain in Navy Intelligence for the ten-year period that Eitan required."

Agee, apparently becoming increasingly uncomfortable with Pollard (if not starting to get downright suspicious of his activities), asked Tom Filkens, another civilian analyst and Pollard's immediate supervisor, to warn Pollard that if the domestic organizations report (dealing with groups opposed to U.S. involvement in Central America) was not soon completed, Pollard would receive an official notice that he was shirking his duties.

The report in question was the one dealing with the surveillance of nonviolent domestic support groups. To Pollard, the report was tailor-made for someone like Filkens. Pollard alleged that Filkens had been forced to resign from an Army counterintelligence unit during the height of the antiwar effort, back in the late 1960s, due to his having conducted several illegal break-ins around Chicago. Charged Pollard, Filkens was quite proud of his previous activities and kept a copy of his discharge papers prominently displayed on his desk as a reminder, he said, of the power of "local subversives." Pollard said Filkens also had a large ashtray on his desk with the word "Auschwitz" written across it in Germanic letters.[4]

According to Agee, Pollard had put yet another nail in his coffin when he was four months late in filling out a routine form used for updating his background for security purposes. Pollard claimed the form was completed on time. "I really can't understand why Agee is lying about things that can be so easily checked out," Pollard said, adding that Agee's accusations sounded plausible enough, "particularly to those people who are unwilling to verify his allegations." But Pollard argued that it is well known within the intelligence community that if an analyst does not submit this document on time, his clearance will be temporarily suspended within twenty-four hours.

"Now, to people who have never worked within the intelligence community, Agee's claim sounds reasonable," Pollard allowed, "since isn't the government known for its inefficiency? But while that characterization might be appropriate for many branches of the federal bureaucracy, it would be incorrect to apply it to those offices which are responsible for updating the background security file of intelligence personnel."

In mid-September, Agee had supposedly again lost his patience with Pollard, following another in what, according to Agee, had become Pollard's all too common disappearing act. Pollard said that when he left his office during the day in question, he left a phone number where he could be reached. "I had left the office with a courier bag and analysts simply do not vanish in thin air," argued Pollard, "particularly when they leave an office with a satchel used for transporting classified material."

In *Territory of Lies*, Wolf Blitzer writes that Pollard, when again confronted by Agee, concocted a plausible story about where he had gone—to a job interview with a nongovernment Washington firm involved in foreign consulting work. But while Blitzer writes that Agee was "only too happy to learn that Pollard was thinking of leaving Navy Intelligence on his own since firing a civil servant can often be quite difficult," Pollard called this just another fabrication on Agee's part. "First of all," said Pollard, "I would have been in a rather awkward position standing there in front of Agee with a bag full of intelligence information. If I had admitted to having met with nonintelligence community personnel for a job interview, NIS security officers would have wanted to know the names of the people who were present during this meeting and exactly where it occurred. For doing what he claimed I did, Agee could have fired me right then and there if he had wanted to. He didn't."

More than ever, though, Pollard was determined to resign from the Navy and get off his tightrope. The fact that the much-publicized raid on PLO leader Yasser Arafat's headquarters had been such a major success— some of the intelligence the Israelis used was provided by Pollard—would nevertheless have no bearing on Pollard's future plans, and was still not enough to entice him to work even harder for Israel.

That brazen raid took place on October 1, 1985. Israeli F-16 fighters had flown an undetected mission of almost five thousand miles round-trip to bomb Arafat's headquarters in Tunis. (Arafat, who wasn't there at the time, was uninjured but the Israelis, making a point, demolished his secret residence.) It was an amazing mission in terms of the stealth required and the distance the bombers had to travel.

Actually, Pollard insisted, the period when he was really "working like a demon" preceded that particular airstrike and did not come after it. That's because right before the airstrike the Libyan army was poised to invade Tunisia, and American, French, and Soviet warships were suddenly pouring into the Gulf of Hammamet. The Algerians, meanwhile, were moving troops and air defense units up to their border with Libya in an attempt to deter Libyan leader Muammar Qaddafi from attacking the Tunisians. So with all this activity in the area, the "threat environment" was changing almost by the hour, which was complicating the Israeli plans to level Arafat's headquarters.

The Israeli air strike against Arafat's headquarters had actually been planned for some time. But when three Israelis were ruthlessly murdered at Larnaca Harbor, it seemed to be the appropriate moment for Israel to retaliate. The Larnaca incident had occurred just five days earlier, on September 25 (Yom Kippur), when a group of PLO terrorists (part of Arafat's Force 17) hijacked a yacht, anchored at Lanarca Harbor in

Cyprus, and shot to death the one Israeli woman and two Israeli men who were aboard.

Pollard—who had sent Israel critical intelligence on Tunisian air defense systems as well as information pinpointing the exact location of Arafat's headquarters—was horrified when, after the murders on the yacht were reported, a gory picture of the female victim was pinned up over the coffeemaker near his office. Next to the photo were the hand-written words: "Force 17: 3—Mossad: 0."

Although Agee didn't know what Pollard was up to—and he probably wasn't yet thinking in terms of espionage—he was continually finding Pollard in what could best be described as compromising positions. But Agee's perceptions no doubt began to change in the weeks following the raid on Arafat's headquarters. Blitzer points out in his book that Agee, along with Lanny McCullah (the agent in charge of counterintelligence at NISC Command in Suitland, Maryland), began to suspect that Pollard may have been working for a country other than the United States. And since almost all classified U.S. military secrets found ordered by Pollard consisted of extremely sensitive documents on Middle Eastern arms shipments—as well as Soviet military technology which was being sent to the Middle East—it was logical to assume that Pollard was working for Israel. He obviously wasn't working for the Soviets, Agee deduced. Why, after all, would the Soviets be interested in buying back their own information?

Pollard said he wishes this point of logic was later introduced into the record during his closed hearings as part of his defense team's rebuttal of the government's claims of damage assessment. "Here we have Agee and McCullah, two veteran Naval Intelligence officers, stating that the Russians wouldn't even be interested in seeing the type of material I was collecting," Pollard said. "In a sense they were right, of course, since most of the intelligence involved Soviet military exports to the Arab world which the KGB presumably already knew about. The Russians were also well aware that most (if not all) of the weapons involved in these transfers are going to be compromised—somewhere along the line—either by being captured by the Israelis or by being sold to Western intelligence agencies."

Pollard added that while Arab security procedures tend to be "rather inadequate," organizations like the CIA and the British MI6 can in fact usually obtain an operator's manual within a few weeks after a given weapons system has been loaded off a Russian merchant ship.

But what the Soviets would have been interested in, Pollard maintains, was the fact that hardly any of the intelligence reports he was collecting were being shared with Israel. "That, in and of itself, I think, would have amazed the Soviets."

In *The Samson Option*, a controversial book by Seymour Hersh, it is alleged that Israeli prime minister Yitzhak Shamir okayed giving Moscow U.S. intelligence on the Soviet Union obtained by Pollard, and that the prime minister—who had always wanted to improve relations with the Soviet Union anyway—therefore gave Moscow a sanitized version of what Pollard had given Israel.

Pollard, although unaware of the validity of those allegations, admits that the KGB did have an interest in knowing the *degree* to which its activities in the Middle East were being monitored by the CIA and other Western intelligence organizations. But did the KGB really need to see the actual material Pollard was providing Israel? "Considering the reams of information the Soviets had received from people like (Soviet spy) John Walker, the Russians had access to things that were completely off-limits to myself as a Naval Intelligence analyst," Pollard said.

According to Pollard, by the end of 1984 the Soviets had also succeeded in building a computer that could crack the National Security Agency's encoding system. "When you add in the fact that the entire CIA apparatus in Russia had been compromised by Clayton Lonetree and Edmund Lee Howard (a former CIA employee who, after offering his services to the Soviet Union, defected there), the assertion that my collection activities represented a potential intelligence boon for the Soviets begins to look rather preposterous."

Pollard concluded that in light of those successful Soviet espionage operations, Agee and McCullah were probably correct, therefore, in feeling that the Russians would basically be disinterested in what he was passing on to the Israelis. Argued Pollard: "It kind of makes the government's case against me look a bit ridiculous."

Jonathan and Anne Pollard began gaining a good deal of weight in the months preceding their arrest, "proof," to some of Pollard's critics, that the two were merrily reaping the benefits of spying for Israel while eating in some of Washington's fanciest restaurants and spending money like drunken sailors. Pollard had a different explanation. He claimed he was working so hard that he didn't have the time to exercise. As far as Anne was concerned, Pollard said her rapid weight gain was due mainly to her illness. (Anne Pollard suffered from a rare stomach disorder that kept her from digesting food properly.)

On November 16, 1985, Avi Sella and his wife, Yehudit, came to Washington and arranged to have dinner with the Pollards. Pollard had previously told Sella about how much the Marrakesh Restaurant would remind him of Israel and Sella was excited about the prospect of eating there. However, Pollard had taken his Saudi contact there for dinner, the evening before, and was hesitant to go back. He especially didn't think it was that wise to again be seen in public, this time with an Israeli air force ace who was known to quite a few of the Air Force and Naval aviators in the Washington area.

Pollard, who for obvious reasons did not want to draw any unnecessary attention to himself, said he explained his concerns to Sella, "over and over, but I could not get him to agree to eat dinner at our apartment which I thought would be far more secure." When he realized that Sella was "absolutely determined to have a night out on my new expense account," Pollard suggested they instead go to La Maree. The reason Pollard chose La Maree, an expensive Washington restaurant, was twofold, he said: Firstly, the owner/maitre d' was a personal friend and would be able to secure them a fairly discreet table; and secondly, La Maree's clientele was "old world," and was unlikely to include any American fighter pilots.

After Sella agreed to this "compromise," the Pollards met the Sellas at their hotel room. They all went down to the hotel's basement garage and for about twenty minutes Pollard and Sella had a private discussion. Although Sella was no longer Pollard's handler, four topics were discussed during the impromptu meeting: the raid on Tunis; the status of the Saudi-Syrian negotiations over the F-15 training; the location of a complete SA-5 missile complex which was then en route to either Syria or Libya; and Pollard's Saudi contact.

"As far as the air strike against the PLO headquarters, Avi described to me, in great detail, how useful the material I had provided Israel had been," Pollard said, "and that he knew exactly where the information had come from the minute he saw it." According to Pollard, the raid was also "a hell of a lot more complicated than people think."

The possibility that the Saudis would actually permit a group of Syrian pilots to familiarize themselves with the F-15—which was the backbone of the Israeli air force—was meanwhile quite troubling to the Israelis. "I assured Avi, however, that between my Saudi contact and the U.S. air attaché in Riyadh, I was in a very good position to monitor this situation," Pollard said.

Another issue that was of major concern to Sella was the destination of the SA-5 missile complex. If the three Russian merchant ships carrying the system crossed the Aegean Sea in an easterly direction, then they were undoubtedly headed for Syria, Pollard reasoned, and Syria would then be in a position to complete its high-altitude air-defense network. On the other hand, Pollard said, if the ships were headed in a southwesterly direction, then Libya was the ultimate destination and the Israeli air force could breathe a little easier—at least for the moment.

Since he hadn't seen any new military construction activity in Syria, Pollard felt that the missile system was probably en route for "storage in Libya." Once again, he promised Sella that he would stay on top of the situation.

The last topic Pollard discussed with Sella was his future plans with his Saudi contact. He had first told Sella about his Saudi contact while he and Anne were in Israel the previous summer. Eitan had evidently been keeping Sella up to date since Sella knew all about the covert Stinger missiles sale and Weinberger's discussions about this with the Saudis. Pollard said Sella had apparently also been talking with Yagur since Sella was "well aware of my plans to resign from the Navy at year's end."

It was at this point, Pollard said, that he told Sella about his intention to repay all the money he had received from the Israelis during the course of his working as a spy.

"Avi just shook his head when I told him this and made a comment that Eitan would probably go through the roof when he learned about my intentions. According to Avi, Eitan couldn't stand agents with morals."

Once again, Pollard said, Sella was trying to tell him something, but he just wasn't listening hard enough. If Sella was trying to let Pollard know that—when push came to shove, and it was every man for himself—Israeli intelligence simply wouldn't be there to take it on the chin and bail the American agent out, it was perhaps something Pollard was not yet ready to hear. Obviously Sella knew something that the somewhat naive Pollard didn't.

During Pollard's trip to Paris, when he first met Rafi Eitan, the Israelis had discussed with Pollard an alternative means of compensation. This was in response to Pollard's concerns regarding how damaging his salary from the Israelis would appear in the event he was captured. Eitan had suggested, at the time, that someone like stockbroker Steven Stern could give Pollard a larger apartment as a wedding gift in lieu of other payment. In this way, Pollard said, his "salary" from the Israelis would take the less sensational form of indirect compensation.

According to Pollard, the idea was mulled over for a while and then abruptly dropped by Eitan, who once again insisted that Pollard receive a straight salary. Pollard said the next time the issue arose was during his visit with Eitan in the latter's hospital room in Israel. Pollard started off by complaining about the unrealistic pace with which he was expected to satisfy his collection requirements. Then, he mentioned how the operation's environment in Washington was becoming much more dangerous due to the Reagan administration's obsession with "leakers" and Communist bloc agents. Finally, Pollard bitterly objected to the fact that no one had bothered to show him the escape plan which was supposed to be activated in the event that he was "found out."

Pollard said he wondered how effective this so-called contingency plan really was. He asked Eitan whether he knew how many entrances there were to his (Pollard's) apartment building and if the place could be modified by contractors without arousing suspicion. Eitan just listened with undisguised amusement to Pollard's litany of concerns without comment. When Pollard finished, Eitan once again reassured him that the escape plan would work, but that, if it made him feel any better, perhaps it would be appropriate for him to look for a more secure place in which to live.

In retrospect, Pollard said, this was merely part of Eitan's effort to keep him working for LAKAM for as long as possible. Eitan, who had no desire to lose his golden goose, even ordered Pollard to find a "safe house" which could also be used by other agents besides himself. Pollard insists this reference to "other agents" was no doubt one of the elements that later convinced the Justice Department that he wasn't working alone.

"Here I was, complaining about my lack of security," Pollard said, "and Eitan wanted me to operate a 'safe house' for Israeli agents. This certainly wasn't what I had in mind. First of all, I wasn't supposed to bring any of my Israeli colleagues home under any circumstances. Second, I really didn't think it was advisable to turn our apartment into a grand salon for Argentine arms dealers, Saudi bureaucrats, and Mujahedin guerrilla chieftains." Furthermore, Pollard said, by September 1985, his Saudi contact had already offered to buy him an apartment—in recognition of their "friendship."

In the weeks preceding his arrest, Pollard continued to pass a great deal of intelligence information to the Israelis. What especially touched a raw nerve with his Israeli handlers, Pollard quickly found out, had to do with the vital satellite photos that Israel wasn't getting but which the Saudis apparently were.

Although this is not classified, the U.S. government never went out of its way to publicize the fact that it had sold a LANDSAT ground station to Saudi Arabia. In an effort to reduce suspicion that the satellite photos being taken were of sensitive military targets in neighboring states, the Saudis were technically supposed to share what they had with any nation in the region that requested to see it—including Israel. "Needless to say," Pollard said, "Israel has been waiting patiently for quite some time for the Saudis to abide by this obligation."

Though bothered by this development, the Israelis were not terribly concerned by this Saudi space-based snooping. The reason was that the imagery derived from the aging LANDSAT system was not considered to be of good military quality. Then Pollard came along and discovered that the Reagan administration had quietly sold a LANDSAT imagery enhancement package to the Saudis which essentially gave them a rudimentary satellite reconnaissance capability.

Making matters worse was the fact that when the Israelis turned around and asked the Department of Defense for a comparable system, they were turned down without so much as an explanation. While it was true that the satellite photos Pollard provided Israel were better than anything the Saudis had been able to obtain through their modified LANDSAT system, the point that was especially disconcerting to the Israelis was that the United States was bending over backward to provide the Saudis, as well as even the Iraqis, with satellite intelligence in the first place, while at the same time denying that kind of assistance to Israel, the one country in the region that needed it the most.

A number of developments actually troubled Pollard during the period of Sella's November trip to Washington. For one thing, Sella wasn't traveling with a diplomatic passport, making him subject to arrest if something unforeseen happened. Then there was the Mistral SAM deal with Lohbeck which, Pollard feared, "was coming apart at the seams." Pollard said he was also genuinely worried over the SA-5 convoy. Sella had more or less intimated that if the SA-5 missile complex arrived in Syria and not Libya, the need for some kind of preemptive strike by the Israeli air force would be given a great deal of consideration. And in the event the Israeli cabinet did decide to knock the system out before it became operational, Pollard's tasking for this operation would make the research for the Tunis raid look like a "walk in the park."

For Pollard, there were other pressures, as well. He felt uneasy about his decision to resign from the Navy, and kept asking himself whether it was right to put his own fears ahead of what he genuinely felt was in the best interests of Israel. Then there was Anne. His wife's illness was becoming more and more acute. She was suffering from "incredible pain which never seemed to end." Pollard struggled with the concept that he had somehow jeopardized his wife's welfare on the altar of his own nationalism.

Pollard remembered a conversation he had had with Sella in Paris. Pollard had told Sella that if "anything happened," Sella should do whatever he could to rescue Anne. "I could have endured anything as long as I knew that Anne would be safe," Pollard said. "It was these kinds of thoughts which continued to haunt me."

Although he knew it was risky, Pollard decided to make one more intelligence "drop" before again meeting Sella and his wife for dinner. At the same time, Agee and McCullah, like two bloodhounds, were now hot on Pollard's trail. Meanwhile, Irit Erb, the attractive young secretary in the Israeli consulate in Washington, was supposed to be waiting for some new material from Pollard. Pollard's instructions were that if Irit was not around during the scheduled drop-off time, Pollard should return the following Monday and try again.

The material Pollard was going to be delivering to Erb that night was time sensitive, however, and had to be passed on as soon as possible. Part of it dealt with the SA-5 complex which, as a relieved Pollard had correctly guessed, was headed for Libya, not Syria. Other material pertained to a new type of SAM guidance frequency that had just been identified at a missile site in northern Syria. Explained Pollard, the Syrians test all their new equipment in the north so as to be as far from Israeli intercept stations as possible. But the "crown jewel," Pollard said, was a complete layout of the MIG-29 cockpit, which would permit the Israelis to create a realistic computer-generated target to "fly" against during video exercises.

After calling his wife on the evening of November 18 to say he was coming home, Pollard—carrying a package containing TOP SECRET documents —left his office at Naval Intelligence. When he got to his car at about 5 P.M., a group of FBI and Naval Investigative Service (NIS) agents were in nearby cars waiting for him. The hounds had finally cornered the fox.

NOTES

1. Pollard's official code name was "Dan Cohen" but this was only known to a handful of senior Israeli officials.

2. According to sources this man has been idenified as Ahmed Tashkandi, a diplomat working in the Saudi Arabian embassy in Washington. Not only was Tashkandi an excellent target of opportunity for Pollard, he also qualified in three out of four categories on the MICE scale. MICE—an American acronym used by all the intelligence services to evaluate an individual's vulnerability to recruitment as an agent—stands for Money, Ideology, Compromise, and Ego. Pollard "false flagged" Tashkandi, meaning he gave him the impression he was working for one country while in reality he was working for another.

3. In *Territory of Lies*, author Wolf Blitzer says court documents reveal that Lohbeck did have a relationship with Pollard and that Pollard gave Lohbeck classified documents. Lohbeck himself admits to knowing Pollard in his book *Holy War, Unholy Victory*, which includes a foreword by Dan Rather of CBS News. However, Lohbeck says it was Pollard who sought him out, and not the other way around. Lohbeck insists he was nothing more than a journalist who had cultivated deep contacts with Afghan freedom fighters and that much of what has been said about him by Pollard and others is a fabrication.

4. Tom Filkins could not be reached for comment to either confirm or deny Pollard's numerous accusations, including Pollard's claim that Filkins had to resign from an Army counterintelligence unit in the 1960s and that Filkins had an ash-

tray on his desk with the word "Auschwitz" written on it. Those I spoke with at Naval Intelligence said they had no record of Mr. Filkins, but could only confirm that he no longer worked there. A number of Navy spokespeople said they also had no forwarding address or phone number for him. My attempts to contact Jerry Agee, to respond to Pollard's charges, were equally unsuccessful. Again, the Navy said it had no record of Mr. Agee, but spokespeople said that he, too, was no longer employed by the Navy.

TRAIL
OF
SECRETS

It was after 7 P.M. when Pollard called his wife. During his conversation with Anne he used the word "cactus," a code word meaning he was in danger. Still being questioned by the FBI and NIS agents, he also managed to concoct a story. He said he actually had been taking the documents found in his possession to Andy Anderson, another Naval Intelligence analyst. The story was, of course, a lie. But Pollard was trying to buy time for both his wife and Sella.

According to Pollard, Anne did not know what the other incriminating documents stashed at their apartment were. But she did know that for her husband's sake the documents would have to be removed from her home. "Anne simply couldn't leave me to my fate," Pollard said. "I know that had our roles been reversed, I could never have abandoned her. Certainly cold-blooded spies can do that sort of thing without hesitation, but we were a married couple whose lives revolved around each other."

Pollard knew that if his wife remained in Washington, she would have no choice but to get rid of those documents as best she could. (She would later be prosecuted because those very same documents were linked to her). One problem Anne had, however, was that it would be difficult leaving the apartment with a suitcase filled with documents while at the same time not drawing unwanted attention to herself. It was quite obvious, Pollard suspected, that his and Anne's apartment was being staked out by FBI and NIS agents.

Anne Pollard could have just thrown the material in the trash. But not knowing whether her husband would need them again, she decided to ask her next-door neighbors—Christine and Babak Esfandiari—for help.

Pollard stressed that although his wife had those documents in her hand, she never had any intention of handing this material over to Avi Sella or anyone else for that matter. Handing the classified information over to Sella could have been logically construed as making Anne an accessory to her husband's espionage activities. But this scenario, Pollard insists, never occurred.

The plan instead was for Babak Esfandiari to bring a suitcase filled with the documents to the Four Seasons Restaurant. (The Esfandiaris wound up contacting Naval Intelligence after they became suspicious of what was contained in the suitcase.) Anne would then stash the documents in a storage locker in either Arlington or Alexandria, Virginia. Pollard admits there was a subsequent meeting between Anne and Sella. "But this was only for two purposes," Pollard said. "The first purpose was to alert Avi that I was in trouble; the second was to get Avi out of the country as fast as possible. At no time, though, did Anne even contemplate transmitting any classified information to him."

Andy Anderson was the "other analyst" Pollard said he was giving his TOP SECRET documents to. Pollard knew his deception would be found out, but he knew also that Anderson was not on watch that night and would—hopefully—be difficult to quickly locate. Continuing to "disemble," Pollard said his story about Anderson broke down at about 10 P.M. "by which time everyone was too tired to continue."

Although Pollard said the government subsequently portrayed this interrogation as "successful," what had to be embarrassing to the government was how easily his wife was able to evade all the surveillance agents who had been posted around their building. If Pollard's objective had been to buy time and not get arrested in the process, then it would seem that he accomplished his goal. "Although the Anderson story was finally discredited," Pollard said, "I did not simply roll over and present my head on a platter to the FBI by bringing Kurt Lohbeck into the picture." (Lohbeck was the freelance journalist who was involved with the Afghan freedom fighters. He was later used by Pollard as a ruse to temporarily get the FBI off Israel's trail.)

Pollard, in reality, had no idea what the government actually knew about his activities. He kept telling himself that the longer the attention of the NIS and FBI agents was focused on him, the easier it might be for Sella to escape—which he did. Also, in the event the Israelis decided to mount a rescue operation for Pollard, he had been able to maintain his freedom of movement long enough—since he had not yet been arrested—for a rescue operation to, in fact, be put together.

Although Pollard's stories began to slowly unravel, he maintains to this day that nothing was ever found in his possession that in any way related to U.S. weapons and military capabilities. "If that was the case, then it surely would have been trumpeted by the prosecution during my trial. It wasn't."

Pollard insists that subsequent interrogations confirmed the fact that his tasking by the Israelis had specifically excluded anything having to do with the United States. The only exception to this rule occurred during the Tunis raid, Pollard admitted. But, in this case, the government was apparently more concerned with the alleged damage Pollard had done to U.S.-Arab relations, by facilitating this operation, than anything else. "True, I had passed on to the Israelis the location of U.S. warships in the Gulf of Hammamet," Pollard said. "But since the Russians had maintained visual contact with every American surface ship in that body of water during the brief crisis between Tunisia and Libya in the fall of 1985, the information I provided Israel could hardly have compromised any ship in the U.S. Sixth Fleet. As these particular ships were literally eyeball to eyeball with the Soviets during that delicate period of time, I'm quite sure Russian Naval Intelligence knew exactly where they were."

Pollard had the opportunity to turn Sella over to the American authorities, but chose not to. If he and his wife had betrayed Sella, Pollard speculated, they might have received far less severe treatment at the hands of the U.S. government later on. Yet betraying a "friend," Pollard said, was never an option.

However, he believed his "true friend" was Yagur. Yagur knew that Pollard was an ideologically motivated nationalist. Yagur also knew how the money received as payment from the Israelis would be perceived if Pollard was caught. Unlike Sella and Eitan, the main thing Yagur was getting out of the Pollard operation, Pollard believed, was the satisfaction of serving the State of Israel. The information Pollard was providing did not figure as prominently in Yagur's professional agenda as it did in Eitan's and Sella's. "For them, I was really just a means to an end when you get right down to it," Pollard said. "For Yagur, on the other hand, I was a friend about whom he cared very much."

Of course, Yagur also fully appreciated the value of the information Pollard was passing on to Israel. But Pollard believed that Yagur was also concerned with his friend as an individual. Said Pollard: "If he did like and admire me, it was probably because he understood both the basis of my attachment to Israel, and the depth of my commitment to her survival."

The next morning, Tuesday, November 19, 1985, Pollard appeared at the NIS office for a scheduled polygraph test and to again be grilled by NIS and the FBI. The test was delayed when Pollard began to talk. He was questioned for over eight hours.

Still stalling for time, and still trying to keep the fresh scent off the Israelis, Pollard began telling the NIS and FBI investigators about his "relationship" with Lohbeck. He explained that Lohbeck was a confidant of Brigadier Hamza, the Pakistani military attaché in Washington. He also gave a very detailed description of Hamza's secure office which he said Lohbeck had told him about several months before.

According to Pollard, when one of the FBI agents returned from checking that story out, there was a look of consternation on everyone's face in the room. They didn't know at the time that this was just another bit of misdirection courtesy of the man they were interrogating. Especially troubling to the FBI was the fact that some of the documents on Pollard's desk dealt with Soviet military options vis-à-vis Pakistan. "One of the interrogators asked me if I had shown any of that material to Hamza," Pollard remembers. "My answer was as ambiguous as possible; my words said 'no' but my whole physical demeanor said 'yes.' " Pollard said the same interrogator later told him that the FBI actually began surveillance on the Pakistani embassy and Brigadier Hamza's personal residence shortly after the November 19 session.

If nothing else, Pollard was beginning to create confusion. During the interrogation held on November 20, Pollard reluctantly substituted Lohbeck for Irit Erb (the secretary at the Israeli consulate who was the conduit through which Pollard passed on classified information to the Israelis), and Hamza for Pollard's handler, Yagur. "This was the day I took the plunge by finally 'admitting' that I was supplying intelligence to the Pakistanis," Pollard said.

That afternoon the FBI drove Pollard to Lohbeck's house (Lohbeck was not home) where Pollard pointed out where he thought Lohbeck was storing the material he had allegedly given Lohbeck to copy. Pollard claimed he even had a floor plan of Lohbeck's house to show the agents that he had, in fact, been inside. "So to say that the FBI, at this time, thought the Israelis were involved with the operation would be way off the mark. The only country mentioned at the time was Pakistan."

Pollard decided to add fuel to the fire. Later that day, he casually mentioned to one of his interrogators that he had met a certain individual at Lohbeck's house several months before, and that the man had invited him to come to East Germany. "I knew that since the man was a suspected East German agent, alarm bells would start going off all over the FBI, thereby complicating the whole interrogation process. But the fact that I had only read about the man in a file was beside the point, since the only thing I now wanted to do was start a jurisdictional struggle over me between competing FBI sections. And that, I thought, would give me two or three more days of freedom before the roof finally caved in."

It was later thought that Pollard might actually have been working with a Warsaw Pact country. According to Pollard, those rumors were little more than a direct result of his attempts to stall for time while leading the FBI down a winding, but fictitious, trail.

Still a free man, Pollard knew he would have to make a bold move. On the evening of November 20, he went to a phone booth and called his friend Yagur. But as had been the case during the previous few days, there was no answer on the other end. Pollard had repeatedly been told by the Israelis that if he ever fell off his precarious tightrope, there would be an Israeli net waiting underneath him. If there was such a net, he was having great difficulty finding it. Later that same evening, Pollard decided it was about time to collect on a debt owed. He went to a phone booth and placed a call to the Israeli embassy in Washington.

The decision to contact the embassy was an act of desperation on Pollard's part. Over the past two days he had repeatedly called the emergency number he had been given by Yagur without success. Yagur never answered his phone and no one had attempted to pass on instructions to Anne Pollard who, recalled her husband, "was literally walking around Washington, not knowing what to do."

When he finally got the duty officer at the embassy, Pollard's plan was to see if he could somehow contact a member of his "team" who could then tell him what in the world was going on. At the time, Pollard was still under the assumption that an escape plan was in the works. But as Pollard mentioned each member of his spy team, the security officer indicated that the person in question was no longer in the United States.

"I was thunderstruck," Pollard said. "Who, I asked, was in charge of getting us out?"

On the other end of the line, Pollard recalled, there was a long pause. Finally, the man answered. "Jerusalem wants you to 'come in.' "

"Come *in*? Come in *where*?" Pollard asked. "The embassy?"

At that point, Pollard said, he realized everything had been virtually turned upside down. Nevertheless, the embassy official was quite clear in his instructions. Pollard was to come to the embassy.

According to Pollard, the last thing he was told was to call back the following morning to coordinate his movements with embassy security. When he called the Israeli embassy on the morning of November 21, Pollard told the security officer that he would be coming to the embassy at around 10 A.M. following his wife's endoscopy. Anne's recurring problem—a stomach disorder known as biliary dyskinesia—was no doubt worsened by the incredible stress caused by the ordeal she was going through with her husband.

"The only things the embassy official asked me were what color and make our car was and whether I thought I could make it to the embassy without being detected," Pollard said. "I told him, quite bluntly, that it would be impossible for us to shake surveillance given the number of agents who would be expected to accompany us to the hospital." The last instruction Pollard said he received was that he should drive all the way down the embassy ramp and park in front of the underground garage.

At this point, Pollard said, it was doubtful that the FBI had suspected that the Israelis were involved with his activities because, if they had been, they would have been monitoring every call into the embassy. "The fact that I was allowed to drive right into the Israeli diplomatic mission while being 'convoyed' by literally scores of FBI agents suggests that my dissembling may very well have been more effective than either the FBI or NIS would care to admit."

In *Territory of Lies*, Wolf Blitzer writes that Pollard was "determined to shake any surveillance," and was "confident that he had done so." Pollard again takes issue with Blitzer. Pollard said the route he took was actually chosen so that his final approach to the embassy would be along a two-lane road, thereby ensuring that the FBI would not be able to have a car alongside his own when he turned onto International Drive, the road leading directly to the embassy. "Surveillance during this trip was extremely heavy and far from subtle," Pollard explained. "As we drove up Wisconsin Avenue, Anne and I could see at least six FBI cars: two in front of us, one to our left, two to our rear, and a communications van further back. So there was no way I was under the impression that I had somehow eluded them."

Blitzer also writes that several unmarked FBI cars followed Pollard, with one dropping off his tail before another picked up the surveillance. Although the FBI description was right out of a movie script, Pollard maintains that the "tail" was far from subtle.

"All the FBI cars assigned to follow us were government-issue Chrysler K-Cars equipped with black sidewall tires and HF antennas on the trunk," Pollard said. "If this wasn't obvious enough, there were four agents per car, each one of whom was wearing sun glasses which was rather odd given the overcast nature of the day. We even thought of waving at some of the agents, but decided not to press our luck."

But Pollard's luck ran out that day just the same. Although the guards at the embassy welcomed him, he and his wife were not going to be allowed sanctuary there. Pollard began swearing at the security officer in Hebrew, but nothing he could say—whether in Hebrew or English—would do any good. It is assumed that the Israelis, caught in an embarrassing no-win situation, decided to leave Jonathan Pollard out in the cold. (An Israeli intelligence source told me he strongly believes that Elyakim Rubinstein, who was in charge of the embassy that day—since Meir Rosenne, Israel's ambassador to the United States, was in Paris—"just panicked, and blew the effort." If Rosenne had been there, my source said, Pollard may not have been turned away. Rubenstein would eventually become Israel's attorney general.[1])

Pollard, now a man without a safety net, or, perhaps, even a country, was arrested the moment he drove off the Israeli embassy's compound.

Jonathan Pollard claims he first met Kurt Lohbeck (a man, Pollard said, whose father had once been a political advisor to Louisiana governor Huey Long) in 1984 when Lohbeck was introduced to him as a freelance journalist who was deeply involved with the Afghan freedom movement. "On the surface," Pollard said, "he appeared to be a legitimate correspondent who was willing to accept great risks on behalf of the Mujahedin—particularly those groups which were being funded by the Saudis and the Pakistanis. However, I soon found out he had another agenda that was less altruistic."[2]

Insists Pollard, a very close friend of Lohbeck's happened to be a Pakistani military attaché in Washington who was letting Lohbeck arrange a number of arms shipments for the Mujahedin on the assumption that both he and Lohbeck would receive a percentage of the action. "From what I understood," Pollard said, "a member of the Saudi military mission in Washington was also involved in this little arrangement."

It was shortly after he began working for the Israelis in the spring of 1984, Pollard claims, that Lohbeck came over to his apartment to ask for some "advice."

According to Pollard, a friend of his had told Lohbeck that Pollard worked for Naval Intelligence and that he was knowledgeable about weapons systems, particularly small antiaircraft missiles such as the Blowpipe and Stinger. Alleges Pollard, when Lohbeck arrived, he had with him a videotape of an ambush in which the Mujahedin's antitank grenades were literally bouncing off Soviet tanks. "Making matters worse was the short range of the antitank grenades which were also wildly erratic in those windy mountain valleys."

Pollard claims Lohbeck got right to the point. "He asked whether I could help him arrange for better weapons to find their way into the hands of the Mujahedin. I told him I couldn't commit to that. I was already working for the Israelis, and I surely didn't want to complicate matters by running guns to Afghanistan."

Nevertheless, Pollard said, Lohbeck was persistent. So Pollard then took the matter up with Eitan when he first met with the Israeli spymaster in Paris. "When I described Lohbeck's connections and interests, Rafi said he would authorize my working with him," Pollard said, "provided I could get my hands on a copy of the MISTRAL—a deadly French equivalent of the Stinger missile, which several Arab armies were then considering purchasing in great numbers."

Pollard said he was told by Eitan that his relationship with Lohbeck was going to be carefully monitored and controlled by his new handler, Yagur, who was replacing Sella. Pollard claimed that in 1985 he therefore worked quite closely with Lohbeck on numerous deals involving Argentina (for guided antitank missiles) and South Africa (night vision scopes). But none of these deals, Pollard stressed, involved any classified information.

During the fall of 1985, Pollard said he finally began to make arrangements, through the French embassy in Washington, for a purchase of several hundred MISTRAL surface-to-air missiles. Israel would now supply goods to the Mujahedin through Pakistan. Alleges Pollard: "The way the deal was put together, Lohbeck was to provide me with valid Pakistani certificates which would satisfy the French that the cargo was being exported to a government rather than a guerrilla organization. Once the missiles had been loaded off in Karachi, Pakistan, Lohbeck was to have 'friendly' stevedores essentially highjack the shipment and forward it to Mujahedin bases."

But at this point, Pollard alleges, things began to unravel. And since this particular operation was a near blueprint for a somewhat parallel transaction that would take place a year later—and would go down in history as the ill-fated "Iran-Contra Affair"—it was not surprising, Pollard mused, that some of the key players were, in fact, the same.

"In order for me to get my hands on the missiles a number of them had to be 'skimmed' in Karachi, which necessarily required Lohbeck's assistance," Pollard explained. "But at the time Lohbeck was also heavily involved with fund-raising for the Contras on behalf of several Conservative PACS. And as luck would have it, I had also made the acquaintance of Contra leader Arturo Cruz's son, 'Arturito,' who apart from living above Anne and myself, was trying to establish a 'southern front' along the Nicaraguan-Costa Rican border with [Lt. Col. Oliver] North."

Pollard claims that when he suggested to Lohbeck that some of the MISTRALS be diverted to North's so-called southern front along the Nicaraguan-Costa Rican border, Lohbeck literally jumped at the idea. "To Lohbeck," Pollard said, "it was an opportunity not only for profit, but for an involvement in yet another anti-Communist crusade."

Eitan ultimately approved this rather complicated plan, Pollard said, then provided the name of a Panamanian "export-import" firm that was being used as a front for Israeli arms deliveries to the Contras. "Once the missiles were received by this firm," Pollard said, "one or two of them would disappear and that would be that."

Pollard insists everything was progressing "quite nicely" until Lohbeck introduced him to the man responsible for highjacking the missiles in Karachi—an Israeli graduate student at Johns Hopkins University who represented himself as a high-ranking Mossad operative. "I nearly died on the spot and hurriedly arranged a meeting with Yossi Yagur to report this bizarre development," Pollard said. "According to his embassy file, this fellow had absolutely no connection to the Mossad. It seems this enterprising 'graduate student' was actually a freelancer who specialized in moving Yugoslavian arms through Karachi via the Sufi Brotherhood in exchange for heroin which he conveniently dumped in Europe." (A top-level Israeli source of mine strongly doubts, however, that the Sufi Brotherhood was in any way involved in heroin trafficking. I doubt it, also. The Sufis are historically Islamic mystics who emphasize meditation and personal piety. They are usually people of great integrity. Former Egyptian president Anwar Sadat, for instance, was said to be a Sufi.)

Suddenly worried about the operation's direction, Pollard claims he told Lohbeck that he was on his own as far as this so-called Mossad agent was concerned.

Later on, Pollard insists, the French, South African, and Argentinean embassies all confirmed "they had dealings with me—but that those dealings were of an unspecified nature."

When Pollard eventually had to defend himself against charges of espionage, the government would make the case that his activities on behalf of Israel had caused some of the most serious damage ever to U.S. national security. But as Pollard's attorneys had argued many times, the government was in no way able to back up this exaggerated claim. The only apparent damage that the prosecution could prove he actually did to U.S. national security, Pollard's attorneys insisted, involved a temporary loss of negotiating advantage with Israel.

Pollard's attorneys were quick to compare his case to that of other spies such as John Walker and Clayton Lonetree. In those cases, they said, the government was quite willing to publicly cite specific instances where the information those spies provided to the Soviets had either endangered American forces or compromised U.S. agents. So why was the prosecution so reticent in the Pollard case to be as equally forthcoming with its evidence?

Perhaps, the attorneys argued, it was the weakness of the government's eventual case against Pollard that prompted Secretary of Defense Weinberger to embellish the classified record with a host of "worst-case scenarios" which involved the Israelis turning over all their "illegally" obtained American secrets to the KGB as payment for some kind of mass release of Soviet and Iranian Jews. Pollard described this scenario as totally absurd.

"Leaving aside the issue of Lt. Col. North's unauthorized transfer of highly sensitive information to Iran during the arms-for-hostages fiasco, the Israeli government has never given any indication that it was prepared to purchase the freedom of Iranian Jews with American supplied intelligence," Pollard said. "And the idea that the Israelis would be inclined to make this trade with a cache of stolen American intelligence reports might happen in third-rate spy novels, but not the real world."

The reason was simple. Once such an exchange had been discovered (as it certainly would have been), the Reagan administration would have immediately reduced whatever amount of intelligence it was officially sharing with Israel at the time. Given the negative impact this would have had on Israel's security, it seems highly unlikely that any Israeli cabinet would have authorized the type of self-defeating behavior that was outlined by Weinberger. "Moreover," said Pollard, "if the material I reportedly passed to Israel was so vital to her survival, why on earth would the Israeli government have passed it on to the Iranians, of all people?" (Actually, the Israelis did have their own Iranian operation going on at this time, "Aliea Capitolina," based in Rome and with the intent of moving Iranian Jews.)

To Pollard, the government's exaggerated accusations against him were in fact based on a true leap of logic. Using this premise, he would later question whether the life sentence in prison—which would be handed out as his sentence—was at all warranted by what he had done. As for his role in the Lohbeck affair, Pollard could argue that that was, ironically, not much different from the role of Ollie North in the Iran-Contra scandal. But while Pollard could not imply that he was taking his orders directly from the president of the United States, as North did, he could easily present the case that he was following the "intent" of a presidential order.

After all, he figured, in 1983 President Reagan had signed a bilateral exchange of information agreement with Israel. And it was the refusal of some of the president's underlings to live by the stated stipulations of that agreement, he could rationalize, that had forced him to become a spy in the first place.

On November 27, 1985—the day the Pollards appeared for a court hearing following their arrest—NSA employee Ronald Pelton and CIA employee Larry Wu-Tai Chin also stood before the U.S. District Court to face spying charges.

It was no wonder that 1985 was dubbed "the year of the spy."[3] However, most of the sentences previously given to persons convicted by U.S. courts of spying for non-Communist countries had been no more than five years. One such case involved a dissatisfied CIA employee (Sharon Scrange) who "compromised all the CIA's clandestine sources in Ghana—most of whom," Pollard said, "were eventually executed by the local regime."

As noted earlier, Scrange's sentence was reduced from five years to two years in 1986.

In 1967, an English court sentenced Norman Blackburn to five years for providing the South African Bureau of State Security with "extremely sensitive" cabinet minutes pertaining to the British government's contingency plans against Rhodesia, soon after that country announced its unilateral declaration of independence. According to a number of accounts, the British never seriously considered undertaking any military operations at the time due, perhaps, to their reluctance to become embroiled in a bitter colonial war with a group of heavily armed white settlers. At the same time, had the British government elected to reestablish crown rule by force of arms, it's clear that the information Blackburn compromised could have conceivably caused the deaths of British soldiers. In spite of this, the British courts chose to draw a distinction between Blackburn and others who had instead spied on behalf of the Soviet Union.

"I can only assume that the issue of Blackburn's motives must have figured prominently in the judge's mind since there was a considerable amount of sympathy that existed in conservative circles for the white

Rhodesians," Pollard said about the case. "Regarded in some ways as 'kin,' the Rhodesian settlers clearly did not constitute a threat to Great Britain in the same way that either the Soviet Union or its satellites did. It's quite likely, then, that Blackburn was seen not so much as an 'enemy' agent as much as he was a 'friendly' one."

A case involving the Israelis occurred in 1968 and centered around Alfred Frauenknect, a Swiss aeronautical engineer. Outraged over the arms embargo that French president Charles deGaulle had imposed upon Israel just prior to the 1967 Six-Day War, Frauenknect decided to give Israel the blueprints for the Mirage jet fighter which was then being produced for the Swiss air force. While the Swiss were extremely embarrassed over this incident, and feared the possibility of French retaliatory sanctions, their courts nevertheless felt that Frauenknect should be treated leniently due to the fact that his intent had not been to harm Switzerland, but to help a sister democracy—Israel. And although the Swiss government was no doubt furious over what Frauenknect had done, the Swiss judicial system still managed to ensure that Frauenknect (who wound up spending five years in a Swiss prison) receive a fair and equitable sentence.

Said Pollard: "I suppose this really illustrates the difference that exists between an independent court, and one which permits itself to be used as a vehicle for political retribution."

The ten-year sentence received by Thomas Dolce, an engineer employed by the U.S. Army's top-secret Aberdeen Proving Grounds, would also compare favorably to the life sentence eventually given Pollard. Argued Pollard, not only did Dolce turn over to the South Africans every piece of intelligence he could lay his hands on that dealt with Soviet military equipment; he also provided the South Africans with classified assessments of U.S. military hardware—which was something, Pollard said, that he never passed on to the Israelis. Moreover, despite the fact that no memorandum comparable to the 1983 U.S.-Israel bilateral exchange of intelligence agreement existed between the Americans and the South Africans, both the Justice and Defense Departments recommended the relatively lenient ten-year sentence.

Pollard has never questioned the leniency of Dolce's sentence, only the difference between that sentence and his own.

"South Africa is . . . an 'informal' member of the Western alliance," Pollard said. "However, I still think there should have been some clear-cut distinction drawn between Pretoria and Jerusalem, since the latter, after all, is a genuine ally of the United States."

Yet if the Reagan administration made a political decision to downplay the seriousness of Dolce's activities in deference to South African "sensitivities," Pollard's supporters have wondered whether Israel's status vis-à-vis the United States may not be as privileged as most Americans have been led to believe. "This could certainly explain why the Justice Department would eventually draw such different characterizations of Dolce and myself," Pollard said, "since by blackening the reputation of an agent, one blackens his cause as well."

Pollard said this belief that the U.S. government was creating a "guilt by association" scenario for Israel was based on more than just gut feelings. He learned how to do such things himself, he said, when he attended a countersubversion class taught by some of the very same Justice Department officials who would later prosecute him at his own trial. If the government seemed to have handled his own case more aggressively than the Dolce case, he insisted, this was definitely done for a reason.

The Helmy case appears to be another instance where the political aspects of an espionage trial have been of paramount concern to the U.S. government.

Abdel Helmy was an Egyptian-born U.S citizen who was accused of funneling highly sensitive ballistic missile technology to his native land. At the time of his arrest, on June 24, 1988, Helmy was a senior jet propulsion engineer who held a "secret"-level security clearance from the U.S. Department of Defense. According to intelligence sources, Helmy's activities were being directed by none other than Caspar Weinberger's close friend Field Marshal Abdel-Halim Abu Ghazala, the Egyptian minister of defense.

Pollard claims that his attorneys had access to a thirty-six-page affidavit filed by the U.S. Customs Service which stated that Helmy also worked with numerous other Egyptian diplomats and intelligence officials, including Admiral Abdel Elaohary of the Egyptian embassy's military procurement office; Lt. Col. Abdel Mahmoud, a member of the embassy's military liaison staff; and Col. Hussam Yussef, a high-ranking Egyptian air force intelligence officer. In addition, the affidavit stated that U.S. Customs agents searching Helmy's trash found handwritten notes outlining how to work carbon-carbon material used in rocket nose cones and "stealth" aircraft like the super-secret B-2 strategic bomber; instructions on building rocket exhaust nozzles; a description of an extremely sensitive microwave telemetry antenna; and a complete package needed to build or upgrade a tactical missile system.

Finally, although there is no public evidence linking Helmy directly with the Iraqis, intelligence sources have indicated that the Egyptians used Helmy's expertise to help Baghdad modify its stockpile of Soviet-supplied Scud-B ballistic rockets.

As for his role in all this, Helmy received a forty-six-month sentence in a minimum-security institution. His sentence was eventually further reduced to three years and ten months.

Helmy's principal responsibility, Israeli intelligence sources say, was to ensure the success of an Egyptian-Iraqi missile program which had encountered some developmental problems. Code-named BADR-2000 by the Egyptians and SAAD-16 by the Iraqis, this Argentine-designed weapon had an estimated range of between five hundred and one thousand miles and figured prominently in Arab strategic planning against Israel.

In what Pollard termed as "one of those ironic twists of fate which seem so commonplace in the world of espionage," he had been working independently on the very same missile as Helmy.

"Back in 1985, when I started collecting information myself on the BADR-2000, I'd decided the best way to cover my activities was to incorporate them in a phony technology-transfer investigation, which I had the authority to open in my capacity as a NIS counterintelligence officer. To all outward appearances, then, I was merely looking into the possibility that the Egyptians might be trying to recruit American engineers for their ballistic missile program. I had no idea that the Egyptians were actually engaged in just such a process.

"Meanwhile, after having been assured by the Reagan administration that no such missile system was under construction by the Egyptians, the Israelis asked me to find out whether or not they were being told the truth. Needless to say, the Pentagon had been monitoring the progress of the BADR-2000 very closely and had amassed an extensive amount of information about its performance characteristics and intended targets. The latter, in particular, did not please the Israelis in the least. It seemed that in spite of the nonbelligerency clauses of the Camp David peace treaty, the Egyptians had specifically insisted that the BADR-2000 be capable of reaching both military and civilian targets in Israel."

Perhaps most troubling of all, Pollard stressed, was the fact that the missile was configured to deliver either chemical, biological, or nuclear warheads with great precision. According to Pollard, this suggested that the Egyptians or the Iraqis might have wanted to use the system as part of a surprise attack against Israeli airfields, mobilization centers, and national command complexes.

"Clearly, if such an attack was successfully carried out," Pollard warned—one year before the modified Scud missiles were actually used in the Gulf War by Saddam Hussein—"it could make the attack on Pearl Harbor pale in comparison."

To put the lid on Pollard—and to keep that lid shut tight—the government often used its "protecting sources and methods" argument as a hammer. To Pollard's legal eagles, that scenario was little more than a smoke screen that had little or nothing to do with the government's tough stand on his turning over satellite photos (which included photos of Iraqi poison-gas facilities) to Israel. Instead, Pollard's attorneys insisted, this particular aspect of the government's case was 100 percent political.

Argued Pollard, perhaps no better proof of this can be offered than the fact that when the administration wanted to generate public support for an air strike against the Rabta industrial complex in Libya, it was quite willing to leak the facts that satellite photos existed which confirmed the construction of a poison-gas manufacturing plant at that facility.

In the instance of the Rabta industrial complex, sensitive "sources and methods" could be compromised because the Reagan administration wanted the world to know what the Libyans were up to. In the case of Iraq, however, the administration—with an eye toward Saudi Arabia —preferred to keep the magnitude of Iraq's chemical-weapons-production capability a secret.

Pollard said, in essence, what he did by passing satellite photos of the Iraqi poison-gas plants to Israel was endanger the Reagan administration's Middle East political agenda, therefore, and not the intelligence community's "sources and methods." The prosecution in his case, Pollard said, would nevertheless "wave its 'sources and methods' argument around like a red flag, due to its inability to specify exactly what damage I had done to U.S. national security." But the problem with Israel having access to U.S. satellite photos may have had little to do with security implications, and a lot more to do with political ramifications.

In *Territory of Lies* Wolf Blitzer wrote that the United States was concerned about a preemptive Israeli air strike against these Arab chemical weapons factories. Some Israeli intelligence sources say the issue was far more complex than that. What the Israelis were actually considering, they argue, was a preventive attack against the Iraqi facilities before they became fully operational. The rationale: Once those facilities went on line, and the Iraqis were able to disperse thousands of chemical munitions around the country, these plants, like the ones in Syria, would have only been targeted during wartime, or in the context of a clandestine sabotage campaign aimed at slowing their production of poisons. (Those fears, of course, would be fully realized during the Gulf War.)

It was this reasoning, Pollard said, that was behind the Reagan administration's desire to bomb the Rabta industrial complex before the Libyans had the opportunity to complete its construction. "The minute Rabta became functional," Pollard said, "Libya's ability to retaliate with chemical weapons would have acted as a powerful deterrent to any American attack against the facility. After all, when the dust had finally settled, Colonel Qaddafi could have wreaked havoc in the West by simply turning over some of his remaining chemical stockpile to a terrorist like Abu Nidal.

"But the crisis over the Rabta plant brings up an interesting question: If the Reagan administration felt justified in its desire to eliminate what it perceived to be an impending Libyan chemical threat to our own national security, why was it so unwilling to grant Israel the same right of preventive self-defense with regard to Iraq's poison gas manufacturing facilities?"

The Reagan administration meanwhile continued to assure the Israelis that Iraq lacked the expertise to produce these substances. The truth of the matter, though, was that the Iraqis had already secretly converted several of their pesticide factories into poison gas manufacturing plants.

Indeed, the Israelis learned through Pollard that the Iraqis were already breaking ground for one of the world's largest chemical warfare complexes. It would be designed by some of the same West German companies that were also involved with the Rabta project in Libya. And their partner, Israeli intelligence would later learn, would be none other than the mysterious Ishan Barbouti himself.

NOTES

1. Contrary to popular belief, there had in fact been a plan to bring Pollard "in from the cold." Back in the Kirya in Tel Aviv (Israel's Pentagon) word had gotten out that there was trouble concerning an operative in the United States. Avi Sella informed his air force boss, who in turn informed Gen. Ehud Barak (the same Ehud Barak who would eventually be elected Israel's prime minister) at AMAN (Israeli Military Intelligence). Officer's in AMAN's Unit 504 had begun to

talk about a rescue contingency. As AMAN hoped, Pollard (although few in Israeli intelligence knew the "Hunting Horse's" real identity) called the Israeli embassy in Washington. The problem was, no one in Unit 504 informed the Foreign Ministry that the embassy should take Pollard in. So Rubinstein, who knew nothing about the rescue effort, ordered the Pollards expelled from the embassy. Rubinstein has never forgiven himself for Pollard's capture, and has long been one of the most vocal voices in Israel demanding Pollard's release.

2. I was not able to reach Kurt Lohbeck to either confirm or deny Pollard's numerous allegations. According to an interview that appeared in *Jewish Week* (New York) on August 28, 1992, Lohbeck (a onetime state representative from Bernalillo County, New Mexico, who was convicted in 1977 of passing a worthless check) was described as the Southern California coordinator for the Pat Buchanan presidential campaign. During the 1992 primaries, I called the Southern California Buchanan headquarters, asking to speak to Lohbeck, or get a phone number where I could reach him, and was told, instead, to call Buchanan's main office in Virginia. When I called there, however, no one said they had a forwarding number for Lohbeck, and no one knew how he could be reached.

3. By the end of 1985 there were seventeen cases of espionage before the federal courts in the United States.

CHAPTER 9

TRUE BELIEVERS

O n March 10, 1995, the Associated Press reported that the root of the various Gulf War illnesses—which according to a number of intelligence sources was affecting more than fifty thousand men and women—remained a mystery. "One in six Persian War veterans suffering postwar ailments still cannot be diagnosed," the wire service story began, "but early tests indicate chemical and biological agents were not involved in any of the illnesses, the Pentagon's top doctor said. . . ." According to the AP story, Dr. Stephen Joseph, assistant secretary of defense for health affairs, stated that there "is no one unique, single, overriding cause of the illnesses that have afflicted thousands of Persian Gulf veterans and have come to be known as Gulf War syndrome."

The timing of the Pentagon's news leak was interesting. Just a few days earlier, on March 6, President Clinton said he was going to begin an investigation into the origins of those ailments that were commonly being lumped together under the Gulf War syndrome umbrella. Words such as "nausea," "fatigue," and "joint pain" had been frequently used by the media in the past in conjunction with the many-faceted disease—words no doubt also taken from Pentagon news releases seeming to indicate that Gulf War syndrome was really more of an inconvenience to its victims than anything else. Rarely did Americans get the impression that the disease was insidious and deadly.

Three months earlier, though, ABC's *Nightline* had aired a show that revealed something perhaps far more sinister. "My service in the Gulf War could be why my son has birth defects," Sgt. Brad Mins told the American public on December 27, 1994. Melanie Ayers, who also served in the Gulf, added: "I pray that it doesn't take hundreds and hundreds of dead children before somebody realizes that this is just not acceptable."

On March 5, 1995, the day before Bill Clinton made his promise to look into the causes of Gulf War syndrome, Carol Pollard, Jonathan Pollard's sister, was one of two guest speakers at the Coral Baptist Church in Coral Springs, Florida. I was the other. We were invited to address the congregation there because the church's pastor, Rev. Herschel Creasman, had been a longtime supporter of those trying to get Jonathan Pollard released from prison. Although I had listened to Carol speak many times—and had even shared a podium with her on a number of occasions—this time she told a story that I had never heard her tell before.

Carol said that she had recently met a former U.S. paratrooper during a cross-country flight. The soldier was in a wheelchair and Carol asked him if he had been injured while making a jump. No, he shook his head. He said he was in the wheelchair because he had become progressively disabled ever since a biological and chemical weapons attack against his unit in Saudi Arabia during the Gulf War. The weapons, he said, were contained in Iraq's Scud missiles and the deadly gases may have been spread when U.S. Patriot missiles shot them down. Carol asked the soldier if there was a cure for his disease and if he would eventually improve. The soldier replied that there was no known cure and that the disease would eventually make its way into his lungs and kill him.

While the soldier was obviously upset about his own fate, Carol recalled that the brave ex-fighting man was even more upset about the fate of his wife and daughter. The soldier's wife had a brain tumor—the result, he believed, of his sexual contact with her. His young daughter was born with a heart twice the size of a normal heart. The child's prognosis was bleak. It appeared that a whole family was going to be wiped out, just like the families of many other thousands of men and women who served their country while the Pentagon continued what, many now suggested, was an unconscionable charade.

The deepest roots of the Gulf War cover-up, William Northrop once told me, were not to be found in the desert sands of Saudi Arabia. Rather, Northrop said, those roots had taken firm hold, some twenty years earlier, in the thick jungle foliage of Vietnam. It was there that the worldview of many of the future Pentagon policymakers was literally molded and shaped.

During the Vietnam War, Northrop was a U.S. Army Special Forces officer who carried out secret operations behind enemy lines. After the war, he would eventually move to Israel where, using some of the unique skills he acquired as a Green Beret, he began working for Israeli intelligence. At the same time, he kept in touch with his old friend William Casey, who, in the 1980s, rose to the position of director of the Central Intelligence Agency.

In his book, *The Mafia, CIA and George Bush*, author Pete Brewton described Northrop as a "key liaison between the CIA and Israel in Central America during the early 1980s." Brewton added: "[Northrop] was pushed out after [Lt. Col.] Oliver North's 'Enterprise' ostensibly took over the Contra war from the CIA. . . . Congressional investigators found that Casey's phone logs showed him in frequent contact with Northrop, according to a May 1988 United Press International story about Iran-Contra."

In trying to explain the dynamics shaping the personalities of him and his fellow covert operators in the 1980s, Northrop reflected that the Vietnam generation of Americans seemed to grow up "in a cusp," a point of time when American society was transitioning away from the black-and-white 1950s and into the 1960s. "Their first great experience in life was the Vietnam War," Northrop said. "Nearly everyone who is involved [in covert operations] on the American side [in the 1980s] has Vietnam in common."

They also had military school in common. Whether it was Reagan National Security Advisor John Poindexter, or Gen. Richard Secord, or Oliver North, their lives were forever changed and their ideas molded by places like the Citadel and West Point. "The military schools make a very simple requirement of every cadet or midshipman," Northrop said, "and that is that he neither lies, cheats, steals—nor does he tolerate anyone else who does."

When this post–World War II generation matured and went to Vietnam, they carried along with them the values inherent in that system. But the Vietnam experience may have also succeeded in perverting some of the more positive values inherent in the psychological makeup of American military strategists of prior generations. Northrop emphasized that when he and his fellow military school graduates first went to Vietnam, they were all "blonde-haired, blue-eyed, all-American boys." Worse, Northrop said, "We were 'true believers.' So Vietnam was a trauma that all of us suffered."

A new generation shaping American foreign policy was in many ways a by-product of the Vietnam debacle. "Within the context of the Vietnam War are your cast of characters," Northrop said flatly. "We are all alike. How we view the world now is what makes the difference; it's what makes us friends or what makes us enemies. Where and when our agendas coalesce or depart is, above all, governed by the passage of history."

As for Jonathan Pollard, Northrop admittedly saw him as a kind of kindred spirit. He has always felt it was Pollard's strong beliefs that forced him into action when he felt that Israel's security was being threatened by an ill-conceived American policy, especially as concerned Iraq. "The Pollard case continues to fester," Northrop wrote in the January 1992 *New Dimensions* magazine, "because it still threatens to expose a secret, potentially controversial U.S. Middle East policy—the 'Level Battlefield Doctrine.' So sensitive is the American government on this matter, that President Bush once equated convicted terrorists being held hostage in Israeli prisons with Americans being held hostage by pro-Iranian terrorists."

But to Northrop, the so-called Level Battlefield Doctrine, which he and others insist has been the covert basis of American foreign policy in the Middle East, was a policy not formulated in the State Department in Washington, but was born in the royal palace in Riyadh, Saudi Arabia. "It was responsible for the Iran-Contra affair," Northrop told me, "and it contributed to the failed end of Operation Desert Storm."

Indeed, while the roots of the Gulf War cover-up may have extended all the way back to Vietnam, the Saudi kingdom—with its massive oil reserves and Bechtel corporation allies—certainly had the ears of the inner circle in the Reagan-Bush White House. Yet it's hardly a surprise that few Americans even knew of the so-called Level Battlefield Doctrine's existence. Secret political agendas are certainly not unheard of in Washington, and this is one that had all the markings of something the American government would not have revealed to Israel—or the American people.

For one thing, the doctrine was based on what many believe to be an inherently false premise: that it was Israel's "reckless use" of military force that destabilized the Middle East in the first place. And the doctrine was perpetuated on the assumption that a misguided American policy had erroneously backed the Israelis, thereby creating a vacuum into which the Arabs were forced to draw the Soviets. On the other hand, the doctrine's backers maintained that if the Jewish state could somehow be "curtailed"—and if the Arabs could be brought to military parity with Israel—then peace would naturally follow, while Soviet influence would be drastically limited.

The Saudis found fertile ground for their ideas in Washington when the Reagan administration took power in 1981. Defense Secretary Weinberger quickly bought into the premise that Israel had to be brought to its knees. Sources tell me that Weinberger gave his stamp of approval to a rebirth of the Level Battlefield Doctrine, which, as we shall see, may have first been "tested" during the presidency of Richard Nixon.

The term "level battlefield" was a fairly benign epithet that in fact masked the policy's truest intentions. The name was akin to the term "incident at altitude" used to describe a crowded jetliner blowing up in midair. Indeed, the Level Battlefield Doctrine's ramifications were anything but benign. Nonetheless, throughout the Reagan-Bush years the doctrine seemed to be the basis of American Middle East policy and resulted in the "cash and carry" sale of sophisticated weapons systems and technology to the Arab oil states.

The obvious shift in American policy manifested itself in numerous large arms deals to Arab governments, perhaps the most well known being the 1981 $8.5 billion AWACS (Airborne Warning and Control System) deal with Saudi Arabia. The deal drew loud opposition, at the time, from the pro-Israel lobby in the United States. One of the eventual results was that the United States also signed a bilateral exchange of information agreement with Israel—partly to mollify the American Jewish community—although, according to most of the sources I spoke to, the Reagan and Bush administrations rarely held up their ends of the bargain.

While withholding a great deal of intelligence from Israel, the United States at the same time provided detailed intelligence assessments of the Israeli Defense Forces (IDF) to Saudi Arabia. The Saudis then passed this information on to the Syrians and the Iraqis, both then "clients" of the Soviet Union (although Iraq later became a client of the United States). This provided a virtual windfall for Soviet military intelligence (GRU) since Israel was an American "client" and her order of battle is American-based.

The United States also purposely withheld information of impending terrorist actions from the Israelis while routinely passing on warnings of the same type to the British, Spanish, and Italian governments. In addition, while looking the other way where Israel was concerned, the United States always seemed intent on enhancing its relationship with Saudi Arabia. It was at the behest of the Saudis that the United States provided detailed satellite imagery of Iranian troop dispositions to Iraqi intelligence during the last three years of the Iraq-Iran War. In addition, when Weinberger was at the helm the Defense Department proposed the sale of long-range strike aircraft and Pershing I missiles to the Saudis. When this created immediate congressional opposition, the Saudis purchased CSS-1 East Wind IRBMs (intermediate-range ballistic missiles) from China. Neither Israel nor the United States Congress knew of their arrival, although the American intelligence community was most certainly aware of it.

Of course, Saudi Arabia was not the only Arab country that had a keen interest in acquiring missiles. When Israel informed the United States that it had received "hard information" that the Egyptians were developing an IRBM known as the BADR 2000 (information that was given to the Israelis by Pollard), Israeli officials were once again stonewalled by Weinberger and his associates in Washington. Since the United States had brokered the Camp David Accords during the Carter presidency—and had guaranteed all parties' adherence to its principles—the Israelis categorically asked the Americans for confirmation of what was a clear violation of that agreement. Reagan administration officials quickly informed Jerusalem—as well as the U.S. Congress—that no such missile system was under development in Egypt.

According to my sources, that, too, was a boldface lie. Not only was the BADR 2000 (later known as the Condor II) under construction by the Egyptians, the program was being developed jointly with the Iraqis and the Argentineans. Technology from that program was actually being used to extend the range of Iraq's Scud-B missiles. Some of those missiles, when later used against American troops during the Gulf War, were alleged by some to also be carrying biological and chemical agents.

While the technology needed to create biological and chemical weapons was being shared with Iraq by the United States, the technology to make the missiles in which they would be contained was simply stolen from this country by Abdel Helmy, the Egyptian-born U.S. jet propulsion engineer. As mentioned in chapters 4 and 8, Helmy, who participated in a scheme to smuggle missile technology to Egypt, was allegedly recruited by Egypt's defense minister, Abdel Halim Abu Ghazala.

There were other toys that interested the Egyptian military. Egypt also benefited when the Reagan administration pushed through Congress a modernization program for the Egyptian army that included the cooperative production of the American M-1 Abrams tank. Congressional opponents of the program were assured by the administration that the Egyptian buildup was necessary because of the "threat" Egypt then faced from Libya. Yet, at the same time, administration officials also had in their possession a top-secret Egyptian planning paper stating that the Egyptian army—equipped with the M-1 battle tank—would require only half the time to deploy in the Sinai for a strike against Israel. That accelerated readiness could be critical, since it requires forty-eight to seventy-two hours for the Israeli army to fully mobilize.

Israeli intelligence was also dismayed when it learned that the United States had proceeded to upgrade the Saudi Arabian LANDSAT ground station with a military-quality photo-enhancement device, giving the Saudis what amounted to direct access to U.S. satellite intelligence on Israel. According to Pollard, Israel's request for the same access was repeatedly denied.

The sale of F-15 "Eagle" aircraft to Saudi Arabia—yet another piece of the Level Battlefield Doctrine puzzle—also did not sit well with the Israelis. When the Reagan administration sold some of its advanced F-15s to the Saudis, it again assured Israel (as well as its congressional critics) that these state-of-the-art weapons posed absolutely no threat to Israel's security. Guarantees were even accepted from the Saudis that the technology of these jet fighters would be safeguarded, while none of the aircraft would be housed in northern Saudi Arabia on bases relatively close to Israel's eastern border. However, not only did the Saudis place the majority of these new fighters on these northern bases; according to a high-level Israeli source, the Saudis allowed a contingent of Syrian pilots to actually study and fly the aircraft as well as copy the planes' technical manuals—a conclusion Pollard also came to while still in the employ of the Navy.

But by far the most ominous suppression of information by the Reagan administration dealt with the Iraqi effort to develop nuclear, biological, and chemical weapons. While the suppression of this intelligence was bad enough, even more frightening revelations—by Peter Kawaja, Alan Friedman, Gary Milhollin, David Dantzic, Louis Campon, Moshe Tal, and many others (see chapter 3)—spoke of an American hand in actually helping Iraq develop these weapons of mass destruction. "Amazingly," says Northrop, "West Nile Fever Virus, used by Baghdad in its manufacture of biological weapons, was in fact sent to Iraq by the Communicable Disease Center in Atlanta. Apparently, these shipments left the United States with permission from the U.S. government." He went on to say: "In instances where American law enforcement officials uncovered such things, their investigations were, in most cases, suppressed; in instances where Congress investigated the export licensing through the Department of Commerce, the subpoenaed records were changed."

While the full details of U.S.-Iraqi trade in nuclear and biological materials and technology were shrouded in a thick haze, the Iraqi efforts to produce and deploy chemical, biological, and nuclear weapons were (and still are) very clear. In addition, a number of intelligence sources charge, around the same time the United States signed its bilateral exchange of information agreement with Israel, President Reagan also agreed to give clandestine support to Iraq. Perhaps not surprisingly, in the spring of 1984—when the Israelis made a direct inquiry to the United States about the Iraqi poison-gas buildup—they were told there was no evidence of such a contention.

Pollard, from his bird's-eye view as a Naval Intelligence analyst with top-secret clearance, was quick to learn otherwise. But it wasn't until the months following the August 1990 Iraqi invasion of Kuwait that the rest of the world was forced to come to terms with what some of the sources I spoke with already knew: that the Level Battlefield Doctrine had been a longtime Mideast and Persian Gulf reality.

When I met personally with William Northrop for the first time, in late 1994, he was one of a number of ex-Green Berets involved in trying to expose the "Gulf War syndrome" cover-up. He was also trying to get needed financial relief for the afflicted GIs and their families, and he told me what it was like to visit some of these veterans who had fought for their country and were now feeling abandoned.

"One of these kids was less than one hundred pounds," Northrop said. "He began buying boys' clothes several months ago. When he walked, the sockets in his hips came apart and his legs came out of joint. His eyes bled when he was under a little stress. It looked as if someone was strangling him. He had a fungus on his tongue and he passed this fungus on to his girlfriend."

Northrop said the once strapping soldier still had the "normal dreams of any twenty-two-year-old kid." He then related an interesting story that the young man had told him. "This particular unit the soldier was part of in Saudi Arabia underwent a raid alert. They put on their gas masks. They went running for shelter after there was an explosion of some sort overhead. The soldier looked up and saw a 'rainbow' above him—which indicated a classic chemical attack. He said by the time they all got to the shelter their skins felt like they were on fire. From that point on they knew they had been gassed. They immediately gave themselves atropine injections [to counter the effects of the poison gas]. They thought they could get through this all right, but they didn't."

In the weeks and months that followed, the soldier would often get sick and report to sick call. He and his buddies were eventually sent back to the United States. They were discharged from the service but their health kept deteriorating. "In that particular unit, not only did they have similar reactions," Northrop said, "but three of them are already dead."

Like the paratrooper who met Carol Pollard, this brave young man was also living on borrowed time. He, too, my sources tell me, was an unsuspecting pawn in a most deadly game.

CHAPTER 10

A
KID
WITH A
LIBRARY
CARD

S ome say Jonathan Pollard was also a pawn. Although no innocent—
he surely knew what he was getting himself into—he was certainly
used to the fullest by his Israeli benefactors, themselves engaged in a life-
and-death struggle for national survival. Ironically, few in Israeli intelligence—aside from LAKAM head Rafi Eitan and a handful of others
including, perhaps, the prime minister—were privy to the exact identity
of their American mole.[1] Prior to Pollard's arrest in November of 1985,
William Northrop, then working for Israeli intelligence, insists he had never
even heard of Pollard. "Frankly, I never crossed paths with him," Northrop
said. "We had no contact."

But the few who did cross paths with Pollard must have known they
had a "deep throat" somewhere, because, as another of my Israeli sources
claims, "The information we received was the highest, most accurate, most
reliable information flow that we had seen."

As covered in great detail in chapter 6, Pollard claims he first made the decision to pass classified U.S. information over to Israel in 1984. Like Julius Caesar had done two thousand years earlier when he defied the Roman senate and caused a civil war, Pollard crossed his own personal Rubicon after attending a lecture by Col. Avi Sella, the charismatic Israeli air force ace who had helped lead Israel's successful air assault against Syrian warplanes in the 1982 war in Lebanon when Israeli pilots shot down close to ninety Syrian MIGS, losing no aircraft of their own. During Israel's bombing raid of the Osirak nuclear reactor in Iraq a year earlier, Sella had also been the raid's lead pilot as well as one of the operation's planners. Sella was lecturing in New York for Israel Bonds when Pollard heard him. After the lecture, Pollard approached Sella and offered his "services" to the Israelis.[2]

The offer appealed to Sella. But before Sella could again meet with Pollard, he had to go through "channels." Sella contacted Yosef Yagur, an engineer who worked at the Israeli consulate in New York. Yagur, in turn, got in touch with his superiors at the Israel Defense Ministry's Office of Scientific Liaison (LAKAM, also called LAKEM), who would make certain that Pollard was who and what he said he was, and that Sella was not, for some reason, being set up.

Rafael "Rafi" Eitan was the head of LAKAM. Short and overweight, Eitan looked nothing like Ian Fleming's depiction of James Bond, but was nonetheless a daring career spy who, in 1960, had participated in the brazen and successful plot to capture Nazi war criminal Adolph Eichmann in Argentina. A man who had fought during Israel's War of Independence, Eitan later joined "Ha Mossad" where, before leaving, he eventually worked his way up to deputy chief of operations.

When Eitan left the Mossad he went into private business with Gen. Ariel Sharon, then also out of government service. In 1977, when Menachem Begin and the Likud Party took over the reigns of Israel's government, Begin named his good friend Sharon to his cabinet—and Sharon took his business partner, Eitan, with him. It was when Sharon later became defense minister that Eitan assumed his position with LAKAM.

It was only after LAKAM checked Pollard out that Eitan gave Sella the green light. Eitan knew the risks. But to the man who helped catch Eichmann—and once even masterminded a scheme (eventually turned down by the Mossad) to kidnap the infamous Dr. Joseph Mengele—whatever Pollard could give him would definitely be worth a role of the dice.

Pollard, in essence, became two different people. Although a spy for Israel—or a "black operative"—he was always a "white operative" for the United States, meaning he officially worked for the Office of Naval Intelligence. As a white operative, he got up in the morning, worked from 9 A.M. to 5 P.M. and everybody knew where he was. His job was essentially to analyze all the data coming in from agent sources via electronic intercepts, spy satellites, and through other means. He would then come to some conclusion about what the data meant.

A black operative differs from a white operative in that while his friends and neighbors know he works for the government, they think he works for a governmental agency such as the Department of Transportation or the Department of State. They don't know that he works for an intelligence-gathering body such as the CIA—or, as in Pollard's case, for another country as a double agent.

The fact that a black operative keeps a part of his life secret allegedly gave rise to the use of the term "the Company" as a buzzword for the CIA in the early 1960s. Ever since the days of Vietnam, however, most operatives have referred to the CIA as the "Agency." Quipped one former spook: "Now, if somebody tells me he works for the Company, it strikes me as an individual who reads a lot of spy novels."

The CIA, meanwhile, is more than just an intelligence-gathering body; it is actually the central collection point of all the U.S. intelligence agencies. Simply put: the other agencies send their reports to the CIA. The CIA, in turn, synopsizes these reports and puts them into a daily intelligence briefing for the president. These reports then go to the commander-in-chief, but only after being reviewed by his national security advisor. At the time of Pollard's arrest, President Reagan's national security advisor was Robert "Bud" McFarlane.

As we know, Pollard began working for Naval Intelligence in 1981 when he was hired as an Intelligence Research Specialist by the Field Operational Intelligence Office of the U.S. Navy in Suitland, Maryland, a Washington, D.C. suburb. From June of 1984 until his arrest in November of 1985, Pollard worked the Caribbean desk at the Navy's new Anti-Terrorist Alert Center (ATAC). Pollard said of ATAC's formation: "When news of it was first announced, virtually every person in NISC with even an ounce of ambition began clamoring for an opportunity to be part of it. Antiterrorism, after all, was properly recognized as a 'growth industry,' and it only seemed logical that those who could get in on the ground floor would have potential for advancement."

By the time Pollard joined ATAC he had already begun "moonlighting." In his other role—as a black operative for the Israelis—he was often tasked by his new friends to go to the Communications Center at Naval Intelligence and check out material.

The resourceful Pollard soon had it down to a science. Part of his routine when checking out material the Israelis wanted was to simply discard the plain brown envelopes that were stamped with the words TOP SECRET and replace them with identical brown envelopes. He would then affix the word SECRET to the envelopes' fronts and backs. Since the guards at the desk were less concerned about secret-level documents than top-secret documents, Pollard considered this repackaging useful in the event that one of the guards actually asked to see what he had in his briefcase.

Pollard always knew there was the possibility that he might get caught, but, as one high-level source explained to me, "Jay's experience with the intelligence community was that he could talk his way out of just about anything." Pollard had talked his way out of trouble in the past, so he must have felt he was on fairly safe ground.

"You have to remember, Pollard was a lot brighter than most of his contemporaries, especially at the terrorist center," my source added. "I don't think he ever thought he would be nailed as badly as he got nailed." That source believes Pollard's cockiness and arrogance didn't help matters any. "This may have contributed to them coming down real hard on Jay," he guessed. "A field agent is trained immediately to go into a very moody response—a feeling of 'shame' that elicits sympathy from his captors."

Pollard never did this. He began to dissemble—which a trained agent is supposed to do—but he was never remorseful. Said the source: "Acting remorseful is the first damned thing you're supposed to do when you get caught."

Pollard has always insisted that he became a spy not because of greed, as some have suggested, but because of American violations of the U.S.-Israel bilateral exchange of information agreement that had been signed by President Reagan. Pollard maintains he had become more and more frustrated over instructions he received from his then boss, Defense Secretary Weinberger, preventing him from giving anything of real value to the Israelis. Contrarily, as for the sharing of technical information with the Arab world, many of my sources agree with Pollard that Weinberger's largesse seemed to have no bounds.

Yet the headline of an editorial that appeared in the New York Times on December 10, 1993—when growing pressure was being put on President Clinton to commute Pollard's sentence—read: "No Special Deal for Mr. Pollard." The editorial began: "Jonathan Jay Pollard sold American intelligence secrets to Israel, motivated, he said, by concerns for Israel's survival and by the attraction of almost $50,000 in cash. Sentenced to life in prison, he has served nearly eight years. The sentence was just and there is no reason to reevaluate the case until he comes up for parole in late 1995."

The way the editorial was specifically worded it sounded like Pollard not only spied for Israel because of concerns over Israel's survival, but that he admitted doing it for the money. Pollard never admitted such a thing, of course, and the editors at the Times had to know that. The question remains: Who was really calling the shots at the New York Times?

An Israeli source of mine bristles at the suggestion that Pollard ever spied for monetary gain. "A study was done by the Israelis that showed that Pollard actually went into debt to run his operation—as opposed to making hundreds of thousands of dollars off it," my source said.[3] "The problem with prosecuting a spy who does it for idealistic reasons is that the argument would have to be made in court of whether or not he was on the moral high ground. If you're only talking about someone who spies for the money, though, then you can write him off as a whore."

In spite of the strong allies Israel seemed to have in the Reagan White House, it is a belief shared by Pollard and many others that Israel's access to top-secret material sent by the United States had begun to dramatically dry up when "Cap" Weinberger became secretary of defense and the "boys from Bechtel" became entrenched in Reagan's inner circle. According to the intelligence-sharing agreement between Israel and the United States, both governments were expected to exchange such sensitive information. But Weinberger and his allies simply refused to honor this joint obligation. The secretary of defense instead sent only heavily censored information to Israel, which turned out to be little better than "open source" information—for all intent and purposes already public knowledge.

Pollard used a summary of an enemy SAM (surface-to-air missile) guidance radar system as an example of the Defense Department's new stratagem: "Say a particular type of enemy SAM guidance radar operated in a very narrow bandwidth between 15.5 and 16.5 kHz," Pollard wrote. "The top-secret level document given the Israelis would only report the guidance frequency as being 'somewhere' between 10.5 and 20 kHz, whereas the top-secret level assessment would accurately identify the exact operating frequency. Nevertheless, most electronic engineers can easily determine the general parameters of an enemy radar system just by looking at the diameter of its reflective dish and the size of its power source. However, to jam a radar system quickly, you have to know the exact bandwidth that system is tuned to.

"Now apply this rule to the Israeli air force, which faces a Russian-supplied state-of-the-art Syrian air defense system that is based upon thousands of variable frequencies. This is why Weinberger wanted to make sure that Israel did not have access to the more precise top-secret numbers. With them, the Israeli air force might be able to destroy the Syrian air defense network so quickly that any Syrian ground offensive would be crushed before it ever got rolling. Simply put, accurate numbers save lives. And by only permitting less accurate secret information to be passed on to Israel, Weinberger was essentially raising the human cost that Israel would have to pay during the next Middle East conflict."

Why not re-tip the scales in Israel's favor? Pollard thought. While he doesn't deny removing a great deal of top-secret information—which he copied and then passed along to the Israelis—he maintains he was actually quite selective in his collection activity. "I never acted like a vacuum cleaner," Pollard insisted. "My tasking was quite precise, and always limited to that material which was either being denied Israel in violation of the bilateral intelligence-sharing agreement, or was, in some way, being distorted by the United States."

Northrop agreed. Essentially, all intelligence is either strategic or tactical, he explained to me in an interview. "When doing a damage assessment report (as was done on Pollard after he was caught) the following questions have to be asked: What kind of strategic damage do we have? What kind of tactical damage do we have?

"And the assessment of the prosecution in the Pollard case was that Pollard did not damage the U.S. in any way accept that he gave the Israelis a negotiating advantage in dealing with the Americans. Defense Secretary Weinberger got the letter saying this from both the Department of Justice and from the Naval Investigative Service. So, in essence, Weinberger made up everything he told to [District Court Judge] Aubrey Robinson. He lied. Now Weinberger was indicted for lying [after Iran-Contra]. He swore up and down to Congress. The man was, and is, a liar. And he would have gone to prison had Bush not pardoned him. Of course, Weinberger made up all the bullshit about Jonathan Pollard, too."

In 1985, the same year Jonathan Pollard was arrested in front of the Israeli embassy, John Walker was charged with selling U.S. military secrets to the Soviet Union. Walker carried on his espionage activities while working for sixteen years as a Navy communications specialist and continued spying for the Soviets even after he retired. In 1985, Jerry Whitworth, a member of Walker's spy ring, was also arrested, as were Walker's son, Michael, and his brother, Arthur, a retired U.S. Navy commander.

Yet in his declaration to the court, just before Pollard's sentencing for the crime of passing U.S. military secrets to Israel, Defense Secretary Weinberger said: "It is difficult for me, even in this so-called Year of the Spy, to conceive of greater harm to national security than that caused by the defendant, in view of the breadth, the critical importance to the United States, and the high sensitivity of what he sold to Israel. In so doing, [Pollard] both damaged and destroyed policies and national assets that have taken many years, great effort, and enormous national resources to secure."[4]

Weinberger in essence defined Pollard's "treachery" by his statements to the judge. The question therefore must be asked: In Weinberger's mind, was Pollard's "crime" of revealing to Israel that Iraq was developing chemical and biological weapons targeted for the Jewish state seemingly worse than what the Walkers did when they sold American military secrets to the Soviets—who, at the time, were still engaged in a cold war with the United States? Did Weinberger actually believe what he told District Court Judge Aubrey Robinson?

That seems a bit hard to swallow. Then again, the Pandora's box that Pollard opened no doubt threatened the financial interests of the Bechtel crowd that was clearly making foreign policy for President Ronald Reagan. At the time of Pollard's early incarceration, the attorney general of the United States was Edwin Meese III. Like Weinberger and Reagan's secretary of state, George Shultz, Meese also had a close connection to the Bechtel Group—a corporation that has enjoyed multibillion-dollar ties to the government of Saudi Arabia—and had been one of the company's attorneys. Weinberger had been a former senior executive of the influential company, while Shultz was a former president. Bechtel, my sources say, was very influential in the Reagan White House.

Pollard, meanwhile, always gave the Israelis the "finished product" to which they felt they were entitled. Ninety percent of Pollard's material would be a report and perhaps would have attachments of some of the raw data. The analysis would be on various subjects. The Israelis would tell Pollard what subjects they wanted, and Pollard would go to the library and take the relevant information out. He admitted that he would then bring it over to Harold Katz's apartment, feed it into the copy machine, pick it up, and take it back to the library.[5] This would not necessarily set off any alarm bells. As was noted by investigative reporter Bob Woodward in *Veil: The Secret Wars of the CIA*, "It was not unusual for busy government employees to take classified documents home."

Pollard in fact had little choice but to leave the library at Naval Intelligence in order to have the intelligence data copied. If he had copied the material at Naval Intelligence he would have then drawn some unwanted attention to himself. "If you as much as check out a piece of paper [from Navy Intelligence] there is a safeguard on that paper," one of my sources explained. "There is a computer listing on that paper. And if you don't check it back in—I mean these people in counterintelligence are not stupid—people will begin to notice."

In the end, people did begin to notice because of the sheer volume of material Pollard began checking out. Northrop insists that the Israelis, aware that Pollard's charade would eventually be discovered, actually tried to get him to cut down on his excessive volume. "Jay didn't, though, because he was such an overachiever," Northrop said. "That's probably the main reason he got caught."

In a letter he wrote to me before the publication of *The Spy Who Knew Too Much*, Pollard said the Justice Department and FBI investigators seemed to be under the impression that he was also being aided by an "inside man" within U.S. intelligence circles—a "Mr. X"—who was somehow advising him as to just what specific documents he needed to obtain. Pollard emphatically denies this, stressing that all that was needed, on his part, was a modicum of common sense. As an example he explained how the Israelis would ask him to obtain certain documents by their precise identification numbers. "The [U.S.] government chose to read something sinister into this, whereas I tried to show them how simple the whole situation really was," Pollard said. "Say the Israelis had officially been given a document with the identification number DIAM/433-72TS. This translated out to a 1972 top-secret level study by the Defense Intelligence Agency (DIA) of a particular missile system. If the Israelis, in 1985, needed the latest top-secret assessment of the missile, all they had to do was ask me to collect a copy of DIAM/433-85TS.

"So, obviously, they didn't need a highly placed mole to explain this kind of thing to them. Moreover, like good academics, the Israelis very carefully scrutinized the citations listed in the back of any study they ordered. If there was something that interested them, all they did was copy down the exact identification number—and pass it on to me."

As simple as this was, Pollard explains, the Navy kept insisting that somebody had to have helped the Israelis understand the citation system used in classified Department of Defense documents. The prosecution in Pollard's case was apparently bound and determined to uncover a high-level Israeli mole.[6]

Pollard maintains that he and one of his Israeli handlers, Yossi Yagur, also used what he called a secret-level compendium of intelligence-community documents to ferret out even more data coveted by the Jewish state. Pollard explained that if the Israelis had been told, through official channels, that a given study "did not exist," then he would be asked by them to get that study anyway, using logical modifications of the original top-secret identification numbers. "What we found out clearly demonstrated to the Israelis just how much vital information the Department of Defense was actually withholding from them," Pollard charged. "According to Yossi, the Pentagon denied the existence of roughly three-fourths of all the documents that should have been made available to Israel under the terms of its bilateral sharing agreement with the United States. Even I was amazed when I heard this figure."

An Israeli source of mine, while insisting he knew nothing about Pollard's identity until after the Jewish spy's arrest, nevertheless explained how the Israelis would put together their wish list. "Let's say we wanted the technical data on a particular kind of SAM-7 missile," this source said. "The CIA must have a thousand reports on the capabilities of the SAM-7—a report of its use in Africa, a report on its use in the Middle East, etc. Well, Pollard would take everything. They'd ask him how come you need all this shit; you're working on the Caribbean desk? He'd say it was background. He never expected to get caught. He thought he was too smart. And he was smarter than most of his peers."

Adds Northrop, in a personal interview: "I think that's what got him into even more trouble. His attitude was at least one reason why there was so much bad feeling about him. Also, Pollard pushed Jerry Agee around. A guy like Pollard is a wonderful thing to have on your side as long as you can control him. Don't forget, Pollard is hypersmart. He's somebody whose intelligence shines even in the company of smart men. And he's a tremendous talent that can be utilized, but can be utilized best only if you can harness him. There are really lots of ways to handle someone like Pollard. Pollard would have been an even more successful spy had he been assigned a real Israeli case agent—because the case agent would have run Pollard; Pollard wouldn't have run him."

Col. Avi Sella was not an Israeli case agent and this caused problems with the whole Pollard operation. While Pollard was a trained intelligence officer, Sella was, in Northop's words, "an airplane driver." Pollard specifically picked Sella for one reason, Northrop said: he could manipulate the Israeli air force ace. Insists Northrop, the operation would have been far better off if Sella had delivered Pollard's material to the Mossad, Shin Bet, or AMAN agents in Washington—anywhere but LAKAM.

"LAKAM essentially wound up with Pollard by accident," Northrop said. "By sheer luck, they hit the glory hole."

Like the attraction of the moth to the flame, Pollard was a temptation LAKAM couldn't resist. The Jewish spy had immediately impressed Sella with the "overheads" of the Osirak operation, especially since Sella—who led the bombing raid against Saddam Hussein's nuclear facility—had been told that the Americans had no overhead photos. "Sella had never seen an American overhead before," Northrop said bluntly. "Pollard was hitting Sella's hot button."

But just how deep was Pollard's well? According to my sources, Pollard was an analyst with top-secret security clearance. He had access to every document in the entire intelligence library of the United States with the exception of documents known as Top Secret Codeword; in other words, documents that were even "above" top-secret. No documents Pollard sent to Israel were ever in that highest classification, therefore, because Pollard simply couldn't have had access to them. As Northrop likes to say about Pollard: "He was just a kid with a library card."

A number of my sources in both Israeli and U.S. intelligence believe that Pollard's admittedly radical solution to the complex problem he faced— since he was literally torn between his loyalty to the United States and to the Jewish people—was not uncalled for, considering what he perceived to be a betrayal of the State of Israel by many of those closest to the president. "He did what he should have done," one of my Israeli sources said emphatically. "He took this information to his superiors and his superiors didn't care because it was the policy of the United States. But Mr. Pollard decided that what he learned about was a clear and present danger to the people of Israel. And it was. There was no question about it. So he took a step—I don't know that I would have had the balls to do it—and this young man basically threw away his life and destroyed his family to save the Jewish people. There's no doubt in my mind: without Pollard's material Israel would have been tremendously vulnerable. Nobody would have helped us. And this could have easily led to a thermonuclear holocaust, because there is just no way Israel would have gone down under clouds of poison gas."

According to Northrop, Pollard's greatest "crime," therefore, was that he warned the Israelis about a secret American policy that genuinely threatened Israel's continued existence. "The reason [the government] is keeping Pollard in jail right now is that they don't want him to expose an overall [pro-Arab] policy that has been on board since 1980—since all those little storm troopers went to Washington," Northrop said. "Pollard spotted the policy right away and he was wrong only about one thing. He worried about Israel. But [Iraq] didn't use the poison gas on Israel. They used the poison gas on those poor kids in the damned Gulf."

NOTES

1. In *Territory of Lies*, author Wolf Blitzer also states that few in Israeli intelligence actually knew of Pollard's identity before his arrest. Notes Blitzer: "The documents obtained by Pollard were forwarded to Rafi Eitan, who had assembled a three-member team of experts in Tel Aviv to analyze and distribute the documents to the relevant offices in the Israeli military. The documents were thoroughly 'sanitized' to make certain that LAKAM's sources and methods of obtaining them were not revealed. Eitan was careful not to reveal Pollard's identity. Indeed, only two of the three members of the LAKAM team were actually aware of him—and one of those two consistently urged Eitan to drop him because the operation was too dangerous."

2. In *The Samson Option*, Seymour Hersh states that Pollard actually began spying for Israel before 1984. According to Hersh, Pollard offered to supply Israel with information as early as 1980 but was not recruited by the Israelis until the fall of 1981, "three years earlier than he and the Israeli government have admitted." In his book about the Pollard case, *Territory of Lies*, Wolf Blitzer does not come to the same conclusion although he writes, "Even before his first meetings with Sella, according to government documents, Pollard had sought to recruit an old friend as a possible courier in taking documents to the Israelis in New York."

3. Pollard was accused of "making" as much as $300,000 for spying for Israel. Actually, as we have learned, a Swiss bank account was supposed to be set

up for Pollard by LAKAM—based on his receiving $30,000 a year over a ten-year period. The Swiss bank account was never activated.

4. See Wolf Blitzer, *Territory of Lies* (New York: Harper & Row, 1989), ch. 12, "The Weinberger Memo." Weinberger also made these statements under oath: see Alan Dershowitz, *Chutzpah* (Boston: Little, Brown, 1991), ch. 9, "In Marion Prison: The Pollard Case."

5. In *Territory of Lies*, Wolf Blitzer describes Harold Katz as an American-Israeli lawyer who has lived in Israel since 1972, and who had worked for the Israeli Defense Ministry for several years as a legal advisor. According to Blitzer, Katz purchased a condo in Washington for $82,500 which was used by the Israelis for part of their spying operation in the United States. Katz, meanwhile, insisted he had nothing to do with Pollard's operation "and if the apartment was used for such, it was without my permission or knowledge."

6. In *The Samson Option*, Seymour Hersh describes the U.S. intelligence search for a "Mr. X." Notes Hersh: "By October 1986, Jonathan Pollard had yet to be sentenced and there were many in the U.S. intelligence community who were convinced that he had one and perhaps many more accomplices inside the government—men or women who were supplying Israel with the identification of highly classified documents that Pollard could then be assigned to retrieve. The hunt for 'Mr X,' as the government called Pollard's alleged accomplice, had only begun."

Former defense secretary Caspar Weinberger appears at a news conference in Washington, December 25, 1992, after President Bush pardoned him and five other former high-ranking government officials for their role in the Iran-Contra scandal. (AP Photo/Doug Mills)

Onetime CIA Soviet counterintelligence expert Aldrich Hazen Ames, who, as a double agent, passed on classified data to his benefactors in Moscow. Was Jonathan Pollard punished for Ames's crimes? (AP Photo/Mark Wilson)

Former Israeli prime minister Benjamin Netanyahu. Did President Clinton make him a promise, during the Wye River Accords (1998), that Pollard would be released? (*Israeli Press Office*)

The late Israeli prime minister Yitzhak Rabin and President Bill Clinton at the White House. Sources say Rabin, who replaced Moshe Arens as Israel's defense minister during the period of the Pollard affair, was against the idea of the incarcerated Pollard being granted Israeli citizenship. (*Official White House photograph*)

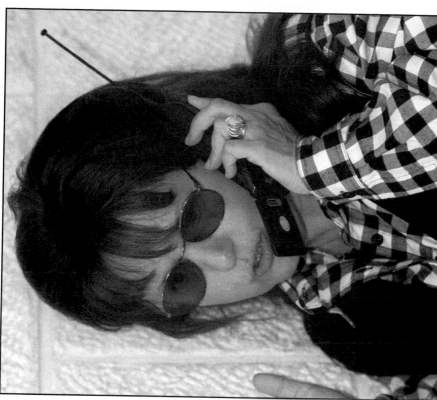

Esther Pollard, wife of former Naval Intelligence analyst Jonathan Pollard, taking a call outside the Israeli Supreme Court in Jerusalem, Monday, November 16, 1998. *(AP Photo/Mati Stein)*

Holding a book celebrating Israel's fiftieth birthday in 1998, Israeli communications minister Limor Livnat visited Jonathan Pollard at the Federal Correctional Institution in Butner, North Carolina. *(AP Photo/Ayala Bar)*

Harvard Law School professor Alan Dershowitz, a longtime Pollard advocate. (*Stu Rosner*)

Former Israeli defense minister Ariel Sharon on the speaker's circuit for the United Jewish Appeal. He has long been a supporter of the Israeli government doing everything in its power to get Pollard freed. (*United Jewish Communities Photo Archive*)

JUGGLING FIENDS

After Jonathan Pollard had spent nearly six years behind bars—much of that time in solitary confinement in Illinois's Marion Penitentiary, often described as the harshest penal institution in the United States—many supporters of the embattled spy finally saw a light at the end of the tunnel. It was September 10, 1991, the second day of Rosh Hashanah, and attorney Theodore Olson, a former assistant U.S. attorney general whose high profile clients included President Ronald Reagan, was scheduled to argue for the vacating of Pollard's guilty plea in front of three appellate court justices in Washington, D.C. Pollard's family and growing network of supporters were buoyed by the prospects.

Still, Pollard—who cut a deal with the government in 1987 (nearly two years after his arrest) but was nevertheless handed a life term in prison—had to know that there was far more to his harsh sentence than the government was willing to admit. In *The Secret War Against the Jews*, authors John Loftus and Mark Aarons gave a hint as to the kind of quagmire Pollard may have inadvertently stepped into while he was trying to help his brethren in Israel.

"To this day, Pollard does not know how sensitive his 'routine' shipping surveillance really was," Loftus and Aarons write. "In the spring and summer of 1984, Pollard noticed a pattern of vessels going back and forth from Greece to Yemen, where the PLO had a major base. Pollard passed the tip to the Israelis, who checked it out with their Interpol and West German sources. In the summer of 1984 the Israelis tipped off the Greek authorities to seize an entire shipload of arms destined for the PLO."

The authors contend that neither Pollard nor the government of Israel was aware at the time that they had smashed then vice president George Bush's first shipment of arms to Iran. The shipment had been arranged by Monzer Khassar, a Syrian contract agent working for the White House. The British secret service had arranged the Greek shipment to ransom American hostages in Lebanon. Pollard, for his part, never realized that he had inadvertently busted one of the most secret White House operations of modern times. Note Loftus and Aarons: "The summer of 1984 Greek shipment was a dagger over George Bush's head."[1]

But from what my own sources tell me, Pollard not only tripped over Iran-Contra, he learned still darker secrets as well—the darkest being the secret arming of Iraq by the United States and the sharing of U.S. technology with Iraqi leader Saddam Hussein. That technology dealt, specifically, with chemical and biological weapons. Those outlawed weapons were to be tested in the field while being used against Iran—after all, the United States was playing both sides against the middle in the Iran-Iraq conflict—yet could also be targeted by Iraq against Israel. As Loftus and Aarons correctly note in The Secret War Against the Jews: "The Israelis had always known that, sooner or later, someone would think about targeting them. The genie of germ warfare had been let out of the bottle by the Nazi laboratory at Auschwitz. During the 1950s and 1960s [Israel] watched nation after nation perfect the technology."

No doubt, the Israelis were already well aware of the potential dangers of chemical and biological weapons when Pollard passed his information along to them in the early 1980s. What Pollard specifically did, however, was help pinpoint just how real (and imminent) the Iraqi chemical/biological threat actually was. Most important to his powerful enemies in the Defense Department and the White House, if allowed to testify in open court—or perhaps even worse, if allowed access to the press—Pollard might have shed some light on the duplicity of the United States.

Not surprisingly, the conspiracy to both discredit and silence Pollard began immediately following his arrest on November 21, 1985. Pollard was literally sequestered from the outside world and was allowed no access to the news media and no visitors other than members of his immediate family. His mail was for the most part restricted and he was rarely granted the privileged communications with his attorneys that lawyer-client relations demand and require. Furthermore, he was not allowed to communicate with his wife, Anne, who, also imprisoned, was suffering from a life-threatening disease. Yet in spite of his harsh treatment, Pollard was never indicted for treason.

The reasoning was clear. "Treason against the United States," the Constitution states, "shall consist only in levying war against them, or, in adhering to their enemies, giving them aid and comfort." Attorney General Edwin Meese needed to find some solid ground since the United States had obviously never been at war with Israel and the two countries had never been enemies.

So, instead, Jonathan and Anne Henderson Pollard were indicted for conspiracy to provide Israel with intelligence information in violation of American security laws. Jonathan Pollard was accused, specifically, of supplying the Israelis with more than one thousand classified documents removed from the files of Naval Intelligence. Before Pollard, no one in the history of the United States had ever been handed a life sentence for passing U.S. intelligence to a de facto ally. Pollard's punishment was unique, to say the least.

Some insist, of course, that there was actually far more to Pollard's crimes. Apart from the alleged political damage he had caused to U.S-Arab relations by "adversely" affecting the Middle East balance of power and making Israel "too strong," Pollard asserts that when the government prosecuted him it also placed great emphasis on his compromising of the U.S. intelligence community's "sources and methods." One way Pollard did this, the government claimed, was by passing along KH-11 satellite photos to his handlers in Israel.

KH-11 satellite technology was a major breakthrough of the 1970s because the KH-11 transmitted its pictures back to earth in radio waves. The Soviets, at the time, were in the habit of monitoring the "ejection of film" to identify a satellite that was taking pictures. The reason was that before the first KH-11 was launched, in December 1976, film had to actually be ejected from a satellite, then retrieved and developed on the ground. With the KH-11, however, not only were the pictures taken nearly instantaneously, but the Soviets didn't even suspect that the passing satellite was taking pictures. Notes Bob Woodward in *Veil: The Secret Wars of the CIA*: "Thus, [the Soviets] failed to conceal or camouflage various military installations and equipment, including missile silo doors, when the satellite passed over. Soviet ignorance had created an enormous U.S. advantage."

Woodward—who interviewed numerous intelligence sources while researching his book, including then CIA director William Casey— stressed that the "great secret" of the KH-11 capability lasted only about one year, however, before William Kampiles, a disgruntled, low-level CIA watch-center employee, sold a copy of the top-secret KH-11 manual to the Soviets for about three thousand dollars. "The CIA knew something had happened," Woodward writes, "when the Soviets began closing silo doors as the KH-11 passed over."

Pollard was no doubt well aware of Kampiles when he passed his KH-11 satellite photos to Israel. Kampiles, after all, was sentenced to prison in 1978—well before Pollard began spying for Israel. Argued Pollard: "In the case of these photos, how could the material I provided Israel have compromised anything? Moreover, what about all the satellite photos going to the Iraqis? Were the Iraqis considered so reliable that

KH-11-derived intelligence could be shared with them without causing any danger to U.S. 'sources and methods'?"

KH-11 photos were also obtained by Iran. This occurred after a number of those photos had inadvertently been left behind at "Desert One," the site of the tragic accident that doomed the Carter administration's ill-fated attempt to rescue American embassy hostages in Tehran.

"When the Iranians later published these photos," Pollard explained, "they effectively eliminated whatever questions still remained concerning the capabilities of the KH-11 system. For all intents and purposes, then, the KH-11 was utterly compromised by the end of 1980. And this was more or less acknowledged by the government in 1981, when a KH-11-derived photo of a Backfire bomber appeared in *Soviet Military Power*."[2]

Still, Pollard admits that while the use of the KH-11 was undoubtedly known to the Soviet military, the knowledge of which targets were actually chosen to be photographed by the National Reconnaissance Office remained somewhat sensitive. Nevertheless, Pollard insists that the sensitivity of the targeting list was also overstated. Pollard reasons that, given the location of the KH-11 satellite in space, the Soviets (and others) could make a fairly accurate determination of what was being photographed. "On the other hand," Pollard said, "I don't know of a single country—especially in the Middle East—that doesn't assume that its military installations can, and will, be photographed by American spy satellites."

The real problem, Pollard has long insisted, was that the KH-11 photos he sent to Israel had alerted the Israelis to the existence of chemical and biological weapons manufacturing plants in Iraq which certain individuals in the Reagan administration would have preferred to keep secret. If no one knew about the facilities, Pollard reasoned, then the State and Defense Departments would not have had to precipitate an embarrassing diplomatic confrontation with Iraq over its violation of the Geneva chemical weapons treaty.[3]

It's important to note that at the time of Pollard's arrest the massacre of Kurdish civilians inside Iraq had not yet occurred, and what little public concern was being raised over the possible use of poison gas by Iraq was largely being ignored by the White House. According to Pollard, if the photos he gave Israel were somehow compromised, this clearly would have jeopardized the administration's policy of calculated indifference toward the proliferation of biological and chemical weapons in the Persian Gulf. "They would have constituted hard, irrefutable proof," Pollard charged, "that Iraq was indeed engaged in the production and use of chemical weapons."

After the gassing of the Kurds, however, the White House was placed in a rather awkward position. While the U.S. intelligence community did not want to be accused of having failed to monitor Iraq's chemical and biological weapons arsenal, neither could the CIA and Defense Intelligence Agency confirm the existence of Iraq's poison-gas plants without running the risk of compromising the Reagan administration's acquiescent policy toward these facilities.

So after a few days of "soul searching" the State Department finally admitted that the United States had indeed intercepted some Iraqi military communications that indicated lethal gas had in fact been employed against unarmed Kurdish civilians. "Of course, had it not been for the Iranians actually bringing in Western reporters to confirm the mass murder," charged Pollard, "I have the sneaking suspicion that the administration would have preferred to maintain a studied silence on the matter."

Pollard believes the Reagan administration was simply outmaneuvered by the Iranians. "I think it's safe to say that the subsequent decision to leak the fact that we were 'reading' Iraqi military communications was seen as being a lesser of two evils," Pollard wrote. "Certainly, confirming the undeniable operational deployment of chemical munitions by the Iraqis was far preferable to describing the exact dimensions of their poison-gas plants—which would have raised some uncomfortable questions on Capitol Hill as to why the administration had done nothing to prevent their construction." Thus, in an attempt to recapture the moral "high ground" from Iran, the White House evidently decided it would be better for the United States—rather than the Ayatollah Khomeini—to be seen as leading the public denunciation of Iraq.

In view of Iraq's penchant for using chemical and biological weapons, Pollard could easily rationalize sending U.S.-originated KH-11 satellite photos of those facilities to Israel. But in his book *The Samson Option*, Pulitzer Prize–winning reporter Seymour Hersh leveled some other serious charges against Pollard as well. According to Hersh—and perhaps unbeknownst to Pollard—a sanitized version of Pollard's intelligence information was turned over to the Soviet Union at the express direction of then Israeli Prime Minister Yitzhak Shamir. Could this have been the real "smoking gun" in the Pollard case?

As his initial source, Hersh had used Ari Ben-Menashe, a former Israeli intelligence operative. "Ben-Menashe's account might seem almost too startling to be believed, had it not been subsequently amplified by a second Israeli, who cannot be named," Hersh wrote. "The Israeli said that the Pollard material was sanitized and dictated to a secretary before being turned over to the Soviets. Some material was directly provided to Yevgeni M. Primakov, the Soviet foreign ministry specialist on the Middle East who met publicly and privately with Shamir while he was prime minister."

Of course, there is no proof that Pollard ever intended for this information to get into Soviet hands. Then again, there is no proof—only Ben-Menashe's word (and that of an unidentified source)—that any of this exchange with the Soviets even took place. Anyone familiar with Ben-Menashe's background would be just a bit skeptical.

In April 1989, Ben-Menashe, an Iraqi Jew, was indicted following a U.S. Customs sting operation during which he allegedly attempted to sell three C-130 Hercules transport airplanes to Iran without the necessary State Department approval. After spending eleven months in jail pending trial, he was acquitted of those charges by a New York jury in November 1990.

Ben-Menashe asserts that in the late 1980s he was part of an elite Israeli intelligence unit run directly out of Prime Minister Shamir's office. Since his arrest, in 1989, he has occasionally been propped up by U.S. intelligence spokespeople as a reliable source—but has just as often been discredited. In the book *The Crimes of a President: New Revelations on Conspiracy and Cover-up in the Bush and Reagan Administrations*, author Joel

Bainerman, who met Ben-Menashe, says of him: "He was simply a mouth-piece, a window into a covert world. It is up to investigative journalists and congressional committees to verify [what he says]."

The U.S. Supreme Court has held that "when a plea rests in any signifi-cant degree on a promise or agreement of the prosecutor, so that it can be said to be part of the inducement or consideration, such promise must be fulfilled" (*Santabello* v. *New York*, 1971). The Supreme Court has also held that when a breach of such a promise takes place, the sentence must be vacated and the case remanded to the court that sentenced the defen-dant. Following remand, the court that initially sentenced the defendant must then either allow the defendant to withdraw his plea or grant the defendant specific performance of the agreement on the plea—in which case the defendant should be resentenced by a different judge. This remedy, the Supreme Court decided in the *Santobello* case, must be granted to a defendant even if the breach was inadvertent and even if the sentencing judge stated that a prosecutor's recommendation did not influence him.

On May 23, 1986, Jonathan Pollard and Anne Pollard signed the plea-bargain agreements they were offered. Pollard wrote me in a letter that "although the plea bargain was blatantly coercive, it was neverthe-less promised that we would be treated leniently in exchange for our complete cooperation."

It was a promise of leniency that U.S. Attorney General Edwin Meese apparently never meant to keep. "I think it's important to stress the fact that the government had essentially presented us with an agreement that we couldn't refuse," Pollard recalled. "On the one hand, Anne was warned that if she rejected the plea agreement, I would receive a life sentence, while I, on the other hand, was told that if I did not accept the government's offer, Anne would 'suffer the consequences.'" Pollard was well aware that the longer his wife remained in prison the quicker her failing health would deteriorate. She would not survive in prison for long.

As a result, Pollard claims he had no choice but to accept a closed hearing, as the government wished, far removed from the purview of TV cameras and reporters. "Anne and I fully appreciated the dangers of a secret trial, but what could we do about it?" Pollard asked, rhetorically. "We were literally caught between a rock and a hard place. It was with great trepidation, then, that Anne and I accepted the plea agreement, hoping the government would honor its promise of leniency."

Pollard noted that the government's true intentions were graphically illustrated, however, during an "impromptu" press conference that U.S. Attorney for the District of Columbia Joseph diGenova held on the steps of the courthouse immediately following the plea session. According to Pollard, while responding to a question posed to him by a correspondent of a Kuwaiti-financed newspaper (*Al-Watan al Arabi*), diGenova blatantly violated the discretionary clauses of the plea agreement by revealing that Pollard had given Israel information that the United States had collected on the military establishments of Jordan, Egypt, and Saudi Arabia. "As a result," Pollard wrote, "the very next day all three of these countries lodged formal complaints with the State Department demanding to know not only what I had passed on to Israel, but also why the United States was spying on them in the first place."

DiGenova simply brushed aside the obvious role he had played in precipitating this diplomatic "crisis," Pollard added, then had the "colossal nerve" to cite these protests as evidence of the "horrendous damage I had caused to U.S.-Arab relations."

To Pollard, diGenova's ploy was the height of hypocrisy. After all, it had been the U.S. attorney's disclosures that caused the diplomatic row in the first place. Moreover, in view of the extremely sensitive nature of the information diGenova discussed during his press conference, it was a fair assumption that he was probably acting under orders. And if diGenova was in fact acting under orders, as Pollard surmised, this would strongly suggest the existence of a high-level conspiracy within the government to undermine the plea agreement.

That conclusion was buttressed, Pollard believed, by the selective way in which diGenova chose to identify the countries Pollard had targeted. Noted Pollard: "Rather than pointing out that most of the information I provided Israel pertained to Syria, Libya, and Iraq, diGenova chose, instead, to spotlight those Arab states that the administration would later be able to portray in its presentencing memoranda as 'allies' of the United States."

Pollard reasoned that perhaps the prosecution may have been frustrated over its inability to show that the man it was prosecuting had either intended to harm the United States or had actually done so. "In an attempt to get around this problem," Pollard explained, "the Justice Department waited until after I signed the plea agreement to charge that by undermining the security of our so-called moderate Arab allies, I had indirectly attempted to injure the United States. And although the transparency of this argument was self-evident, Judge Robinson went right ahead and embraced it as gospel. What the government had done, in effect, was redefine the case in such a way that the judge would be able to sentence me for a crime I had never committed."

Pollard has repeatedly stated that the circumstances under which the government linked his guilty plea with his wife's well-being clearly undermined his free will, and, as a result, should have rendered his plea an involuntary one. David Kirshenbaum, an attorney and friend of Pollard's, also maintained that U.S. District Court Judge Aubrey Robinson—who sentenced Pollard to life in prison—had failed to properly inquire into the voluntary nature of Pollard's plea agreement as required by Rule 11 of the Federal Rules of Criminal Procedure. "The Supreme Court has held, in McCarthy v. The United States, that a defendant whose plea has been accepted in violation of Rule 11 should be afforded the opportunity to plead anew," Kirshenbaum wrote.

In his decision, however, Robinson cited the statement of Pollard's then attorney, Richard A. Hibey, that, at the time of his sentencing, Pollard came before the court and "knowingly and voluntarily entered his plea."

As I noted in *The Spy Who Knew Too Much*, the following brief exchange between Robinson and Pollard took place.

Robinson: "Do you know of any reason why I shouldn't accept your plea?"

Pollard: "No sir, I don't."

Yet, Kirshenbaum said, Rule 11 provides that a court "shall not accept a plea of guilty without first, by addressing the defendant personally in open court, determining that the plea is voluntary and not the result of force or threats or of promises apart from the plea agreement."

Even though federal rules required that inquiry be made into the voluntary nature of a defendant's plea, the court never asked Pollard whether he was entering his plea voluntarily or whether the plea was actually the product of force, threats or promises. Consequently, Kirshenbaum noted, "Judge Robinson's failure to inquire of Pollard directly whether his plea was voluntary, as opposed to giving him the opportunity to raise the issue on his own, is not merely a technical defect. Federal law provides that when a defendant's plea is made in consideration of a third party's receiving a lenient sentence, special care must be taken and a higher standard must be applied to assure the voluntariness of the guilty plea."

Kirshenbaum maintained that the government also implied that it would not ask for a life sentence but, rather, would limit its recommendation to asking for a "substantial" sentence.

Notwithstanding, Defense Secretary Weinberger submitted two declarations to the sentencing court (the first being classified and detailing the nature and extent of the purported harm Pollard may have caused to national security) that could plainly be interpreted as advocating a life sentence. Weinberger wrote in his declaration to the court, prior to the sentencing of Pollard: "It is difficult for me, even in the so-called Year of the Spy, to conceive of greater harm to national security than that caused by the defendant." In a separate statement to the court Weinberger also declared: "Punishment, of course, must be appropriate to the crime, and, in my opinion, no crime is more deserving of severe punishment than conducting espionage activities against one's own country."

With his allusion to the "Year of the Spy," Weinberger seemingly put Pollard on the same plane with a number of other American spies arrested in 1985, including John Walker, who spied for the Soviet Union for seventeen years. In stating to the court that Pollard caused even greater harm to national security than the likes of Walker, Weinberger was sending Judge Robinson a crystal-clear message: If Walker got life and Pollard caused as much or greater damage to national security, then Pollard should receive a life sentence as well.

According to Alan Dershowitz, a longtime advocate for Jonathan Pollard (although never his attorney of record), Weinberger also tried to pander to the sensitivities of Judge Robinson, an African American, about the apartheid government of South Africa. Dershowitz found out about this only after his old friend, former Supreme Court Justice Arthur Goldberg, wrote a letter that appeared in the September 12, 1989, edition of the *Jerusalem Post*. In that letter Goldberg stated that the Jewish community shouldn't get involved in the Pollard case because of the "terrible offenses" that Pollard had committed.

Upon reading the article, Dershowitz called Goldberg, then sent him some comparable sentencing data, whereupon Goldberg promised to make some inquiries of his own regarding the case. Dershowitz later said in a sworn affidavit that Goldberg contacted Robinson himself, who told Goldberg that he (Robinson) was informed by the government that Pollard gave Israel extremely sensitive satellite photographs of South African military facilities.

Dershowitz carefully checked out what Goldberg told him, then— when thoroughly convinced there was no truth whatsoever in the government's charges—relayed to Goldberg what he had found out. It's reasonable to assume that those secret charges, which were part of the Weinberger memo to the judge, were made in this "ex parte" (one-sided) fashion for only one reason: so that the defense would not have the chance to respond to them in court.

Dershowitz recalled that Goldberg was quite upset by all this and promised "to get to the bottom of it." Unfortunately, Goldberg never got the chance. On January 19, 1990, four days after his last phone call from Der-showitz, the eighty-year-old former Supreme Court justice died in his sleep.

Standing before U.S. Circuit Court Justices Laurence H. Silberman, Ruth B. Ginsburg, and Stephen F. Williams, on the morning of September 10, 1991, attorney Theodore Olson—a Washington "insider" who surely had to sense that he might be playing poker against a card shark with a stacked deck—presented Pollard's case as follows: The U.S. government decided to avoid what would have been an awkward, potentially embar-rassing situation and inconvenient trial. The government then promised to relay to the court the fact that Pollard's cooperation had been of consid-erable value. Finally, in exchange for Pollard's guilty plea, the government would agree not to seek a life sentence.

Unfortunately, Olson surmised, the government's actions during the sentencing process "were intended to have precisely the opposite effect." According to Olson, Defense Secretary Weinberger's use of the word "treason," and a reference by the lead prosecutor, Joseph diGenova, to the term "traitorous conduct" were, indeed, deliberately designed to convey to the district court the government's views that Pollard had com-mitted a much more serious crime than that for which he was indicted by the grand jury. Olson called the tactic "an outrageous abuse of power," adding: "Although the government didn't use the words 'life imprison-ment,' it certainly moved in for the kill at sentencing time."

Even Assistant U.S. Attorney John Fisher, who argued against Olson, had to at least partially agree. While insisting that Pollard was "fully aware" that his plea agreement in no way precluded Judge Robinson from imposing a life sentence, Fisher acknowledged it was "regrettable" that a secret Weinberger memorandum—delivered to the judge immediately before he handed down Pollard's sentence—had implicitly accused Pol-lard of treason, a crime with which he was never charged.

Judge Silberman, the most vocal of the appellate court justices, appeared concerned by what he heard from both Olson and Fisher, and

173

said it "troubled" him that the government, "through winks and nods," seemed to almost suggest that Pollard get life. Silberman then turned to Fisher and coldly asked: "How in God's name could you justify Weinberger's use of the word 'traitor' in the memorandum?" He added: "The message the prosecutors seemed to convey in the Pollard case was that you'd better be damned careful when you deal with the United States government."

In retrospect, it would be naive to assume that Olson's arguments and Silberman's comments made much of a difference. Six months later, on Friday, March 20, 1992, the appeals court for the District of Columbia Circuit, by a 2-to-1 margin, rejected Pollard's claim that the U.S. government violated the terms of the plea bargain it had offered him. Judge Silberman—in an opinion he wrote for both himself and Judge Ginsburg—acknowledged that the government's dealings with Pollard had been "hard-nosed," but noted that Pollard had "not mounted a sufficient challenge to the government" to overturn his life sentence.

The dissenting opinion was written by Judge Williams (ironically, the only non-Jew of the three), who said there had nevertheless been a "fundamental miscarriage of justice" in Pollard's original sentencing. Williams concluded that Pollard's prosecutors had not only violated the spirit but also the letter of the agreement they had made with him when the Jewish spy gave up his right to a trial.

"Pollard's sentence should be vacated and the case remanded for sentencing," Williams wrote as part of his lengthy opinion. "This should occur before a new judge, as the *Santobello* case indicates, even though the fault here rests on the prosecutor, not on the sentencing judge.

"Though I do not wish to be too critical of the government, and though the analogy is inexact on some points, the case does remind me of Macbeth's curse against the witches whose promises—and their sophistical interpretations of them—led them to doom."

Williams ended his eloquent dissent by quoting from the bard:

And be these juggling fiends no more believ'd,
Then palter with us in a double sense;
That keep the word of promise to our ear,
And break it to our hope.

NOTES

1. In an opinion piece he later wrote that appeared April 23, 1995, in the *Miami Herald*, Loftus noted that in the last four chapters of *The Secret War Against the Jews* he and Mark Aarons document each of the shipping manifests, bank accounts, and arms transactions and corroborate them with cross-citations to matching entries in Lt. Col. Oliver North's diaries. Loftus and Aarons add that Monzer is identified in North's declassified diaries as "M-the-Mediator" for the release of hostages in Iran. The authors contend that North's Swiss bank records also confirm that the White House paid Monzer millions of dollars to purchase arms for the Contras.

2. *Soviet Military Power* was a U.S. government document put out annually by the Department of Defense.

3. At the time he wrote this in a letter to me, Pollard was not aware that the United States had possibly even helped Iraq violate the 1976 London Accords on Chemical and Biological Weapons.

THE McFARLANE CONNECTION

I n *The Celestine Prophecy* author James Redfield maintains that there really are no coincidences. My intelligence sources have often told me the same thing. I wondered whether it was a mere coincidence, therefore, that Judge Laurence Silberman—the jurist whose comments made him appear most likely to rule in Jonathan Pollard's favor in September 1991, then seemingly had a change of heart the following March—was linked to the 1980 arms-for-hostages scandal by Gary Sick in his book *October Surprise.*

I also wondered whether it was just a coincidence that on June 14, 1993, Judge Ruth Bader Ginsburg—who also ruled against Pollard—was nominated by President Bill Clinton for the United States Supreme Court.

It was while I was completing the last chapter of *The Spy Who Knew Too Much*—only days after Judge Silberman's majority opinion denying Pollard a new trial was made public—that I literally stumbled over the fact that Silberman had been indirectly connected by Gary Sick to the first "arms-for-hostages" deal with Iran. That agreement was said to have immediately pre-ceded the 1980 election of President Ronald Reagan and ensured that, in exchange for secret U.S. arms dealings with Iran, the mullahs would wait until after the 1980 presidential election before releasing their hostages, thereby assuring a Reagan victory over an "impotent" Jimmy Carter. Although its existence has been denied for years by Republicans—espe-cially Republicans with ties to the Reagan and Bush administrations—Sick, who served on the National Security Council staffs of presidents Ford, Carter, and Reagan and was a principal White House aide during the hostage crisis of 1979–81, believes that such a deal did, in fact, take place.

According to Sick: In late September (or possibly early October) 1980, Silberman, then a member of the Republican National Committee, together with Richard Allen, who would become President Reagan's for-eign affairs advisor, and Robert "Bud" McFarlane, a longtime friend of George Bush, Reagan's vice-presidential candidate, met with an "uniden-tified Middle Easterner" at the L'Enfant Plaza hotel in Washington, D.C., who subsequently offered to "arrange the release of the American hostages to the Republicans."

According to Sick, no deal was actually consummated at this time and the proposal was rejected outright by Silberman, Allen, and McFarlane. However, Sick's book also suggests that people close to the Reagan-Bush campaign, intent on delaying the release of the fifty-two American hostages until after the presidential election, did, at some point, make a deal with Iranian leaders. That deal, Sick maintained, involved illegal arms shipments to Iran by way of Israel.

The twisting road of the Pollard case, meanwhile, apparently also cut through the rugged mountains of Afghanistan. The so-called Afghan freedom fighters, who were involved in a long, drawn-out conflict with the Soviet Union, were the cold-war beneficiaries of American military aid, much of it covert. Following the 1979 Soviet invasion of Afghanistan, the Carter administration—and later the Reagan administration—searched for any means by which they could supply guns and money to the Mujahedin.

Yet while Washington labeled the Afghans as "freedom fighters," most Americans were kept in the dark concerning their sheer brutality. Recalled an intelligence source of mine who spent some time in Afghanistan: "The Afghan mountains are brown and very sparsely vegetated. The wind always blows and it's always cold. During the war the Afghans would come up to a Russian position in a valley. The Afghans developed a tactic. The Russians would call in their HIND-24 gunships, everything you would want in a helicopter. Now the best way to get them is to hit them in the engines but you can't really get at them from underneath. So the Afghans developed a technique of getting higher in the mountains and would hit [the helicopters] with their Stingers—heat-seeking missiles that would go to the exhaust system of the engine.

"But the aircraft wouldn't explode. It would normally crash to the ground. And the chopper was so well constructed that often times the crew would survive. The Afghans loved this because they really got a big kick out of torturing the crew."

Pollard, among his other extracurricular activities while working for Naval Intelligence, was also once linked to a deal involving secret arms shipments to Afghanistan, although he insists the U.S. government did not want this revealed during his 1987 closed hearing. The reason, Pollard believes, had to do with his indirect connection to a particular Afghan resistance commander—and Robert McFarlane's connection to that same person.

Pollard has tried to connect the dots. As noted earlier, he said that while working as an intelligence analyst he was asked by Kurt Lohbeck, a freelance journalist, to help deliver arms to certain Mujahedin "freedom fighters" in Afghanistan. Pollard charges that Lohbeck was more than just a freelance journalist, however, and was actually involved in covert operations involving Afghanistan that were being run directly out of the National Security Council in Washington. In addition, Pollard noted in Wolf Blitzer's book, *Territory of Lies*, that those operations were personally being handled by then National Security Advisor Robert McFarlane—the same man who had apparently worked in close association with Silberman in the days preceding President Reagan's election.

Pollard portrayed Lohbeck as more or less a go-between who was mainly into arms trafficking for the money and was trying to cut himself in on a piece of the action. But why did Lohbeck come to Pollard in the first place? I asked one of my sources who was close to Pollard. Why didn't he just go through channels to the National Security Council? My source said he didn't know for sure, but stressed that Pollard, who had a relationship with Lohbeck, was very knowledgeable about certain types of handheld missiles, had lots of contacts, and had developed a "taste" for arms dealing—especially if the deal could benefit his friends in Israel.

Pollard has insisted that the reason his connection with Lohbeck was never brought up at his closed hearing was simple: He was quite emphatic in letting Assistant U.S. Attorney Charles Leeper know that if Leeper did charge him with passing military secrets to Afghanistan through Lohbeck, then he would tell a grand jury everything he knew about McFarlane's connection, also through Lohbeck, with Abdul Haq, the Afghan resistance commander.

My intelligence sources give little credence to the McFarlane connection, however. They tell me that Pollard knew far too much about both Iran-Contra and the illegal arming of Iraq to be allowed to testify in open court where he could have been put on the witness stand and would have had uncensored access to the public and the press. That, they say—and not any link to McFarlane—is why a government-arranged plea bargain was essential.

It was at the same time also essential to his enemies that Pollard receive as lengthy a prison term as allowed by law. A free Pollard—especially a free Pollard living in Israel—would have been a reporter's dream but a virtual nightmare to the inner circle of Bechtel graduates who helped shape American policy during the Reagan-Bush years.[1] The need to effectively muzzle Pollard is the real reason, my sources insist, why Pollard was tricked into agreeing to a plea bargain, then watched as the government locked the door and threw away the key.

Nevertheless, the McFarlane angle does bring up some interesting questions. For instance, could Silberman have had a predisposed prejudice toward Pollard because of Pollard's threats to "expose" Silberman's colleague, McFarlane, in yet another possible scandal? (McFarlane, after all, was a central figure in the Iran-Contra debacle which many believe was spawned by the so-called October Surprise.*) If so, did Silberman's participation as one of three appellate court justices hearing arguments for a new Pollard trial present a conflict of interest?

When I spoke to Gary Sick, the former National Security Council staffer said that he only had a "general knowledge" about the Pollard case, but stressed that, from what he did know, Silberman probably should have disqualified himself from sitting in judgment of Pollard. "I have felt that Silberman should have disqualified himself from a number of other cases he was involved in as well, such as the [Lt. Col.] Ollie North case," Sick told me. "It's not the first time [Silberman] has been accused of participating in a case that he should have excused himself from."

When I called Silberman at his Washington office, to ask him if he may have been prejudiced in the case, he chose not to speak to me. After a woman I believed to be his secretary told him I was waiting on the line for his response, she came back to the telephone and said: "The judge can't comment on that opinion." Asked if that was the judge's comment, her reply was the same. "The judge can't comment," she said.

I immediately faxed a letter to Pollard's (and Ronald Reagan's) attorney, Ted Olson, informing him of the link I felt I had possibly uncovered between Pollard and McFarlane. I also wrote an op-ed piece on the subject that appeared in the *South Florida Jewish Journal* on April 20, 1992. Described by Carol Pollard, Jonathan's sister, as the "ultimate political insider," I was anxious to know Olson's opinion on the whole matter.

From his office at the Washington law firm of Gibson, Dunn and Crutcher, Olson sent me a return letter dated April 30, 1992.

"Dear Mr. Goldenberg: Thank you for sending me your article concerning the Pollard case," Olson's letter began. "Although it may be true

---

*Both the "October Surprise" and Iran-Contra involved trading arms to Iran for American hostages. Because of all the arms we gave the shah, Iran's order of battle was American-based and Iran therefore needed our spare parts.

that Judge Silberman, Richard Allen, and Robert McFarlane had a meeting in October of 1980 (long before Judge Silberman's appointment to the bench) with 'an unidentified Middle Easterner,' at L'Enfant Plaza in Washington, the participants in that meeting, as I understand it, have all contradicted the version of that meeting that is being advanced by Mr. Gary Sick. In any event, I am not aware of any relationship between Judge Silberman and any of the events relating to the arrest, conviction, or sentencing of Jonathan Pollard.

"Judge Silberman's name was drawn by lot to participate as one of three judges to handle the Pollard appeal. While we do not concede that the majority of that panel reached the correct legal conclusion in the Pollard case, we do know that both Judge Silberman and Judge Ginsburg, who constituted the majority, are honest, able, conscientious, thoughtful, and respected members of the judiciary. . . . We have no basis for imputing any improper motives to either of them. . . . Speculation concerning anything other than entirely proper motives on behalf of Judge Silberman is both unwarranted and not constructive to Mr. Pollard's quite legitimate objections to the prosecution's conduct in this case.

"Very truly yours,

"Theodore B. Olson."

Olson apparently believed that even if there was some kind of Pollard-McFarlane connection, it had no bearing on Pollard's treatment by the appellate court. Olson may have been right. At the same time, I couldn't help but think of a conversation freelance writer Craig Unger said he once had with former Israeli intelligence operative Ari Ben-Menashe—the same Ari Ben-Menashe who had been one of Seymour Hersh's inside sources when the Pulitzer Prize–winning journalist wrote *The Samson Option*.

Ben-Menashe (who, according to my sources, also worked the Afghan connection) seemed to provide a missing piece to the complicated puzzle. Indeed, what Unger told me about his conversation with Ben-Menashe made me wonder whether Pollard had unknowingly sealed his own fate the moment he first mentioned McFarlane's name.

Carol Pollard has claimed for years that her brother told her he believed that Joseph diGenova, the U.S. attorney for the District of Columbia, was under "enormous pressure" to provide evidence of some kind of extensive Israeli spy network in the United States. According to Carol Pollard, her brother said the government was especially interested in a mysterious "Mr. X." Pollard claims he was repeatedly asked who this "Mr. X" was, yet has always insisted that he was working alone and, as far as he knew, there was no "Mr. X"—an important Jewish leader or Reagan administration official who was also feeding information to the Israelis behind Defense Secretary Weinberger's back.

Yet Carol Pollard recalled her brother saying something that stuck in my mind. Not necessarily describing any intelligence relationship with Israel per se, she said her brother once told her of a somewhat flippant remark he made to his inquisitors after he was first arrested. "There are much bigger fish to fry here," Pollard told her he said to them.

Perhaps Pollard was speaking in generalities, perhaps not. But in his magazine article also entitled "October Surprise," which appeared in the October 1991 issue of *Esquire* magazine, Craig Unger wrote: "In a sworn affidavit signed by [former U.S. Attorney General] Elliot Richardson on behalf of one of his clients, [Ari] Ben-Menashe, states that [National Security Advisor Robert] McFarlane had a 'special relationship' with Israeli intelligence, McFarlane having been recruited by Rafi Eitan. . . ."

This was the same Rafi Eitan who Pollard took his orders from as a "walk-in" when Eitan was the head of LAKAM, the special scientific intelligence-gathering unit of the Israeli Defense Ministry.

Unger went even further. He also quoted Ben-Menashe as stating that "McFarlane was the infamous 'Mr. X' in the Pollard case." When I spoke to Unger over the telephone, he said he was told this, personally, by Ben-Menashe. Not surprisingly, Unger told me he was also being sued by McFarlane for $25 million.

In a 1988 interview with *Playboy* magazine, PLO Chairman Yasser Arafat also linked McFarlane to the Israelis. Pollard has admitted passing U.S. satellite data to Israel showing the exact location of Arafat's headquarters in Tunis, which the Israelis subsequently bombed. Could someone else have done the same thing without Pollard knowing about it? During the *Playboy* interview Arafat told the interviewer, Morgan Strong: "We know that the United States supplied Israel with sensitive information, satellite photographs of our headquarters in Tunis, before they bombed it in 1985. Robert McFarlane did this."

"The same McFarlane who was, at the time, using the Israelis as intermediaries in the Iran-Contra deal?" Strong asked.

"Yes," Arafat replied. "We know it is true."

McFarlane, meanwhile, made a well-publicized suicide attempt in 1986 after the Iran-Contra story broke. Trying to piece all this together, I wondered whether there was a growing concern among McFarlane's friends in Washington over his well-being. I also wondered about some other elements that may have somehow factored into the Pollard case. If Ben-Menashe was correct about the alleged connection of McFarlane to Israeli intelligence (and this of course has never been proven), was the government fearful that Pollard's testimony in an open courtroom might have brought McFarlane into the espionage equation along with Pollard, thereby creating an embarrassing situation for both the United States and Israel? Were the Israelis especially worried about this, necessitating their allowing Pollard to face the full consequences of his actions while they worked behind the scenes to secure his eventual release? And if McFarlane was involved in working for the Israelis—obviously he worked in close association with them in connection with Iran-Contra as did many top advisors to President Reagan—could this have been a key element in the secret Weinberger memorandum sent to Judge Aubrey Robinson immediately preceding Pollard's sentencing?

As for McFarlane's having some kind of special relationship with Israel that went beyond the bounds of his role as U.S. national security advisor, there are a number of interesting scenarios. One, of course, is that there was no role—and that Ben-Menashe was merely making one up for reasons known only to himself. Another is that McFarlane, like Pollard, was sensitive to the plight he believed Israel faced while McFarlane's colleague,

Caspar Weinberger, was secretary of defense. Perhaps McFarlane was like Lord Percy in *The Scarlet Pimpernel*. In that classic book, Percy, who played a fop, continually risked his life to rescue French aristocrats condemned to the guillotine during the French Revolution. Was McFarlane trying to help save Israel from Weinberger's condemnation?

Reagan's inner circle should have known that history has a strange way of repeating itself. More than a decade earlier, some allege, a true American hero, Gen. Alexander Haig, had literally saved Israel from the mistakes made by President Richard Nixon and his secretary of state, Henry Kissinger. Those mistakes, sources say, nearly resulted in the first implementation of what Seymour Hersh called the "Samson Option," as Israel inched ever closer to that dangerous precipice where it would have had no choice but to play its nuclear hand as a last means of self-defense. (More about this in the next chapter.)

Notwithstanding, throughout this book there are clear indications that Weinberger and his cohorts—seemingly unconcerned about Israel's ability to ensure its survival by unleashing its growing arsenal of nuclear weapons—may have overseen a secret policy that not only caused the countdown to Armageddon in the Gulf states and the Middle East; it nearly resulted in its horrifying consequences.

NOTE

1. The Bechtel Corporation, described by John Loftus and Mark Aarons in *The Secret War Against the Jews* as "one of the most notorious anti-Semitic companies in the United States," adhered to the long-standing Arab boycott of Israel that began after Israel won the 1948 war against its Arab neighbors. According to Loftus and Aarons, "Bechtel absolutely carried out the provisions of the boycott to the letter; even when offered extremely lucrative contracts to do business in Israel, the company declined to deal with Jews."

CHAPTER 13

NIXON'S
AND
KISSINGER'S
BLUNDER

The exclusion of Israel from U.S.-held information deemed vital to the Jewish state's security was clearly not an invention of the Reagan administration and its secretary of defense. As alluded to in the last chapter, there were many black marks in that regard even before the Weinberger era, the blackest of which may have come during the presidency of Richard Nixon.

Still, a number of intelligence sources and investigative reporters dispute that Nixon's foreign policy decisions were ever meant to be damaging to Israel. In *The Samson Option*, Seymour Hersh seems to suggest that, in Nixon, the Israelis actually had a true ally in the Oval Office—and a friend who "turned a blind eye toward Israel's growing nuclear capacity" while paying lip service to the goal of nuclear nonproliferation. Notes Hersh: "Richard Nixon and [Secretary of State] Henry Kissinger approached inauguration day on January 20, 1969, convinced that Israel's nuclear ambitions were justified and understandable. Once in office, they went a step further: they endorsed Israel's nuclear ambitions."

According to Hersh, Nixon's and Kissinger's support for Israel's nuclear-weapons program "was widely known" to the Israeli leadership. "The Nixon administration made a judgment that would become American policy for the next two decades," Hersh wrote. "Israel had gone nuclear, and there was nothing that the United States could—or wanted to—do about it."

Many American Jews also remember the decision by Nixon to authorize a massive emergency airlift of supplies to Israel during the darkest hours of the Yom Kippur War. It was October 1973, and the besieged Israelis were engaged in a life-and-death struggle against Arab armies led by Egyptian President Anwar Sadat. Going by the commonly held belief, it was a gutsy Nixon, and his brilliant secretary of state, Kissinger, who literally "saved" the ill-prepared Israelis—perhaps reluctant to use their few nuclear weapons—from possible annihilation. Nevertheless, the sources I spoke with see Nixon's and Kissinger's roles during the fierce conflict in a far less flattering light.

In letters he sent to me from his prison cell, Jonathan Pollard stated his own conclusions about what he described as Nixon's and Kissinger's blunders. "American Jews assumed that the United States loyally abided by its security commitments to the Jewish state [during the Yom Kippur War]," Pollard wrote. "But Israeli leaders, in contrast, have a much less positive view of American behavior at the time."

Eventually, a supply airlift to Israel did take place and Israel survived the Arab onslaught. But, going by materials he read at Naval Intelligence, Pollard surmised that the only reason Nixon gave the okay for the airlift was that the Israelis had indeed begun assembling a nuclear weapon in response to their initial reverses on the Suez and Golan fronts.

Hersh's own sources seem to agree. In *The Samson Option* he notes that the Israeli leadership, faced with its "greatest crisis," decided to arm and target its nuclear arsenal while demanding that the United States begin an emergency airlift of replacement arms and ammunition.

So the implementation of the "Samson Option"—the option of last resort—may in fact have been given the green light by Israeli leaders. "Had this not occurred," Pollard noted, "from what I've heard, the Nixon administration would have been quite content to have watched the Israeli army run out of ammunition, thereby forcing the Meir cabinet to accept a cease-fire under conditions that would have left the Arabs with their first battlefield victory in twenty-five years."

Pollard wrote that Kissinger, although a Jew himself, was apparently of the opinion that there would be no peace in the Middle East until the Arabs had erased the military humiliation they collectively suffered in 1967. Once Arab "honor" had been satisfied, the assumption went, the Arabs would finally be able to negotiate with the Israelis from a position of equality.

"Oblivious to the fact that this policy would cost the lives of fellow Jews," charged Pollard, "Kissinger went ahead and privately assured Sadat, in the spring of 1973, that the United States would not be that upset to see the area 'heated up a little.' It was therefore no coincidence that, shortly after this exchange took place, the Egyptian general staff was ordered to set a certain date for what it called 'Operation Badr.'" (The Arabs call it the Ramadan War; Israelis and Americans call it the Yom Kippur War.) Pollard argued this was the real reason why the Nixon administration never bothered to alert the Israeli government about the Egyptian army's subsequent preparations for its surprise offensive against the Bar-Lev line (a fortified defense line to protect Israeli troops on the banks of the Suez Canal)—even though that buildup was being monitored extremely closely by U.S. intelligence. (Israel's dependence on American satellite overheads at the time caused Israel to go on a crash program to launch its own spy satellites—which it eventually did in 1992.)

However, in her book, *My Life*, Golda Meir, the Israeli prime minister at the time of the Yom Kippur War, blamed herself, and not Nixon or Kissinger, for the Israeli government's lack of preparation. "On Friday, October 5 [1973], we received a report that worried me," Meir wrote. "The families of Russian advisors in Syria were packing up and leaving [Syria] in a hurry. It reminded me of what had happened prior to the Six-Day War and I didn't like it at all. I asked the minister of defense and the chief of staff and the head of intelligence whether they thought this piece of information was very important. No, it hadn't in any way changed their assessment of the situation. I was assured that we would get adequate warnings of any real trouble anyway."

"Not only that," Meir added, "but foreign sources with which we were in constant touch agreed absolutely with the assessment of our experts."

Meir, diplomatically, never said who those foreign sources were who reassured her experts. But she gave accolades to both Nixon and Kissinger. Of Nixon she noted: "However history judges Richard Nixon— and it is probable that the verdict will be very harsh—it must also be put on the record forever that he did not break a single one of the promises he made to us."

Of Kissinger's role in the cease-fire to end the Yom Kippur War, Meir wrote: "At this point, the outstanding personality in the Middle East became not President Sadat or [Syrian] President Assad or [Saudi Arabia's] King Feisal or even Mrs. Meir. It was the U.S. secretary of state, Dr. Henry Kissinger, whose efforts on behalf of peace in the area can only be termed as superhuman. My own relationship with Henry Kissinger had its ups and downs. At times, I know I annoyed and perhaps even angered him—and vice versa. But I admired his intellectual gifts, his patience and perseverance were always limitless, and in the end we became good friends."

CNN political analyst Wolf Blitzer, in interviews done years later for the *Jerusalem Post*, said he spoke to both George Carver, who had been the CIA's deputy for Naval Intelligence at the time, and Joseph Cisco, who had been assistant secretary of state for Near Eastern and South Asian Affairs during the days leading up to the surprise attack against Israel. According to Blitzer, both Carver and Cisco maintained that Israel's "intelligence failure" in not anticipating the surprise attack "has had a lasting [negative] impact on the overall U.S.-Israeli intelligence relationship." Blitzer quoted Sisco as saying: "The lesson we drew from it was that we could not rely exclusively on Israeli intelligence and that our own independent means had to be provided."[1]

To Pollard, however, nothing could be further from the truth.

"The fact is," Pollard wrote, "Kissinger reassured the Israelis—right up until the last minute—that the Egyptians were only conducting 'large-scale exercises' on their side of the canal, and nothing more." (Those assurances were seemingly confirmed by then White House chief of staff Alexander Haig in his book *Inner Circles: How America Changed the World*. Writes Haig: "Prime Minister Golda Meir apparently believed U.S. intelligence reports that confidently argued that no Arab attack was imminent despite the enormous buildup of Soviet military aid to Israel's most dangerous enemies.")

Pollard charged that Kissinger also warned the Israelis that if they initiated an "unprovoked" attack against any Egyptian units moving toward the canal, Israel would be "left alone" to face the consequences of such an act. Pollard also stressed that several hours after Kissinger communicated this message to Jerusalem, one hundred thousand Egyptian troops stormed the Bar-Lev line, which was defended by a mere six hundred Israeli soldiers.

"As the casualty reports started pouring in," Pollard continued, "it didn't take the Israelis long to realize that their would-be 'friends' in Washington had essentially been willing participants in Egypt's prewar deception efforts against them. What we should never forget about this tragedy is that the four thousand Israelis who ultimately lost their lives in the Yom Kippur War were victims of the Nixon administration's cold-blooded betrayal of our people."

Bruce Brill, who from 1971 to 1974 was working for the National Security Agency as a Mideast analyst, confirms much of what Pollard alleges. States Brill, in an article that appeared in the *Jerusalem Post* on October 31, 1992: "While at the [National Security] Agency as an Arabic and 'Special Arabic' traffic analyst in the early 1970s, I learned of the planned October 6, 1973, invasion of Israel, by Syria and Egypt, thirty hours before the United States notified Israel." According to Brill, "upper-echelon NSA personnel knew of the planned attack hours, if not days, prior to that." Not passing this vital information along in time, Brill insists, "resulted in the unnecessary deaths and maiming of thousands of young Israelis."

When I personally met with Brill, prior to the publication of that article, he told me essentially the exact same thing.

In *The Secret War Against the Jews*, authors John Loftus and Mark Aarons also punch holes in the theory that Israeli intelligence somehow broke down, thereby allowing the Arabs to launch their simultaneous sneak attack on the eve of Israel's most holy day. What really happened, Loftus's and Aarons's sources told them, was the following: First, Kissinger failed to appreciate the danger of the Saudi-Egyptian alliance against Israel. Second, in order to curry favor with the Arabs, the White House ordered the National Security Agency to suppress information that a sneak attack against Israel would take place on October 6, 1973. And third, Kissinger's initial strategy was to let Israel get "bloodied" a bit and then force both sides to the peace table.

However, in a total miscalculation, the authors charge, Kissinger underestimated the consequences to Israel of delays in intelligence, mobilization, and resupply, which nearly caused a military catastrophe. Notes Seymour Hersh in *The Samson Option*: "Kissinger made no secret of his initial strategy in the war, telling James R. Schlesinger, the secretary of defense, that his goal was to 'let Israel come out ahead, but bleed.'" Loftus and Aarons put it more succinctly: "The unwitting Kissinger, intent on letting the Jews bleed a little, had opened an artery instead."

What nearly turned out to be the White House's worst-case scenario began unfolding because, by the fall of 1973, Kissinger was eager that Israel be forced to comply with UN resolution 242, which would reverse all the territorial gains that Israel had made in 1967, thereby returning the Israelis to the days when they were most vulnerable to an Arab attack. So while Israel was in the midst of losing its desperate fight for survival— three days into the war the Israelis were already running out of ammunition—stalling was seemingly the policy of the Nixon administration. And instead of rushing arms to the Israelis, Loftus and Aarons argue, Defense Secretary Schlesinger cautioned that the United States had to keep a "low profile in order not to create an Arab reaction in the oil markets."

The outbreak of hostilities gave the Arabs at the Vienna oil negotiations "a great moral boost," Loftus and Aarons continued. "The oil companies offered a 15 percent price increase, but the Arabs wanted to double their take. The Arab armies were winning for once, and the time was ripe to squeeze the West."

And squeeze they did. On October 12, six days after the war had begun, the oil companies sent a letter to Nixon via lawyer John McCloy suggesting that the Arab producers should receive some significant price increase. Already, several thousand Israeli soldiers had died and over five hundred Israeli tanks had been destroyed. Israeli Prime Minister Golda Meir desperately pleaded to the White House for help— help that had still not arrived. Help would soon arrive, of course, but only because the Israelis had a guardian angel: not Nixon or Kissinger, but White House Chief of Staff Alexander Haig.

According to Loftus and Aarons, Haig actually made national policy behind the slow-moving Kissinger's back. On October 6, during the first day of the war, Haig told Israeli intelligence that there was a weapon that could stop any Arab tank onslaught, and that if the Israelis could get a team to the United States, he would give it to them. The secret weapon was the new TOW missile which could be fired from a foxhole and could destroy a moving tank from up to three kilometers away. Its kill ratio was 97 percent.

When the Egyptians attacked the Israelis with their huge offensive on October 14, in hopes of delivering the knockout blow, it was those same TOW missiles, received courtesy of Al Haig, that turned the battle (and the war) in the Israelis' favor.

In his book *Inner Circles*, Haig credits Nixon, however, for turning the tide. Notes Haig: "By October 12, I had been informed, and had reported to the president, that the Israelis had already lost five hundred tanks, or nearly one-third of their inventory. I also briefed the president on the unacceptable delays in the airlift. That same day, Nixon called Kissinger and Schlesinger into the Oval Office, and, in a rare, but to me highly gratifying, display of personal domination, banished all excuses. He asked Kissinger to itemize the arms and materiel Israel needed, and Kissinger read out the list. 'Double it,' Nixon said. 'Now get the hell out of here, and get the job done.' "

Nixon, in public at least, had always described himself as a strong supporter of Israel. During an interview with Ted Koppel that was broadcast on January 7, 1992, Nixon reiterated that he never would have betrayed Israel—and, in fact, admonished the Reagan and Bush administrations for appearing to lean in that misguided direction.

As a guest on ABC's *Nightline*, when asked by Koppel whether any American president would actually desert Israel, Nixon responded sharply, telling the American public exactly what he told congressional leaders during the 1973 Yom Kippur War: that no American president, Democrat or Republican, would ever let Israel go down the tubes. "It's not an issue," Nixon said.

When Koppel, playing devil's advocate, then asked why the United States would continue to burden itself with huge loans to the Israelis, since Israel obviously no longer had the same strategic value to the United States that it once had, Nixon was again firm in his reply. He explained that the United States is concerned by more than strategic values. "That's maybe a weakness," the former president went on, "but it's the way we are."

There are also moral issues involved, Nixon continued. He said that while Israel isn't an ally of the United States, "at least in the technical sense," the United States has a "bond" to Israel that is much stronger than any alliance. To Nixon, that bond was a moral one "because of what happened during the Holocaust," and because Israel is the only democracy in the Middle East. Under the circumstances, Nixon said confidently, future American presidents would have few qualms about ensuring the survival of Israel if Israel were attacked.

Koppel seemed just a bit skeptical. Describing Nixon as a "very tough, pragmatic man," he said he wondered if Nixon was the prime minister of Israel, instead of a former U.S. president, and heard Richard Nixon, or any sitting American president, say, "there's really no strategic value anymore," how much faith would he then place in that kind of moral commitment if push really came to shove?

Nixon refused to budge. He said that if he were an Israeli leader he'd put a great deal of faith in that moral commitment because of the track record of the United States.

Koppel pressed on, stressing that the "track record" was established at a time when the Soviet Union tended to be allied with Israel's ene-mies—but that the Soviet Union no longer existed. Quickly changing gears, Koppel then began to probe Nixon about Israel's ultimate insurance policy—her nuclear capabilities.

"You also state, categorically, that the Israelis have atomic weapons," Koppel said. "You know that the Israelis have never admitted this publicly. But since you state this as a former president of the United States, you must know what you're talking about."

"I'm not going to divulge any of my so-called secret information and so forth," Nixon replied, "but I will say this: If I were an Israeli I wouldn't indicate that I had them and I wouldn't indicate that I didn't have them. Let me just say, most experts in the area assume that the Israelis have nuclear weapons."

"But you don't qualify it here this evening," Koppel said, "and you didn't qualify it in your book—"

Nixon—as if he knew something that Israel's enemies couldn't be sure of—interrupted before Koppel could finish his thought. "Because," Nixon warned, "the Israelis will use them."

NOTE

1. The story appeared in the American Jewish press on December 8, 1989.

CHAPTER 14

BAGHDAD GLOWING
IN THE
DARK

I n his 1991 book, *The Samson Option*, Seymour Hersh alleges that when Iraq attacked Israel earlier that year with its Scud missiles, Israel had again gone on full nuclear alert, ready to launch its nuclear-armed missiles against Saddam Hussein. It was not the first time Israel had gone on nuclear alert, since (as noted in the last chapter) the Israelis had also begun a nuclear countdown, eighteen years earlier, during the near-disastrous Yom Kippur War. But while Israel's nuclear capability in 1973 was quite limited, by 1991, my sources tell me, Israel had become a true nuclear power.

While the Israeli embassy in Washington was quick to dismiss as "totally nonsense" a number of the charges Hersh made in his book—including charges that Israeli prime minister Yitzhak Shamir had handed Moscow sanitized U.S. intelligence information provided by Jonathan Pollard—an embassy spokesperson would not comment on Hersh's other charges related to Israel's nuclear readiness.[1]

My intelligence sources also scoffed at Hersh's assertions regarding Pollard and Shamir. Former Israeli intelligence operative William Northrop says Hersh called him for a confirmation regarding Pollard's information winding up in the Kremlin. "I told him, 'It never happened,' " Northrop said.

Those same Israeli sources were not reticent, however, about commenting on Israel's reliance on its Jericho missiles—armed with nuclear warheads—as a prime deterrent against her enemies.

"There is an old saying," Northrop once told me. "Question: What is three feet deep and glows in the dark? Answer: Baghdad, five minutes after an Iraqi chemical and biological weapons attack against Israel."

Frank Gaffney is the former Reagan administration Deputy Assistant Secretary of Defense for Nuclear Forces and Arms Control Policy. If any Washington insider knew how close Iraq had come to being the target of nuclear-armed Israeli Jericho missiles during the Gulf War, one of those people certainly should have been Frank Gaffney, who later became the director of the Center for Security Policy, a Washington watchdog organization whose membership is a who's who of Reagan-Bush Republicans.

Gaffney had been among a number of speakers addressing a large audience at Temple Beth Israel, a synagogue in Sunrise, Florida, when I met him in early December of 1993. (One of the other speakers was Dan Raviv, author of *Every Spy a Prince*.) Speaking as a guest of the Middle East Network—a group that closely monitors what it considers blatantly anti-Israeli press coverage by the media—Gaffney appeared that day to be an unswerving supporter of Israel, was highly critical of Israel's enemies in the Arab world, and, as expected, was extremely well received by the audience. Indeed, Gaffney sounded far more like a member of Israel's Likud Party than America's Republican Party.

"I believe the people of Israel were actually hoodwinked," Gaffney told the crowd of mostly senior citizens. "It's not a question of if [the peace process] will turn out to be a problem for Israel. The real question is how grievous a problem it will turn out to be."

Gaffney said the much talked about handshake between PLO

Chairman Yasser Arafat and Israeli Prime Minister Yitzhak Rabin conjured up a comment made by eighteenth-century British wit Samuel Johnson about second marriages. "Johnson once called second marriages a triumph of hope over experience," Gaffney quipped. "Unfortunately, the peace accord seems less a reason for hope, and has more to do, I believe, with Israel's weariness of the *intifada** and the costs of maintaining its troops [in Gaza]."

Gaffney added that while the recent deaths of Israelis at the hands of Arab hard-liners during terrorist attacks had been blamed on the splinter group Hamas—considered more radical than the mainstream PLO—both groups were in fact basically the same. "I don't see any appreciable difference between Hamas and the rest of the PLO," Gaffney stressed. "Although Hamas is more bellicose, up until this point, at least, it has actually committed fewer violent attacks against Israel than has the PLO. So the distinction is without a major difference. And even if Arafat were miraculously transformed from the terrorist thug he has been, to a genuine man of peace, it's still hard to determine what's going to happen when he's eventually removed from power."

Gaffney then said he hoped that, in the final analysis, Israel does not have to use its nuclear arsenal in order to defend itself from its enemies.

"If Israel has to rely on its nuclear weapons—which could happen—then the whole world will rue Israel's agreeing to such a risky peace," Gaffney warned.

Unlike Nixon and most Israeli leaders, Frank Gaffney, President Reagan's nuclear arms expert, publicly admitted that Israel had nuclear weapons. And, if necessary, Gaffney implied, the Israelis would be ready, willing, and able to play their ultimate trump card.

After the roundtable discussion ended, someone introduced us and we walked together to Gaffney's car. After we exchanged business cards I told my new acquaintance that I was the author of *The Spy Who Knew Too Much,*

---

*A Palestinian uprising that took place on the West Bank (in Israel) and the Gaza Strip. The Palestinians there considered this to be an Israeli "occupation" of their land.

which I explained was about the Jonathan Pollard spy case. I then asked Gaffney a loaded question: Was his ex-boss, Caspar Weinberger, actually the man behind Pollard's stiff sentence?

The affable Gaffney politely smiled but wouldn't (or couldn't) answer. He did put me on his mailing list, however. To this day I continue getting mail from his organization, and invitations to Center for Security Policy events (including Ronald Reagan's birthday party in Washington).

I asked Gaffney about Weinberger because while the Reagan administration certainly had more than its share of strong pro-Israeli voices—perhaps the most notable being Alexander Haig's—Weinberger's voice clearly wasn't among them. Besides, according to some of my intelligence sources it was Weinberger who appears to have been the high-level Reagan administration official most responsible for overseeing the secret sharing of technology with Iraq dealing with the development and testing of chemical and biological weapons—a misguided policy that nearly caused an Israeli nuclear response in the Persian Gulf. My sources also insisted that it was Weinberger, through his good friend U.S. Attorney General Edwin Meese, who made sure that Pollard—the man who informed the Israelis of that secret American policy—would be shackled in silence for the rest of his life.

On October 30, 1990, meanwhile, Weinberger was honored when he received the prestigious Center for Security Policy's Keeper of the Flame Award, given each year to an individual who has "exemplified the ideals of freedom, democracy, economic opportunity, and American strength to which the center is committed."

Along with his business card, Frank Gaffney had also handed me a folder that included a number of brochures and flyers. The headline atop the first page of one of the flyers stated in bold print: "Here we go again: After the Iraqi debacle, will Syria be let off the state sponsors of terrorism list?" The article stressed that President Bill Clinton was making a serious mistake by allowing his then secretary of state, Warren Christopher, to give certain concessions to Syria in exchange for a Syrian commitment to get back to the peace table with Israel. The author of the article, whom I assumed was Gaffney (or at least shared Gaffney's views), wrote: "Secretary Christopher is said to have pledged that Syria would be removed from the official U.S. government list of state sponsors of terrorism, a status that precludes listed nations from receiving certain preferential trade benefits and access to sophisticated, militarily relevant technologies."

According to the writer, the initiative "bore an appalling resemblance to an earlier, misbegotten decision by the U.S. government. In 1982, the Reagan administration decided—at a time when it was legitimately concerned that Islamic revolutionary Iran might prevail over Iraq—to tilt toward Saddam Hussein. Central to the implementation of that decision was the removal of Iraq from the list of state sponsors of terrorism, despite Baghdad's continued, vigorous support to international terrorist organizations."

This condemnation of Clinton seemed ironic since Weinberger—the 1990 Keeper of the Flame award-winner—may well have been the chief architect of that same "pro-Iraq" policy. At the very least, he certainly did little to oppose it. The "preferential trade benefits" that Iraq received included that country being given the technological assistance to produce biological and chemical weapons. Those weapons, my sources tell me, were to be "field-tested" against Iran. And as Jonathan Pollard quickly learned from his "catbird's seat" at Naval Intelligence—Israel was in Iraq's sites as well.

"What kind of moron gives Sarin to Saddam Hussein?" William Northrop rhetorically asked during a taped conversation I had with him at the Bimini Boatyard Restaurant in Fort Lauderdale. The Germans, in 1939, came up with a new kind of poison gas that, instead of attacking the blood system or the circulatory system, attacked the human nervous system, Northrop told me. "This, the father of all nerve agents, is called Taubun," Northrop said. "Taubun was the first real workable nerve gas. Sarin was developed later and is about twenty times as powerful.

"So nobody in their right mind gives that kind of technology to Saddam Hussein. They just don't do it. But [the Reagan administration] did. And they approved it. And the Commerce Department sent the precursors, the chemicals. Pollard, meanwhile, was like the mama spider sitting in the center of the web. All this input was coming down the line and he was the one who saw how it all fit together."

About nine months after my conversation with Frank Gaffney I received a "Fall Report" from the Center for Security Policy. The second paragraph of the first page read: "The Center joined forces with other concerned organizations and individuals—such as former secretaries of defense Caspar Weinberger and Donald Rumsfeld—in alerting the American people to an alarming, but little known fact: The U.S. government is currently unable to protect its people, troops overseas, and allies, from ballistic missiles equipped with nuclear, chemical, and biological weapons."

We did have a serious problem, of course, as many of the soldiers who fought in the Persian Gulf—and were now watching their health rapidly deteriorate—already knew. As for Weinberger being put on the Center for Security Policy's "concerned individual" list, I couldn't help but think that this was a bit like the French physician J. I. Guillotin suddenly feeling remorse over how many French citizens were being beheaded by the deadly contraption that was in fact named in his honor.

Just as all roads once led to Rome, all Reagan administration policy decisions involving the Arab "allies"—decisions that, more often than not, appeared biased against Israel—seemed to lead to Caspar Weinberger's doorstep. With the tough-minded secretary of defense at the helm, the marriage of convenience that took place between the Arab world and the United States during the Carter administration seemed to blossom into a honeymoon during the presidency of Ronald Reagan. As has been well documented, the gaining of U.S. prestige and influence in the Arab world—too often at Israel's expense—was of course an old policy and not the brainchild of Weinberger. He and some of the other "Bechtel boys" within the Reagan administration merely continued the policy and refined it.[2]

Indeed, the apparent anti-Israeli tilt in Washington began well before Weinberger even got there. In an article that appeared in the *Los Angeles Herald Examiner* on August 22, 1982, entitled "Back Door to the PLO: How Cap Sold Defense to the Arabs and Israel Down the Road," the authors, Stephen B. Zatuchni and Daniel Drooz, wrote: "Caspar Willard Weinberger did not reverse U.S. policy by himself. In January 1981, when [Weinberger] became secretary of defense, there was already an anti-Israel bias within the Joint Chiefs of Staff."

In fact, the Joint Chiefs' chairman Gen. George S. Brown had already made national headlines when he publicly condemned the influence of American Jews when it came to U.S. foreign policy making. Weinberger no doubt agreed with Brown's assessment, at least in private. Surely, it would not have been difficult for Weinberger to justify any negative attitudes he may have had about Israel in the name of American economic interests. As of 1982, Saudi Arabia alone had as much as $300 billion invested in the United States and the West. The Saudis had also spent billions of dollars by that time on military hardware, much of it coming from the United States.

But Weinberger, many argue, brought a truly "pro-Arab" disposition to the Defense Department, and his impressive resumé included his tenure as vice president, director, and legal counsel of the Bechtel Group, an engineering firm that had greatly profited from its multibillion-dollar ties to the Saudi Arabian government. Bechtel had steadfastly refused to do any business with Israel, or Israeli companies worldwide, ever since the Arab boycott of Israel began in 1948. A suit was eventually brought against Bechtel by the Justice Department, charging the company with complying with the Arab boycott in violation of U.S. law.

Zatuchni and Drooz went on to state in their article that an anonymous senior member of the Senate Foreign Relations Committee staff had bluntly told them: "Weinberger believes that what's good for Bechtel is good for the United States. A lot of people in the Defense Department look at Israel as a pain in the ass. This is a dominant way of thinking in the DOD. They think Israel will get the United States in trouble and hurt business."

In his book, *Twin Pillars to Desert Storm: America's Flawed Vision in the*

Middle East from Nixon to Bush, Howard Teicher, a top director at the National Security Council during the Reagan administration, argues that Weinberger was hostile to Israel mainly because of his eagerness to please Arab leaders. Besides chronicling Weinberger's ongoing feud with Secretary of State George Shultz, Teicher noted that Weinberger often ignored direct instructions from his president regarding Israel.

Angelo M. Codevilla, a former intelligence officer who was once on the staff of the Senate Select Committee on Intelligence, was also highly critical of Weinberger's behind-the-scenes posturing concerning the Jewish state. "The management of foreign policy requires, above all, the instinct to prefer friends to enemies," Codevilla wrote. "From Weinberger's book *Fighting for Peace* (which Codevilla reviewed in the September 1990 issue of *Commentary* magazine), one learns that Weinberger lacked such an instinct."

To Codevilla, Weinberger erroneously saw the major problem in the Middle East as being the State of Israel and its stubborn leaders. "Consider U.S. policy in the Middle East," Codevilla stated. "About all the countries, but one, Weinberger's feelings are friendly or nuanced. About Israel and Israel's leaders they are unbelievably hostile."

Codevilla noted, for instance, that Weinberger denounced Israel for requesting, in the summer of 1982, that the Syrian forces—which had entered Lebanon and were camped outside Beirut—be withdrawn simultaneously with its own troops. According to Weinberger, this simultaneous withdrawal would have suggested a "legal and moral equivalent" of the Israeli presence with the Syrian presence. For Weinberger, Codevilla explained, Syria apparently stood on a higher "legal and moral plane." When the Israelis finally dropped their insistence on a parallel Syrian withdrawal, and left unilaterally as the Americans had asked, security in and around Beirut deteriorated rapidly. It was after the Israelis honored the U.S. request that, on October 23, 1983, 241 U.S. Marines were killed when fundamentalist Shi'ite terrorists set off a bomb in the Marine headquarters in Beirut.

Codevilla asked: "How does one reconcile Weinberger's punctilious refusal to hold accountable the Syrians, self-declared enemies of his country, with his eager credence of the darkest rumors about Israel and the lowest construction of Israel's motives? Surely not in terms of state-craft. For a statesman, even the worst of states that supports your basic interests and stands with you in the crunch is to be preferred to a state that opposes your basic interests, kills your people, and sides with your enemies. And where the United States is concerned, how much more should this be the case when the state that is your friend is a democracy, and the state that is your enemy is a tyranny."

Lt. Col. Oliver North, in his book *Under Fire*, also leveled harsh charges against Frank Gaffney's ex-boss, stating that the former defense secretary "seemed to go out of his way to blame the Israelis for every problem in the Middle East." Noted North: "In our planning for counterterrorist operations, [Weinberger] apparently feared that if we went after Pales-tinian terrorists, we would offend and alienate Arab governments—par-ticularly if we acted in cooperation with the Israelis."

According to North, Weinberger's sensitivity about his alleged Jewish ancestry may have been one cause of his seeming disdain for Israel. North alluded, also, to Weinberger's close association to the Bechtel Group. A former general counsel of Bechtel, Weinberger was joined in the Reagan administration, in mid-1982, by George Shultz, a former Bechtel president who replaced the pro-Israeli Alexander Haig as secretary of state.

Weinberger, for his part, has long claimed that all the anti-Israeli charges levied against him have been spurious. In a 1983 speech to the American Jewish Committee, he strongly denied any of the allegations that he had "some kind of personal animus" against the Jewish state. "I am a strong supporter of Israel," Weinberger said at the time, "and an admiring witness to the democracy [the Israelis] have built and preserved under the most trying conditions."

But Lawrence J. Korb, a director of the Brookings Institute—and, like Frank Gaffney, a man who once worked directly under Weinberger as an assistant secretary of defense—disagreed. In a letter he wrote to

Jonathan Pollard's father, Dr. Morris Pollard, Korb said of Weinberger: "I know that Weinberger had an almost visceral dislike of Israel and the special place it occupies in our foreign policy."

North also took issue with Weinberger's glowing portrayal of himself as a "friend" of Israel's. In addition, North stated in his book that there were many others in Washington—particularly in the State Department—who apparently shared Weinberger's antipathy toward the Jewish state. "There seemed to be a constituency [in the State Department]," North wrote, "that actually relished any antagonisms that could be fostered between us and the Israelis."

Besides literally handing Saddam Hussein the technology to make chemical and biological weapons—as some of my sources charge—Weinberger and his colleague Deputy CIA Director Bobby Inman were at the same time reluctant to give Israel any satellite data about Iraq, especially after Israel bombed the Osirak nuclear reactor located about ten miles outside of Baghdad.

William Northrop described to me how that particular attack took place. He said there were two sections of Israeli jets that were flying extremely close together, four in a formation. "If they fly close enough," Northrop said, "on radar it looks like one jetliner, like a 747." Northrop said there was a "top cover" or "cap" of American-made F-15As that flew as protection for the bombers, while the lower-flying American-made F-16s were "carrying the big iron."

The jets approached the target from a low altitude. Northrop said the Iraqis finally "painted" them with radar, but only after the F-16s, flying at about 3,000 feet, had already hit the Osirak reactor's dome. "The dome went in on the first hit and collapsed and went into the building," Northrop recalled. According to Northrop, a Frenchman working for the Israelis was inside the Osirak facility and was killed during the attack. It was the only Israeli casualty.

To the Israelis, the raid was a smashing success. It's important to stress that then CIA director William Casey—whom Bob Woodward notes in *Veil* was "pleased that the Israelis had disposed of the problem"—was not nearly as reticent about working closely with Israel and sharing information with Jerusalem as were Weinberger, Inman, White House Chief of Staff James Baker, and Vice President George Bush.

In his book *Crimes of a President*, investigative reporter Joel Bainerman states that while Weinberger has often been thought of as being the most "anti-Israeli" of all the members of Reagan's cabinet, his sources told him that Bush, in fact, may have even been more so. Bainerman notes that Alexander Haig allegedly claimed—in the discussion in the cabinet following the bombing raid—that it was Bush, not Weinberger, who actually demanded that the United States cut off all aid to Israel because of an "outrageous" breach of international law.

It was Weinberger, though, who then proposed canceling a proposed F-16 aircraft sale to Israel, insisting that some sanctions against the Jewish state were essential.

Reagan and Casey, although privately delighted with the attack, nevertheless went along with Weinberger's suggestion.

NOTES

1. Reported by David Friedman for the Jewish Telegraphic Agency. The Israeli embassy spokesperson, Friedman noted, was Ruth Yaron. Yaron reportedly described Hersh's source, Ari Ben-Menashe, as a "low-level translator."

2. A number of members of President Ronald Reagan's cabinet at one time or another served the Bechtel Corporation in various capacities. Former Bechtel officials or legal advisors included Secretary of Defense Caspar Weinberger and Secretary of State George Shultz.

THE
BOYS WERE
IN THE
OIL BUSINESS

W hile President Reagan and CIA Director William Casey privately applauded the Israeli attack on the Osirak nuclear reactor in Iraq, the Reagan administration nevertheless had at least two main reasons for solidifying its relations with Saddam Hussein during the decade leading up to the Gulf War.

The first reason was a fear of the growing strength of Islamic fundamentalists and the legitimate threat they posed to peace in the Mideast and Persian Gulf regions. As Dr. Walid Phares, the author of *The Iranian Islamic Revolution*, noted in an article: "Fundamentalist Moslem doctrine states that any time, by any means, the forces of Islam may attack, subdue, and conquer."[1] A strong Saddam Hussein, on the other hand, would have acted as a major buffer against Islamic fundamentalism while keeping Iran's dangerous expansionist designs at bay.

A second reason, however, may have had more to do with administration insiders looking to line their pockets. In 1984 the United States was importing 60,000 barrels of crude oil a day from Iraq. By July of 1990—on the eve of the Gulf War—that figure had risen to approximately 1.6 million barrels a day. As one of my sources told me, "The boys were in the oil business."

Indeed, by 1990 the United States was purchasing about 25 percent of Iraq's total oil production. Said my source: "Now all these boys—Weinberger, Schultz, Baker, Bush—they all had very heavy holdings in oil. And it was the companies in which they had those holdings that were importing the Iraqi crude. Bechtel even had a project to build a pipeline from Iraq to the port of Aqaba, in Jordan, to carry the Iraqi crude oil to ports where it could then be shipped out of the range of Iranian bombers. Remember, [from 1980–88] we had a war going on."[2]

In 1989, then president George Bush signed a top-secret order, National Security Directive 26, permitting the secret transfer of sensitive weapons technology to Iraq. Through sources I received a partial copy of NSD 26. It had officially been sent to the vice president, the secretary of state, the secretary of defense, the director of Central Intelligence, and the chairman of the Joint Chiefs of Staff, as well as to a number of other agencies and advisors. My copy was stamped UNCLASSIFIED and was dated October 2, 1989. It read, in part: "Access to Persian Gulf oil and the security of key friendly states in the area are vital to U.S. national security. The United States remains committed to defend its vital interests in the region, if necessary and appropriate through the use of military force, against the Soviet Union or any other regional power with interests inimical to our own. . . . Normal relations between the United States and Iraq would serve our longer-term interests and promote stability in both the Gulf and the Middle East. The United States should propose economic and political incentives for Iraq to moderate its behavior and to increase our influence with Iraq. At the same time, the Iraqi leadership must understand that any illegal use of chemical and/or biological weapons will lead to economic and political sanctions, for which we would seek the broadest possible support from our allies and friends."

In spite of what NSD 26 officially said, however, billions of dollars worth of loans guaranteed by American taxpayers went to Saddam Hussein even after U.S. intelligence agencies reported that Saddam was still building up his chemical and biological weapons arsenal.

Jonathan Pollard, meanwhile, was far more interested in Israel's security than he was in helping to maintain the decade-long quid pro quo relationship that had developed between Saddam Hussein and two Republican administrations. It was Pollard who first passed on the U.S. satellite photos of the attack on the Osirak facility to Col. Avi Sella, the Israeli pilot who had led that raid. And it was Pollard whose testimony before a court of law could help prove that Iraq was not only attempting to produce its own chemical and biological weapons, but was apparently doing so with American help.

Back in early 1984 the Reagan White House had made the decision to suppress any news of Iraq's burgeoning chemical and biological weapons-production capability, regardless of the fact that this would place Israel at great risk. When questions were later raised by the media concerning the origin of Iraq's mustard gas, for instance, they were invariably deflected by the administration in such a manner as to leave the impression that whatever few chemical arms the Iraqis were "thought" to be using had been obtained from either Egypt, North Korea, or the Soviet Union.

The Israelis didn't quite buy this story. For one thing, they had seen no evidence of large-scale transfers of chemical munitions to Iraq from any outside suppliers. It was at this point that Israeli intelligence began to suspect that the Iraqis were actually manufacturing their own poison gases.

Still, the Reagan administration continued to assure Israel that Iraq lacked the expertise to produce these substances. The truth, meanwhile, was that the Iraqis had already begun secretly converting several of their pesticide factories into poison-gas manufacturing plants. They were also breaking ground for one of the world's largest chemical warfare complexes which had been designed by some of the same West German companies involved with the Rabta project in Libya.

Pollard's firsthand knowledge of all this—and his knowledge of the

White House's duplicity concerning Iraqi efforts to further develop and refine these outlawed weapons—were among a growing list of reasons why his enemies in the U.S. government considered him such a threat. Pollard could link Iraq to the German company Imhausen-Chemie; he could link Imhausen Chemie to Dr. Ishan Barbouti (who helped build the chemical weapons plant at Rabta); and he could link Barbouti to the CIA.

"Pollard was the first person to actually identify Imhausen-Chemie as being the prime supplier of the chemical weapons plant at Rabta," one of my sources explained. "And he identified Barbouti, as well. Actually, something like ninety or ninety-five German companies were in some way involved in the mass production of chemical and biological weapons. The Germans looked at this as a very positive cash flow."

The reluctance of the United States to tackle the threat of Iraq's poison-gas manufacturing head-on may have also been due to Washington's long-time friendly relations with Saudi Arabia. In *Veil: The Secret Wars of the CIA*, Bob Woodward writes about the relationship between U.S. and Saudi Arabian intelligence: "It was impossible to determine where Saudi interests in these arrangements ended and American CIA interests began."

Pollard agreed. "Sanity," he once wrote in a letter to me, "is in short supply whenever Saudi Arabia is involved with U.S. policy making."

Through sources, Pollard said he learned that the Saudis had told some Reagan advisors that, without the use of chemical weapons, the Iraqis would have had great difficulty in containing the Iranians along the Shatt al-Arab waterway during the war between the two countries. Pollard said the administration was warned by Saudi Prince Sultan that Iran's Revolutionary Guards would have also had clear sailing into downtown Kuwait City. "Of course, the fact that the Iraqis could have easily thrown back any Iranian offensive without dousing the battlefield with poison gas was totally disregarded by the White House and the Defense Department," Pollard argued. "So, in early 1984, the White House made the decision to bury any news of Iraq's growing chemical warfare production capability."

That same year the Reagan administration assured the Israelis that there was no evidence to support their contention that Iraq was building a major poison-gas complex with the assistance of several West German companies. "So as you can well imagine," Pollard recalled, "the Israelis were utterly flabbergasted by the information I subsequently made available to them."

In *Territory of Lies*, author Wolf Blitzer correctly points out that among the first documents Pollard gave Israel—and which so impressed Pollard's handlers—involved the details of Iraq's chemical warfare factories. "This information I provided the Israelis didn't so much impress them, though," Pollard insisted, "as it shocked the hell out of them."

Saudi Arabia has actually been closely linked to the shaping of U.S. foreign policy going as far back as the 1920s when Western oil companies used American and British spies to prop up Ibn Saud as king of the oil-rich Gulf state. But in the November 1991 issue of *Mother Jones* magazine, Scott Armstrong—a former *Washington Post* reporter and coauthor (along with Bob Woodward) of *The Brethren*—argued that, by 1979, the national interests of Saudi Arabia had become even more closely intertwined with the national interests of the United States. Explained Armstrong, when Iranian militants seized the U.S. hostages in Tehran on November 4, 1979, and Soviet troops invaded Afghanistan a month later, President Jimmy Carter suddenly became the first American president to face the real prospect of having to move a rapid-deployment force into the Persian Gulf. However, as Carter and his aides "scrambled to consider contingencies," Armstrong wrote, "they found the Pentagon's bag of tricks virtually empty."

There was a shortage of port facilities in the area, no easy access to the Persian Gulf, and no prepositioned equipment. In addition, Armstrong charged, the virtual absence of sophisticated electronic and technological support—on which the U.S. military had become so dependent—made it difficult (if not impossible) for the United States to plan operations of more than hours or days duration. "Conflicts requiring weeks or months of combat were beyond anyone's imagination," Armstrong concluded. "In

the phrase of the day, the rapid deployment force was a joke. It was neither rapid, deployable, nor forceful."

A desirable option, Armstrong noted, was to have American bases
already in place in the Persian Gulf—specifically in Saudi Arabia, which,
historically, had enjoyed extremely warm relations with the United States.
The Saudis, after all, needed American protection and the Americans
needed to protect the flow of Saudi oil. Except for a handful of small airfields, however, Saudi Arabia was generally devoid of a usable military
infrastructure. To change all that—and to create what would later become
a vast network of "superbases" extending throughout the sheikdom—
would require a mammoth U.S. investment to create modern facilities,
ports, air bases, and air defense equipment, not to mention command,
control, and communications facilities.

In the past, although always willing to do business with the United
States, the Saudis had nonetheless wanted to keep a safe distance from
their would-be American benefactors. That all changed in 1979. While
up until that time the Saudis had never shown any inclination to offer
the United States even temporary use of their bases, a number of
events—including the fall of the shah, the emergence of a hostile
Shi'ite theocracy under the Ayatollah Khomeini, a coup attempt in
neighboring Bahrain, the Soviet invasion of Afghanistan, and the seizure
of the Grand Mosque in Mecca—caused the Saudis to undergo a
drastic reevaluation in their thinking.

The Carter administration soon began working quietly behind the
scenes with the Saudi royal family in order to implement gradual weapons
purchases supported by large-scale investments in airfields and ports.
Reluctantly, though, Carter had to put his ambitious plans on hold until
after the 1980 presidential election. A Democrat, he needed Jewish votes,
not to mention Jewish financial support. And American Jews might have
been put off, to say the least, if news leaked out about what Carter was
doing in Saudi Arabia.

When Carter was soundly defeated at the polls, however, the Reagan
administration immediately picked up where the Carter White House had

left off. With an obvious mandate from the voters behind them, President Reagan's new national security team also approved the plan, conceived by Carter's advisors, to sell the Saudis the linchpin for what was to be a grand network of superbases on Saudi soil: the Airborne Warning and Control System (AWACS). According to intelligence sources, the two main lobbyists for the AWACS were Gen. Richard Secord and Lt. Col. Oliver North. Secord confirmed his own lobbying efforts in an October 1987 interview with *Playboy* magazine. "I headed the drive for the sale to the Saudis of the AWACS aircraft in 1981," Secord told interviewer Morgan Strong.

The decision to sell the AWACS touched off heated opposition, meanwhile, from the powerful pro-Israel members of Congress. The AWACS, after all, were capable of directing offensive actions against Israel while neutralizing the Israeli air force. Not surprisingly, the strong backers of the Carter plan within Reagan's inner circle wanted to keep the "superbase" deal out of congressional debate. The way to do that was to have no formal agreement. "By keeping the agreement oral," Armstrong reasoned, "both sides had the 'understanding' they wanted without anything in writing which could be reviewed—and possibly rejected—by the U.S. Congress."

Armstrong alleged that the Reagan administration figured out a simple way to get the job done while at the same time maintaining the flow of weapons and technology to Saudi Arabia. "The key to maintaining secrecy lay in minimizing congressional review of Saudi requests to purchase U.S. arms other than the AWACS planes themselves," Armstrong wrote. "By breaking additional military purchases into smaller packages that fell below the dollar limits requiring congressional review, the Reagan administration made it difficult for Congress or the media to track the course of the new relationship."

Years later, when Saddam Hussein marched into Kuwait and then amassed his forces on the Saudi border, he possibly underestimated what he was getting ready to face. The United States, after all, had been quietly making Saudi Arabia into a nearly impregnable U.S. military outpost—prepared to more than match any Soviet or Iranian-inspired attempt to overthrow the Saudi regime and threaten American oil supplies. Saddam, of course, had a trick up his own sleeve. He had amassed an arsenal of chemical and biological weapons which, as he promised, he would not hesitate to use.

Interestingly, as the allied forces gathered for the defense of Saudi Arabia and the rescue of Kuwait, America's erstwhile ally predictably turned its eye away from Iraq and toward Israel. Having been pulled from the fire by the rapid deployment of American forces, the Saudis—who had always feared Israel mainly because of its Western ideas that could threaten their own backward feudal monarchy—not only demanded that Israel not retaliate should it be attacked by the Iraqis; they hinted that they might join Iraq in a new war against the Jewish state.

It was probably all bluster. The United States knew it could handle Saudi Arabia and that the coalition was not about to fall apart in spite of any Saudi posturing. The real concern was that if Iraq used its chemical and biological weapons against Israel, my sources tell me, Israel might have retaliated with a nuclear strike.

Bush, although perplexed about how Israel was going to play its nuclear hand, was not about to be cowed by an out-of-control Saddam Hussein. During the war's first day, things in fact went well for the American president. Bush was delighted as Air Force and Navy planes struck targets in downtown Baghdad at will. Reality set in during the war's second day, however, as the Iraqis fired eight Scud missiles at Israel, two of which landed in Tel Aviv and another of which landed near Haifa. According to early reports—that later turned out to be erroneous—the missiles contained deadly nerve gas.

It seemed conceivable, Seymour Hersh stated in *The Samson Option*, that Israel could enter the Gulf War by simply sending its air force and specially trained commando units into western Iraq where the Scuds were located. Of course, there was a far greater element of danger not known to the public, but which was easily detected by an American satellite then orbiting around the earth. Noted Hersh: "The satellite saw that [Prime Minister Yitzhak] Shamir had responded to the Scud barrage by ordering mobile missile launchers armed with nuclear weapons moved out into the open and deployed facing Iraq, ready to launch on command." (According to Israeli intelligence sources, a strike force of more than one hundred Israeli aircraft was also on its way toward Iraq.)

Former Israeli intelligence operative William Northrop confirmed how perilously close Israel came to making Baghdad "glow in the dark." The Israelis, Northrop said bluntly, had "pulled their [nuclear] weapons out and put them in their launch mode."

So while the White House was officially apprehensive about the coalition against Iraq falling apart if Israel declined turning the other cheek, behind the scenes Bush's advisors were obviously far more worried about something else—that an unprovoked chemical and biological attack against Israel would trigger a nuclear holocaust in the Persian Gulf.

NOTES

1. Appeared in the *Fort Lauderdale Sun Sentinel*, June 1, 1995.

2. John Loftus and Mark Aarons write in *The Secret War Against the Jews*: "It is a matter of public record that many former members of the Reagan-Bush administrations had such heavy investments in oil companies that they had a clear conflict of interest in determining U.S. policy in the Middle East. George Bush secretly waived the federal conflict of interest policy. Many members of his administration have enriched themselves in the Gulf states after leaving government service. Even Bush's son, George Jr., was awarded a lucrative oil contract in the Gulf."

ARAFAT
IN THE
CROSSHAIRS

On September 13, 1993, PLO Chairman Yasser Arafat shook hands with Israeli prime minister Yitzhak Rabin outside the White House as President Clinton and much of the world looked on. The signing of a peace treaty between the PLO and Israel was indeed a historic moment. "We, the soldiers who have returned from battle stained with blood, we who have fought against you, the Palestinians, we say to you in a loud and clear voice: Enough blood and tears," Rabin said in a solemn tone. Arafat—who like Rabin knew what a hard road covered with Hamas and Hezbollah land mines lay ahead—echoed the Israeli prime minister's sentiments. "My people are hoping this agreement marks the beginning of the end of a chapter of pain and suffering which has lasted throughout the century," Arafat told the throng seated before him that included past U.S. presidents, foreign dignitaries, members of Congress, and high-ranking cabinet members from four American administrations.

To Arafat, the moment had to be as sweet as it was triumphant. After all, he had spent much of his adult life waging a guerrilla campaign against his hated enemy, Israel. And he had done so while at the same time avoiding relentless Israeli assassins.

On October 2, 1985, the *Jerusalem Post* reported that key buildings in the PLO headquarters in Tunis were destroyed and more than sixty people were killed during an air raid the day before by the Israeli air force. Arafat was not in his office as scheduled, and escaped injury. According to Israeli sources, this was the farthest the IAF had ever flown on a bombing raid. Israeli F-16s traveled more than 5,000 miles, round-trip, to accomplish a mission considered noteworthy in terms of both the stealth required and the distance the bombers had to travel to carry the mission out.

The attack on the PLO headquarters was successful because of information given to LAKAM by Jonathan Pollard, an Israeli operative later told me. That information fell into two categories: radar and sensor coverage; and weapons capabilities of the Soviet-manufactured air defense systems that were employed along the route by the Arab countries. Said my source: "When the pilots returned, many of them had to be pulled out of the aircrafts. It was such a long and arduous flight, they could barely walk."

Then defense minister Yitzhak Rabin stated that the air raid was given the green light in Jerusalem in response to increased acts of terror by the PLO, culminating in the murders, on September 25, of three Israeli tourists who had been vacationing in Cyprus.

The Israeli strike had actually been planned for some time. But when those three Israelis were killed five days earlier at the Cypriot port of Lanarca, it seemed to be the appropriate moment for the Israel Defense Forces (IDF) to retaliate. The Lanarca incident began when three PLO terrorists—part of Arafat's "Force 17"—boarded a yacht anchored in the harbor. An Israeli operative recalled that after the terrorists entered the boat, an Israeli woman, Esther Paltzur, was immediately shot down. Jonathan Pollard later wrote to me in a letter: "A wire service photo showed the body of the female victim draped over the bow of the yacht like some type of grotesque figurehead."

After killing Paltzur in cold blood, the terrorists then took the two remaining Israelis as hostages. After negotiating with the Cypriot government for more than twenty-four hours—and obviously not getting what they wanted—the terrorists shot the two men in the back of the head before finally giving themselves up.

Upon hearing the news of the executions, the anger in Israel manifested itself in one united voice. Yet Israelis also asked, "Where were the boys?" one of my sources recalled. "I mean, where was Israeli intelligence? And how come these terrorists got so close to Israelis, no matter where they were? The Israeli people are hard taskmasters in what they require from their secret services."

Jordanian television reported that Mohammed Natour (Abu Taef), the head of the PLO's Force 17, was killed during the retaliatory raid on Arafat's headquarters, along with other top PLO leaders. Said Rabin: "We have shown the terrorist groups and the world that there is no place where terrorists organizations can be immune to blows from our forces. The long arm of the IDF can reach wherever terrorist forces are deployed. And Israel will not tolerate acts of terror by Arafat's PLO which are initiated to undermine the prospects of peace in the region."

The same day, Wolf Blitzer wrote in the *Jerusalem Post* that President Reagan appeared to condone Israel's air strike rather than condemn it. Blitzer noted that when Reagan was asked whether the Israelis had picked out the right people responsible for the killings in Cyprus, the president responded: "I've always had great faith in their intelligence."

The raid at his headquarters in Tunis was not the first time Arafat's life had almost come to an end at the hands of his Israeli tormentors. Three years earlier, during the 1982 war in Lebanon, Arafat had also been a target. "I know for a fact that one of the Israeli sniper teams had Arafat in the crosshairs as he was departing aboard a ship in Beirut harbor," William Northrop told me. "One of the snipers could have squeezed the cap on him at that point, but orders came down to the sniper not to kill him."

It didn't matter whether those orders came from Israel or the United States. Arafat, although long perceived as a terrorist, was nevertheless a highly intelligent man with a Westerner's mind whom many felt could be reasoned with. A practical man, he was a Palestinian nationalist, not a radical fundamentalist like the mullahs in Iran. Even well before his signing of the peace treaty with Israel, many American leaders believed they could deal with Arafat—and had been secretly doing so since Carter was in the White House. The Israelis may have felt this way as well, in spite of Arafat's many terrorist escapades and public pronouncements that Israel should be "driven into the sea."

In his 1988 *Playboy* interview Arafat showed he also had a sense of humor when he made a joke about his dark image in the West. As a young man from a relatively affluent family, Arafat had been accepted for admittance at the University of Texas as an engineering student (he almost went), and told *Playboy* of the carefree way in which he used to travel around the world before his name became synonymous with the PLO.

"You traveled as a tourist?" interviewer Morgan Strong asked.

"Yes, as a tourist," Arafat replied, laughing loudly. "Not as a terrorist, as a tourist."

What happened in Beirut a decade earlier, however, was anything but a laughing matter. The PLO, under Arafat's leadership, gradually began expanding its power in this onetime picturesque capital of Lebanon after the Palestinians were expelled from Jordan, in the early 1970s, by King Hussein's forces. As Ze'ev Chafets notes in *Double Vision*, the PLO's power base in Lebanon soon became the hundreds of thousands of Palestinian refugees there who joined forces with radical Moslem groups in a rough alliance against the Christians. Embroiled in a bloody civil war, by 1982 Beirut had become a quagmire that was literally a microcosm of the dangerous political entanglements that made the whole of the Middle East so volatile. Encircled by an army of Arafat's PLO fighters, ruthless Moslems fought sometimes equally ruthless Christians while the Syrians and Iranians sat in the background like hungry jackals waiting for their turn at the kill.

The Israelis—wanting to do away with a PLO stronghold so close to Israeli territory—were getting ready to invade the war-torn country themselves. In *Veil: The Secret Wars of the CIA*, Bob Woodward recalled defense minister Ariel Sharon telling CIA Director Casey that Israel "wouldn't tolerate" having neighboring Lebanon as an outpost for terrorists who wanted to destroy Israel. On June 6, 1982, after months of watching and waiting from its northern border, Israel made good on its threat, sending its troops into Lebanon and declaring its intention of "driving the PLO terrorists out."

In their article "Back Door to the PLO," in the August 22, 1982, *Los Angeles Herald Examiner*, Stephen Zatuchni and Daniel Drooz wrote about how, four months earlier, the Department of Defense had put together an "Interagency Contingency Operations Plan" calling for three levels of response in case the anticipated Israeli invasion came to fruition. The first response would be the application of strong pressure on Israel to withdraw; the second would be to introduce Soviet pressure; the third, if all else failed, would be to allow for a limited U.S. military action against Israel.

By the time the Israelis made their expected move, President Reagan was in Europe with Secretary of State Alexander Haig. According to Zatuchni and Drooz, with the president gone the news was "leaked" by the Defense Department that Israel had rejected the PLO's offer to lay down its arms and withdraw from Lebanon if Israel also pulled back its forces. The Israelis, for their part, maintained that this so-called offer was never even conveyed to them until after it was already publicized by the American media.

The leak seemed to have Weinberger's fingerprints all over it. Zatuchni and Drooz charged that the defense secretary immediately went behind Haig's back and opened his own channel of communication to the PLO. The authors noted that, according to an authoritative source on the Senate Armed Services Committee, while Haig was trying to arrange a cease-fire through Philip Habib, the president's special Middle East envoy, Weinberger was undercutting Haig by dealing directly through the Saudis who were telling the PLO to "hang on."

On June 10, 1982, Soviet pressure—the second level of U.S.

response—was also applied when Prime Minister Menachem Begin received a letter from Reagan. It began: "Today I received a message from President Brezhnev which expressed serious concerns that a most serious situation has been created which contains the possibility of broader hostilities."

Zatuchni and Drooz insist that a limited military action by the United States against Israel was also a possibility if all else failed. They say the United States went so far as to try to instigate a confrontation between the two countries that the Weinberger camp believed could result in a drastic reversal of U.S. public support for Israel. The confrontation began when an unmarked U.S. helicopter took off from the U.S.S. *Forrestal*. The helicopter not only bore a strong resemblance to helicopters sold by the French to the Syrians, but no flight plan had been filed with the Israeli control center, established expressly for the authorization of flights into the active war zone. An Israeli gunboat subsequently tracked the helicopter, which did not answer routine requests for identification. Israel then ordered two jets to make a close visual inspection. When the helicopter landed in Lebanon, Israeli troops took the unprecedented action of searching the U.S. personnel on board.

Fortunately, Israel never opened fired on the unidentified aircraft. If she had, there would have been a public furor while a total arms embargo against Israel might have been the very least of the punishments expected by the Israelis—all because of an action precipitated by the United States solely to provoke America's so-called ally.

Administration insiders hostile to Israel also used the major American television networks which were eager to play Washington's game in order to pump up ratings. News footage continually came back from Beirut that deliberately exaggerated the destruction to the city as well as the human carnage allegedly caused by the Israeli invaders. On NBC, anchorman John Chancellor reported after a limited Israeli offensive which was more of a surgical strike against the PLO than anything else: "What will stick in the mind about yesterday's savage Israeli attack on Beirut is its size and scope. Nothing like it has ever happened in this part of the world."

Buoyed by the cooperation of much of the news media, Weinberger not only wanted Israeli troops out of Lebanon; my sources tell me he also wanted Alexander Haig out of the White House. Weinberger's opportunity to rid himself of Haig came when the secretary of state publicly attacked the White House policy of trying to get the Israelis to pull back—a policy which, Haig believed, would leave Lebanon dangerously vulnerable and unstable. Although Weinberger and George Shultz had a well-documented icy relationship, Shultz nevertheless became the logical choice to replace Haig. After all, Shultz, like Weinberger, was a team player with a Bechtel pedigree.

On June 25, 1982, Haig, the "hero" who literally saved Israel during the Yom Kippur War, was forced out of Reagan's cabinet. By July 16, 1982, the pragmatic Shultz had replaced him.

In *Territory of Lies*, Wolf Blitzer stresses that there is a clear difference between "unobtrusive" intelligence-gathering operations and the actual running of paid spies, such as occurred in the Pollard case. "Yes, there is always some spying going on, even among very close friends and allies," Blitzer wrote. "But that is a far cry from actually planting a 'mole' in a friendly country's intelligence community." Nevertheless, CIA Director Casey had accepted an Israeli military walk-in during the war in Lebanon in 1982, as was later revealed by Sen. David Durenberger of Minnesota, a former chairman of the Senate Select Committee on Intelligence. "It was the United States," Durenberger said bluntly during a 1987 speech, "that actually broke the rules of the game first."

Shortly after stepping down as chairman of the Senate Select Committee, Durenberger was at a Palm Beach, Florida, fund-raiser when he told his mainly Jewish audience that CIA Director Casey had in fact employed an Israeli military spy after Israel invaded Lebanon in 1982. Durenberger—who did not reveal the spy's name—raised the issue because the United States was prosecuting Pollard for spying against the United States. When his comments at the private fund-raiser were leaked to the media, Durenberger said he was merely indulging in "speculation" and was not disclosing classified information. Despite his clarification, Durenberger was publicly blasted by Weinberger who called Durenberger's remarks "very damaging and very wrong."

Yet, although Weinberger categorically denied that the United States had ever recruited an Israeli spy, a news report appearing June 5, 1993, in the *Los Angeles Times* stated that Israeli sources, earlier that week, had officially identified the spy referred to by Durenberger as Maj. Yosef Amit. According to the news report, Amit was handed a twelve-year prison sentence. Noted *Los Angeles Times* reporters Robert Jackson and Ronald Ostrow: "Israeli government spokesmen have refused to provide any details of Amit's case, although the government suggested that he had contacts with foreign agents in 1982, both inside and outside Israel." (My own intelligence sources told me that an American immigrant, who became an Israeli battalion operations officer, was also arrested by Shin Bet for spying against the Israelis in Lebanon. The man, whose name was never made public, was debriefed and deported back to the United States.)

Before Amit's name had been made public, Blitzer opined in his 1989 book that there were "limits within which friendly countries are supposed to operate." Blitzer noted that Durenberger had been referring in his comments to "a very modest, onetime incident with no money changing hands." Added Blitzer: "With Pollard, Israel would go way beyond those limits."

Pollard strongly disagreed. In a letter he wrote to me—also before Amit's true identity was revealed by Israeli intelligence—Pollard noted that at the height of the 1982 Lebanon campaign this U.S.-born agent had actually passed on "extremely sensitive information" to the CIA pertaining to Israeli dispositions, intentions, and communications codes. "For men who are literally fighting for their lives," Pollard insisted, "this unauthorized release of such tactical information to a foreign intelligence service is not considered to be a 'minor matter' by any stretch of the imagination."

Making this situation even more dangerous, Pollard believed, was that the CIA leaked a great deal of what it obtained from this spy to the media—which, Pollard insisted, was how the Israelis finally identified who the agent was. "From what I understand," Pollard wrote, "the CIA's objective in leaking this material was to increase the number of Israeli casualties to the point where Israel's cabinet would be forced to withdraw the Israeli army from its positions around Beirut."

According to Howard Teicher in *Twin Pillars to Desert Storm*, Weinberger not only schemed to get the Israelis out of Beirut, but wanted the American presence in the war-torn country to be drastically reduced as well. Teicher claims that Weinberger basically took it upon himself to order the Marines to leave Beirut, in September 1982, before alternative security arrangements could be made. As a result, intelligence sources suggest, the Syrians were encouraged to "take out" Lebanese President Bashir Gemayal.

These sources, in both Israeli and American intelligence, confirm that Christian Phalangist leader Bashir Gemayel had developed close relations with Israeli Defense Minister Gen. Ariel Sharon as well as the Mossad. As Bob Woodward noted in *Veil*: "The CIA had played matchmaker, putting the Christians and Israelis in touch with each other, making Gemayal a shared CIA-Mossad asset."

Two and a half months after the Israeli invasion of Lebanon, Gemayal was elected as Lebanon's president. His glory was short-lived. On September 14, 1982, nine days before he was to take office, a bomb blast in an East Beirut Phalangist Party office killed the president-elect along with many other Lebanese Christians.

Israeli intelligence sources believe that the Syrians were most likely behind the assassination. President Hafez el-Assad considered Lebanon as little more than a Syrian province, while a potential U.S.-Lebanese-Israeli alliance behind Gemayal would have been a strong blow to Syrian influence in the area. In addition, the planners of the attack were linked by the CIA to the Syrian president himself. Notwithstanding, the White House was unwilling to make what it knew public.

Revenge against the Moslems was swift. Within days of Gemayal's death, Phalangist units entering the Sabra and Shatilla Palestinian refugee camps in Beirut massacred more than seven hundred inhabitants, many of them women and children. Regardless of the fact that Israeli troops did not take part in the slaughter, much of the world, including Israeli citizens, held the Israelis culpable for allowing the Phalangists to go into those camps.[1] As attorney and Jewish activist Arnold Forster noted, remnants of the PLO had been hiding in those camps, among the civilians, in violation of the cease-fire and withdrawal arrangements the PLO had agreed to. Still, Forster wrote in *Penthouse* magazine, "The Knesset, Israel's parliament, shook in angry debate. Public and private soul-searching was in evidence everywhere. Four hundred thousand Israelis gathered in Tel Aviv to protest the bloodshed, demanding atonement."

Two weeks later, U.S. Marines, trying to keep a lid on the Beirut powder keg, took up a strategic location in barracks near Beirut's airport.

On May 17, 1983, Israel finally signed an agreement with Lebanon and its new president—Amin Gemayal, Bashir's brother—to remove Israeli troops from Lebanon's borders. In *Veil*, Bob Woodward notes that Secretary of State Shultz, an ex-Marine, urged that a 1,600-man Marine peacekeeping unit remain in Lebanon. CIA Director Casey went along, Woodward noted, while Weinberger and the Joint Chiefs objected strenuously. "But the president did not want to seem to back down, so the Marines stayed."

But the withdrawal of the Israelis proved to be the death knell for any real security in the region. While the toughened Israelis were in Beirut to crush the PLO, the American troops were there mainly as "peacekeepers." If at all possible, the White House did not want them firing on Palestinians or Syrians.

Peacekeepers or not, by October 17, 1983—the day Robert McFarlane replaced William Clark as National Security Advisor—six U.S. Marines had already been shot and killed in Lebanon. Then, on October 23, at 6:22 A.M., a truck drove into the Marine compound and, armed with the equivalent of more than 12,000 pounds of TNT, exploded, killing 241 Marines who were stationed there. The Iranian-backed Islamic terrorist group Hezbollah was most likely behind the suicide mission.

"The explosion rattled all of Beirut," a source of mine who was there told me. "It felt like an earthquake. We looked over and there was a large column of smoke that sort of reminded me of those pictures of Nagasaki after the atomic bomb had been dropped. It was a long, tall, black column of smoke that climbed up thousands of meters into a crystal blue sky. We didn't know, at that point, that it was the Marine barracks, but we knew it was in the American section."

When the Israelis ascertained that it was the Marines' barracks that had been the target, Israeli command immediately put Rambam Hospital, in Haifa, on alert. The Israeli hospital had one of the best trauma teams in the world and was only sixteen minutes south of Beirut by air. Yet the wounded Marines were never flown to Israel; instead they were placed aboard a U.S. C-141 and transported to the American Armed Forces Hospital in Wiesbaden, West Germany—a well-equipped hospital, but four hours away from the scene of the bombing.

"We later found out it was Weinberger who had given the direct order that none of the Marine casualties were to be moved to an Israeli hospital," my source said. According to a number of sources I spoke with, the secretary of defense—ever wary of Saudi sensibilities—chose to risk the lives of the wounded Marines rather than offend his Arab friends.

Two Marines died enroute to the West German hospital.

NOTE

1. The 1983 Kahan Commission of Inquiry in Israel concluded that Sharon was indirectly responsible for the massacre.

CHAPTER 17

THE
WAKE
OF THE
ACHILLE LAURO

Unlike the quagmire in Beirut, the *Achille Lauro* incident, during which an American Jew, Leon Klinghoffer, was murdered, would turn out to be a rare victory by the Reagan White House over terrorism. The victory was a Pyrrhic one for Israeli intelligence, however, costing the Israelis one of their top agents-in-place. In addition, if not for the *Achille Lauro* affair, my sources tell me, Jonathan Pollard's broadening activities on behalf of Israel may, in fact, never have been uncovered.

Once robust, Klinghoffer, sixty-nine, who owned an electrical appliance business in Queens, New York, had suffered a stroke that left him partially paralyzed and confined to a wheelchair. When four young Palestinian thugs, part of a PLO splinter group, hijacked the *Achille Lauro*—the Italian cruise ship they boarded as "tourists" on October 3, 1985—Klinghoffer became the hijacking's first (and some would say the only) fatality. The Jewish businessman and his wife Marilyn, fifty-eight, were among a group of 748 passengers taking part in the ill-fated voyage. Many of those passengers (including two Israelis) had disembarked in Alexandria, Egypt, just days before, to see the pyramids.

Alarm bells perhaps should have gone off when the terrorists—who looked "different" than most of the other passengers, the majority of whom were either middle-aged or elderly—boarded the ship in Genoa, Italy. Their passports said they were from Argentina, Canada, and Norway. But, as one of the passengers, a shoe-store owner from New Jersey, would later comment, "They certainly looked like Arabs to me."

Nevertheless, to the Italian authorities, at least, the documents presented by the Palestinians "seemed to be in order." There were no metal detectors aboard the ship and their luggage also was never X-rayed. Inside the suitcases the terrorists brought with them were AK-47s and hand grenades.

According to sources in the PLO, the Palestinians were to pass as ordinary tourists, cruise to the Israeli seaport of Ashod, and then strike at a military target. The attack was supposed to be in reprisal for the Israeli attack, only weeks earlier, on the PLO headquarters in Tunis—a mission for which some of the intelligence was supplied by Jonathan Pollard.

The terrorists' plans for revenge quickly went awry, however; their mission was thwarted when a steward aboard the ship noticed the quartet cleaning their weapons in their cabin. Discovered, the bungling terrorists felt they had no choice but to take over the ship.

Once they did, their tactics were brutal. To show they meant business, during the first few hours of the hijacking one of the hijackers kicked a fifty-three-year-old Austrian woman (she walked with a cane since one of her feet had been amputated) down a staircase. The terrorist would later say he felt the woman "was moving too slow." The hijackers also checked the nationalities of the tourists still aboard. Of the 438 passengers left, fourteen were Americans and six were British. The hijackers separated them from the others. Two Austrians, whom the hijackers mistakenly believed to be Jewish, were added to the group. Among the "games" the hijackers played with them was to have the group sit next to cans of gasoline while bullets would be sprayed sporadically over their heads. Recalled

Marilyn Klinghoffer, "The hijackers kept popping their guns and playing with grenades on their belts, like little kids."

Midway through the second day of their takeover, the hijackers moved Leon Klinghoffer to the ship's rail. One of the hijackers held his automatic rifle to the wheelchair-bound man's head and opened fire. Blood splattered over the terrorist's pants and shoes. Another terrorist walked to the area below, where the other passengers were being held, and ordered Joaquim Piniero Da Silva, a Portugese cabin steward, and Ferrucio Alberti, the cruise hairdresser, to go up on the deck, and then gestured for them to throw Klinghoffer's body overboard. From another holding area below, Marilyn Klinghoffer would later say she heard the splash—but she didn't know it was her husband.

The blood-splattered terrorist walked up to Captain Gerardo de Rosa on the bridge. "We have killed a man," he calmly told the captain.

The hijackers immediately broadcast the news around the eastern Mediterranean. Their hasty plan was that they would be allowed to land at the Syrian port of Tartus (just north of Lebanon). All night and into the following morning Captain de Rosa had a gun held to his ribs as the ship headed toward Syria, long a haven for terrorists on the run. Upping the ante, the hijackers told the Syrians that if they weren't allowed to take refuge in that country, "there would be more dead bodies." In addition, they informed the Syrians that they wanted an international diplomatic team to be present to hear their demands for the release, by Israel, of fifty Palestinian prisoners. They also asked that they receive diplomatic asylum in Syria.

Syrian president Hafez el-Assad wasn't moved. Since this escapade didn't fit into his political agenda, his government refused all the hijackers' requests. Deflated, the terrorists ordered that the *Achille Lauro* steam toward Beirut.

Perhaps seeing that there was no upside to killing any more hostages, the terrorists never followed through on their threat. When the Lebanese also closed their ports to them, they changed course for Libya, then Cyprus, but, still, they were refused safe harbor.

Finally, they turned back to Egypt, where President Hosni Mubarak said his government would deliver them into the hands of the PLO, but only on one condition: that they give up their hostages. At the same time, the Egyptians tried to get international support in this effort. The ambassadors of the United States, Great Britain, West Germany, and Italy were reluctant, however, since they correctly believed that the terrorists had, in fact, killed at least one of the passengers.

Meanwhile, U.S. and Italian warships and Israeli gunboats continued to tail the *Achille Lauro* as it slowly moved across the eastern Mediterranean. Washington's message to all the governments involved was not to give an inch to the terrorists. According to U.S. government sources, the Reagan administration feared that if the *Achille Lauro* was allowed to dock at any of the ports, the terrorists would surely be free to "disappear."

The *Achille Lauro* would spend that evening just fifteen miles off the Egyptian coast. The four hijackers—edgy and dangerous—demanded to talk to Mohammed Abul al-Abbas, leader of the Palestinian Liberation Front (PLF), and, less than an hour later, Abbas came aboard the ship. It was hardly surprising to intelligence analysts that Abbas would be the hijackers' negotiator of choice; after all, the Palestinian terrorists who commandeered the *Achille Lauro* were part of a splinter group of the PLO loyal to Yasser Arafat—and headed by Abbas himself.

Abbas's star in the world of international terrorism had begun its meteoric ascent in 1983, after the PLF had split into three rival factions, only one of which remained allied with Arafat. One of the other two factions was pro-Syrian, while one claimed to be independent. Arafat found it politically expedient to reward Abbas at the time, and made sure he was elected to the Palestine National Council's Executive Committee.

As for any direct involvement by Arafat in the bungled operation that led to the *Achille Lauro* hijacking, there are two scenarios: first, that this was done without Arafat's authorization; and second, that Arafat felt forced to resort to the terrorism of the 1970s, since his hold on the PLO was seemingly beginning to weaken.

It is doubtful, though, that the shrewd Arafat ever felt completely comfortable with the bungling Abbas. After all, the Haifa-born "freedom fighter" had more past embarrassments on his terrorist résumé than he had successes. Six years earlier, in a 1979 raid on the Israeli port town of Nahariya, four PLF guerrillas accomplished little when they murdered young Danny Haran and his five-year-old daughter, Einat. When the two surviving terrorists later surrendered to the Israelis—the third was killed by a South African immigrant who was armed with a pistol, while the fourth was killed by Israeli soldiers—they were sentenced to life in prison. (One of those two men was among the fifty prisoners whose release would be part of the *Achille Lauro* hijackers' wish list.)

Another misadventure for Abbas came in 1981 when his guerrillas tried to infiltrate Israel and attack a Haifa refinery by hang glider. A month later, Abbas attempted to attack the same refinery again, this time by hot-air balloon from southern Lebanon. That mission was botched as well.

Arafat, to this day, has never fully acknowledged his involvement in the operation that led to the *Achille Lauro* hijacking. Notwithstanding, Israeli and American intelligence sources suspected that Arafat, at the very least, was not opposed to it, especially since the hijackers may have been part of Force 17, a corps of trusted PLO terrorists who also moonlighted as Arafat's personal bodyguards.

According to Israeli sources, Arafat began building Force 17 into an elite commando group in 1983, the same year Abbas began to ally himself more closely with the PLO leader. Those chosen to be part of Force 17 were trained for seaborne assaults against Israel, and Israeli intelligence sources said the group was tasked with carrying out "maximum casualty" terrorist attacks on Israeli civilians. It was no secret, and it has been confirmed by U.S. sources, that the gunmen who killed three Israelis aboard a yacht in Cyprus, a month before the *Achille Lauro* incident, were Force 17 members. Soon after the *Achille Lauro* hijacking, Maj. Gen. Ehud

Barak, chief of Israel's military intelligence (who fourteen years later would become the prime minister of Israel), said Israel had "irrefutable proof" that Arafat had been directly involved in all the "recent acts of terrorism" plaguing Israel and the Mediterranean. Barak did not make his evidence public, however.

As noted in the last chapter, Arafat, a cat with nine lives, had nearly been "taken out" by the Israelis on a number of occasions. In 1972, Prime Minister Golda Meir vetoed a secret plan to have the Mossad hunt Arafat down and kill him. (Meir decided it would be prudent not to make a martyr out of the charismatic PLO leader.) Then, during the siege of Beirut in the summer of 1982, Prime Minister Begin actually did authorize Arafat's assassination, but, as we know, at the last moment orders were given to spare him as part of the U.S.-negotiated cease-fire. On a number of occasions Israel had also dropped "smart bombs" on various locations in Beirut where Arafat had been known to hide out. Each time, the slippery Arafat barely escaped.

Captain de Rosa, a gun still at his head, radioed a message to the Egyptians that, in spite of what they might have heard, all the Achille Lauro's passengers were safe and unharmed. Buoyed by the news, West German and Italian ambassadors signed the document approving the hijackers' deal with Egypt. U.S. Ambassador Nicholas Veliotes was certainly leery of the validity of the message, but the deal was nevertheless okayed. Waving in triumph, the four Palestinians got onto a tugboat that headed back to shore while the relieved passengers remained on the ship.

U.S. officials, meanwhile, weren't convinced that the Italian captain had told the truth. For the next few hours, those officials demanded access to the Achille Lauro to make sure that all the Americans still aboard were alive and well—especially since rumors were rampant that at least one of the hostages, possibly an American, had been executed. U.S. intelligence agents also wanted to keep tabs on the terrorists once they were on Egyptian soil.

It was approximately eight hours after the hijackers had surrendered to the Egyptian authorities that U.S. Ambassador Veliotes announced, from aboard the *Achille Lauro*, that an American national was dead. In Rome, at around the same time, Italian Prime Minister Bettino Craxi exclaimed, "Thank God it's over." Ten minutes later, he learned about Klinghoffer's murder. Craxi's government did a quick turnabout, and said it would seek extradition of the terrorists to Italy since the crime had occurred aboard an Italian ship.

Mubarak now had a major problem. He would have to weigh his fear of Arab extremists on the one hand (Anwar Sadat, after all, was assassinated after making peace with Israel), against his economic dependency on Washington on the other. Added to that, his country's relations with Israel had become increasingly chilly after Israel's invasion of Lebanon in 1982. And while he had tried to put some distance between himself and the United States, Egypt, in 1985, was (next to Israel) the second largest recipient of U.S. aid. Egypt was also set to receive $1.3 billion in military aid in 1986, and more than $1 billion in economic assistance, not to mention the fact that a large percentage of Egypt's $30 billion foreign aid debt was still owed to Uncle Sam.

Washington at first accepted Mubarak's story that, at the time his government made the deal with the hijackers, no one in Cairo knew that Klinghoffer had been killed. The next day, however, Mubarak's credibility began to unravel. A guest on NBC-TV's *Today* show, he said that when news of the murder reached him, the hijackers had "already been sent out of my country."

Where to? the Egyptian president was asked.

"Perhaps to Tunis," Mubarak replied.

Later, when questioned again, Mubarak said he wasn't even sure that Klinghoffer had been executed. "Maybe he wasn't aboard the ship," Mubarak said, defensively.

There was now little question that Mubarak was lying. With the knowledge, through an unnamed intelligence source, that the terrorists were still in Egypt, Secretary of State George Schultz angrily told the Egyptians to "hold these people—and prosecute them."

The October 21, 1985, issue of *Newsweek* magazine quoted one U.S. official as bluntly stating: "They lied to us from top to bottom. They did everything they could in order to mislead us." Also, according to *Newsweek*, it was this same unnamed intelligence source who not only allowed the United States to know that the terrorists had never left Egypt; he allowed Navy Intelligence to pinpoint exactly where they were. It's the identity of who this "deep throat" was, however—and how the Egyptians eventually found out about him—that would become a part of the *Achille Lauro* affair that many in the Reagan administration would never want revealed.

Convinced that the *Achille Lauro* hijackers would leave Egypt by air, a bold plan was set in motion to bring them to justice. Charles Allen, the CIA's national intelligence officer for counterterrorism, reported to his superiors in the CIA that the four hijackers were still on Egyptian soil and that neither Egyptian leaders, nor the PLO, knew exactly what to do about them. It was National Security Council terrorism expert Col. Oliver North who, according to *Newsweek*, came up with the idea of having U.S. fighter jets force the terrorists' plane down after they would try to make their getaway. It was also North who called Vice Admiral Arthur Moreau, who then told North that the U.S. Sixth Fleet would be able to do the job. North and Moreau were joined by Pentagon officials who quickly put together a plan. At the same time, a steady stream of intelligence data kept coming in.

"North was one of the facilitators, one of the staffers," a high-level intelligence source told me. "North contacted Amiram Nir."

Nir, at the time, was the Israeli prime minister's special advisor on terrorism. My source, who worked extremely closely with Nir, said, "North had a close relationship with the Israelis. At that point, North and everybody else at the NSC was 'jonesing' hard for the release [by Egypt] of the *Achille Lauro* hijackers."

According to this source, the U.S. Navy was tasked with the deal. "ATAC (the Navy's Anti-Terrorist Alert Center) was at the epicenter of the intelligence flow," my source said. "Jonathan Pollard, who was one of the Middle East experts at ATAC, certainly had conversations with Israeli intelligence on this. He had to. He was trying to establish where the hijackers were, and where they were headed."

The Israelis, meanwhile, wound up exposing the identity of the "unnamed intelligence source" who was feeding Israel highly sensitive data that was, in turn, being handed over to the Americans. This extremely important Israeli agent-in-place was situated in a position of great prominence in Egypt. Just how important was he? According to a high-level Israeli source of mine, this spy had risen to the rank of an Egyptian *general*—and was serving in the Egyptian high command!

The "official" CIA version of how the United States found out about the terrorists' whereabouts, as told by Bob Woodward in *Veil*, is that Mubarak was uncomfortable with the secure voice system that had been supplied to him by the United States. Mubarak was in the habit, the story went, of using an ordinary phone when contacting his aides—even when discussing delicate matters of state that required complete secrecy. Noted Woodward, "Early on the morning of Thursday, October 10, a Mubarak phone call was intercepted, and the information arrived at the White House situation room within half an hour in a top-secret code-word message." Woodward said that what the White House received was a short transcript of a conversation between Mubarak and his foreign minister. In that conversation, Woodward said, Mubarak told his foreign minister that the terrorists were still in Egypt. "North knew that such precise intelligence was a rarity, and in this case an opportunity that would not last," Woodward wrote.

While the CIA's explanation sounds plausible, one of my Israeli sources tells a far different tale. He insists it was through the close cooperation of Israeli intelligence—and not the result of any intercepted messages—that U.S. Naval Intelligence learned where the terrorists were, and where they would be going. And he insists that the intelligence data had been supplied to the Israelis by their spy in Egypt, a confidant of Mubarak himself.

As for precisely what Amiram Nir, a link in this chain, may have provided for his good friend Oliver North, it's only speculation at this point, and may never be known since Nir was killed in a mysterious "plane crash" in 1988.

"All I can say for sure is that North was in the loop when American intelligence received the name of the agent-in-place," my Israeli source told me. "North obviously took what he had, and ran with it."

Newsweek, meanwhile, had made its reference to a mysterious "source" telling American officials that the terrorists hadn't yet left that country. According to my own sources, while putting the pieces of the puzzle together the identity of the Egyptian general was eventually deduced by the Egyptians—and he was summarily executed for treason.

Was it North who inadvertently exposed this agent, thereby costing him his life? Or worse, was this leak to *Newsweek* done on purpose by someone in Reagan's inner circle, perhaps to appease the beleaguered Mubarak?

"Well, the reason that North gets the blame, in my mind, is because it was quite obvious that the *Newsweek* article exposed this person, and who he was, and he was then killed by Egyptian counterintelligence people," one of my sources told me. "The fact was, nobody knew who really exposed him. But the Israelis were hot as hell, and American counterintelligence was hot. Because, guess what, you don't get that kind of cooperation again once something like that happens. I don't care what the excuse is."

On the night of October 10 it was confirmed that the *Achille Lauro* hijackers were still trying to get out of Egypt. Intelligence sources located the specific plane the terrorists were going to use—a Boeing 737 on the runway at Al Maza Air Base, just northeast of Cairo. The terrorists were presumably going to fly to Tunis, while North's plan for intercepting them called for radar planes and F-14 Tomcats to be launched from the aircraft carrier *Saratoga*.

At 11:30 that evening North contacted National Security Advisor

Robert McFarlane, traveling aboard Air Force One with President Reagan. The president agreed to the plan in principle, but wanted to know more of the specifics.

There were a number of fears in the White House, not the least of which was what effect this would have on Mubarak, who had to deal with the Arab radicals and hard-liners within his own country. As expected, Defense Secretary Weinberger was the advisor who seemed the most worried about the operation and how it would affect America's standing in the Arab world, especially in Egypt. Nevertheless, the president gave his stamp of approval to the operation. Politely brushing Weinberger off, the president said he wanted the mission carried out.

Less than two hours later, the plan began. Intelligence sources produced the flight number of the plane that would be transporting the terrorists. Then, the Navy's EA-6B Prowler electronic warfare plane surveyed every plane headed out of Egypt until they found the right one. President Reagan immediately cabled Tunisian President Habib Bourgiba, telling him that the hijackers would be headed for Tunis—and that under no circumstances did the United States want them to be allowed to land.

The Egyptian flight was right on course. As the F-14s stayed behind the Egyptian plane, flying without lights, it's doubtful that the plane's pilot ever knew he was being followed. Suddenly, the trap was sprung, and the F-14s closed in along both wings of the airliner.

The Egyptian pilot began radioing Cairo for instructions, but his radio signals were jammed by the Prowler: No matter what frequency the pilot tried, he couldn't get through. Intimidated by the F-14s, and not sure he wouldn't be shot down—although Reagan certainly wanted to avoid the loss of Egyptian lives—the pilot felt he had little choice; he would follow the instructions he was being given, and would land in Italy.

A crewman aboard the *Saratoga* would later tell a reporter from *Newsweek* (October 21, 1985): "I don't know if you ever saw a Tomcat with all its lights on going like hell, but it's an awesome sight. I guess we just scared them down."

It wasn't until the planes reached Italian airspace that the Italians were actually informed of what was going on. Then, after the plane holding the *Achille Lauro* hijackers landed at Sigonella Air Base in Sicily, there was the question over whether the Americans, or the Italians, had the final jurisdiction over them. The Americans had flown their "Seal Team 6" into Sicily from Rota, Spain, and were proceeding on orders from the White House to take the terrorists into custody. Waiting outside the Egyptian plane, however, the Navy Seals were immediately surrounded by Italian military personnel. When Major Gen. Carl W. Stiner saw that the Italians did not plan to surrender custody of the terrorists to the Americans, he and an Italian colonel got into a heated debate. According to a U.S. official, the Seals were "pulling back the bolts on their rifles," but were ordered by Washington to "stand down." Secretary of State Shultz reluctantly yielded to the Italians when Italian officials promised that the terrorists would be prosecuted to the full extent of the law and charged with murder.

Already pleased with their bounty, when they boarded the 737, U.S. and Italian officials found an added bonus. Seated next to the four terrorists was Abul Abbas, himself. Days later, though, when the United States started extradition proceedings against the terrorist leader, the Italians refused to cooperate. After all, not only did the Craxi government have close ties with the PLO; the Italians depended heavily on Arab oil.

Playing hardball, President Reagan strongly suggested to Prime Minister Craxi that Abbas be extradited to the United States. Maxwell Rabb, the U.S. ambassador to Italy, then delivered a formal request to the Italian Justice Ministry for Abbas's arrest on charges of complicity in hijacking and murder. It would never come to fruition: While American officials were trying to serve a warrant on Abbas, he somehow "slipped out" of Italy— and back into the bowels of the Arab world.

For Prime Minister Craxi, the gamble of allowing Abbas to escape would turn out to be a costly one. Craxi's removal from office was ensured, days later, when Defense Minister Giovanni Spaldolini, a staunch supporter of Israel, pulled his "Republican Party" out of Italy's coalition government.

As for Mubarak, some say he was forced to play the hand he was dealt. He saved face in the Arab world by not appearing to cave in to the American demands to hand over the terrorists. He expressed "outrage" at American "piracy" when the 737 was forced down in Italy. Notwithstanding, it's been a popular theory that Mubarak, all along, had secretly kept the United States informed about the terrorists' true whereabouts.

Not everyone agrees, however.

"Mubarak was incensed," an Israeli intelligence source of mine said. "Remember, any order to execute the Egyptian general would have been given by Mubarak, and only Mubarak. No one else in Egypt could have given that order."

The United States, meanwhile, still wanted the fugitive Abbas brought to justice. One U.S. intelligence official told a reporter at *Time* magazine in 1986: "The world is getting very small for Abbas. His days as a free terrorist are numbered."

He was wrong. To this day, Abul Abbas remains at large.

The suspected intelligence leak that caused a valuable Israeli agent-in-place to be "burned" and executed had a number of repercussions. Among them, it resulted in greater general security at the Anti-Terrorist Alert Center, and a closer scrutiny of its analysts. That tightened security net quite possibly resulted in the arrest of one of its employees, Jonathan Pollard, only five weeks after the dramatic capture of the *Achille Lauro* terrorists.

Concerning Amiram Nir, is it possible that his own fate—he was killed in an airplane accident on a runway in 1988—was sealed as a result of his close ties with U.S. intelligence, especially his connection to Oliver North? Did he know too much about the exposing of the Egyptian general, or was it some connection with Iran-Contra that made him both dan-

gerous and expendable? Much has been speculated about Nir's mysterious death, by conspiracy buffs, among others, but the truth has
remained elusive. I asked an Israeli intelligence source, who had worked
with Nir, whether Nir might have been the target of an assassin, and, if so,
why? My source said he did not want to speculate. But he grudgingly
added: "Look, there were six people on that plane, and Amiram, who had
his neck broken in the accident, was the only one who was even hurt. All
the plane did was slide off the runway. I mean, it didn't even crash. I guess
you can come to your own conclusions."

CHAPTER 18

KHOMEINI'S LEGACY AND THE SHANGHAI SURPRISE

After Jonathan Pollard began working for Israel, Shin Bet, for security reasons, wired his Washington apartment—something Pollard was never aware of. But the Israelis could not only hear everything going on in Pollard's residence; they could hear everything going on in the apartment directly above that was rented by a young man named Arturo Cruz Jr., whose father, Arturo Cruz, was one of the most vocal Nicaraguan Contra leaders. When the Israelis ran their security route around Pollard's apartment they found out that one of the persons going upstairs to spend time with young Arturito was none other than Fawn Hall.[1]

The strikingly beautiful Hall's name would soon surface in connection with the Iran-Contra affair when she allegedly shredded secret documents for her boss, Col. Oliver North, while stuffing other documents in her bra. However, the questions that have most often been asked ever since the Iran-Contra story broke—and Hall, during her fifteen minutes of fame, became fodder for the tabloids—was, first, whether President Reagan was actually involved in the Iran-Contra cover-up, and, second, why was the United States selling arms to the government of Iran in the first place?

Little about Iran-Contra made sense on the surface. Indeed, a main impetus for peace between such disparate elements in the Middle East as Israel, the Palestinians, and Syria remains, to this day, their common fear of the spread of Muslim fundamentalism—the center of which exists in Tehran. As Benjamin Ben-Eliezer, a retired general who was once Israel's military governor in the West Bank and Gaza, noted in a 1993 speech before Jewish leaders in New York: Israel and its Arab neighbors recognize the "common threat of Iranian-backed fundamentalism." In addition, Ben-Elizer stressed that the "rise of fundamentalist extremism in the region, supported mainly by Iran, threatens all Western nations."

As a result, the United States has secretly backed regimes hostile to Iran—including Saddam Hussein's regime in Iraq—knowing that any power vacuum left when these dictators fall could be immediately filled by Islamic fundamentalists who would not only be hostile to the United States, but could seriously threaten American oil supplies.

And like Iraq, Iran, too, may not be all that reluctant to use biological and chemical weapons in order to achieve its ends.

On March 24, 1995, the Associated Press reported Defense Secretary William Perry's comments that Iran had installed chemical weapons and six thousand troops near the mouth of the Persian Gulf in a military buildup capable of crippling the flow of oil in the region. "We really do not know why Iran would choose to deploy chemical weapons there, but we consider it to be a very negative factor," Perry said. Added Perry, the chemical weapons—housed in several batteries of Iranian Hawk surface-to-air missiles—gave Tehran the capability to harass shipping in the Strait of Hormuz through which one-third to one-half of the world's oil is transported.

A number of my intelligence sources dispute Perry's claims, however. They maintain that the Hawk missiles are not engineered to carry chemical and biological weapons. In addition, they insist that Iran's favorite brand of terrorism is economic, not political. An example, one source said, was that the Iranians wound up with the original U.S. plates needed to print perfect

$100 bills. It was for this reason, that source alleges, that the United States began printing $100 bills with a larger Ben Franklin and a watermark.

Notwithstanding, Iran was apparently also renewing its efforts to acquire four nuclear reactors which could help make it easier for that government to one day build nuclear weapons.

Perry obviously didn't take these threats lightly. After all, the State Department, in its 1994 annual report on "Patterns of Global Terrorism," called Iran "the most active state sponsor of terrorism." And Clinton's secretary of state, Warren Christopher, blamed the July 18, 1994, bombing of a seven-story building in Buenos Aires housing Jewish organizations—during which dozens of people were killed—on Hezbollah, the radical Lebanese-based "Party of God" that, Christopher said, is financed and largely controlled by Iran. (Not everyone in the intelligence community agrees here, as well, concerning the amount of control Iran actually maintains over Hezbollah. When, in the mid-1980s, Gen. Richard Secord negotiated with the Iranians for the release of U.S. hostages in exchange for weapons shipments—an arrangement that later became known as the "Iran-Contra Affair"—he said his Iranian contacts didn't tell him what he had hoped to hear. "[The Iranians] laid it right out on the table that they didn't necessarily command the Hezbollah, which was holding the American hostages in Lebanon, and couldn't automatically get them released," Secord recalled in his 1987 *Playboy* interview.)

Nevertheless, it's been widely promulgated that the United States has been the major bull's-eye in Iran's terrorist sights. In the introduction to *Target America: Terrorism in the U.S. Today* Congressman Bill McCollum (R-Fla.), then chairman of the Congressional Task Force on International Terrorism, notes that the World Trade Center bombing in New York City "brought into sharp focus what a select group of experts have been warning for years: that the United States is a prime target for terrorism by militant Islamic fundamentalists." In his preface to the same book, published in 1993, author Yossef Bodansky, at the time the director of the House Republican Task Force on Terrorism and Unconventional Warfare, writes that the explosion that shook the World Trade Center was "only the beginning." Argues Bodansky: "Islamic terrorism has embarked on a holy war—Jihad—against the West, especially the United States, which is being waged primarily through international terrorism." Radical Islamic fundamentalists would in fact seem to agree. In an interview with an Arabic daily during May of 1995, Hezbollah's mentor, Sheik Hussein Fadallah, matter-of-factly predicted, "What you see right now is just the spasms that precede the earthquake."

In his book, *Holy Terror*, Amir Taheri, an Iranian-born former newspaper editor, quotes the Ayatollah Fazl-Allah Mahalati who explains his rationale for terrorist acts against Israel and the West in the name of Islam: "He who takes up a gun, a dagger, a kitchen knife, or even a pebble with which to harm and kill the enemies of the faith has his place assured in heaven." Taheri noted that many fundamentalist clerics also believe that Muslims have the right to "lie and deceive their adversaries, and that a promise made to a non-Muslim can be broken whenever necessary." He quoted fundamentalist theoretician Mostafa Chamron as having offered the rationalization: "We are not fighting within the rules of the world as it exists today. We reject all those rules."

Concurred Dr. Walid Phares, who has written extensively about the Iranian Islamic Revolution: "Islamic fundamentalists do not operate under the same set of values advocated in the West—meaning agreements and treaties have a different perception in the fundamentalist vision of the world, and that radical Islamists intend to wage a world-wide campaign of domination."

Muslim extremists also seem to have a genuine disdain for what they perceive as the weaknesses of their enemies. When President Reagan gave the Ayatollah Khomeini's successor, Hashemi Rafsanjani, a Bible as a gift, Rafsanjani reportedly sneered, "This is one more evidence of how Islam has humiliated the Great American Satan, forcing its chief to crawl on his knees and beg us to take notice of him."

Dr. Walid Phares believes that twentieth-century Islamic fundamentalism was, above all, a movement that called for a return to the original teachings of Islam. This particular dimension of "Islamism," Phares says, does not pose a threat to non-Moslems or to Western democracies. It is a second dimension, however—that allows that by any means the forces of Islam may attack, subdue, and conquer—that poses the real threat.

According to Phares, this twofold vision of world politics is more or less the end product of a grand design formulated back in the seventh century at the eve of the great Arab-Islamic conquests. Those conquests were for the most part brought to a sudden halt by the military defeat at Tours, France, in 732, at the hands of Frankish leader Charles Martel. "Despite changes in world history and international relations during the following thirteen centuries," Phares said, "today's 'Islamists' basically preach a return to the golden age of those early conquests that began when the prophet Mohammed won the first battle of Islam by uniting the tribes of the Arab peninsula into one 'nation.' "

After centuries of Arab domination, the Arab hierarchy would later be controlled by the Ottomans, a Turkish dynasty from Central Asia. By the end of the nineteenth century, though, the Turkish empire had lost most of its European possessions while North Africa was occupied by the French, the British, and the Italians. The first wave of a new fundamentalism—launched by the Wahabi tribe of Arabia in the nineteenth century—came as a response to this hated Western colonialism. In the wake of the Ottoman collapse, one particular Wahabi tribe, the Saudis, founded their own kingdom which soon became a main source of Sunni fundamentalism.

In the 1920s, Hassan el-Banna, an Egyptian scholar, initiated the second wave of fundamentalism by creating the Moslem Brotherhood. The members of the Brotherhood, well-educated and organized, spread across the Arab world into countries such as Syria, Jordan, Lebanon, Algeria, Sudan, and Iraq.

The third wave of fundamentalism was the result of the Khomeini revolution in Iran in 1979. For the first time, a Shi'ite-inspired form of fundamentalism had swept into the Persian Gulf. The subsequent fundamentalist tidal wave—which led to the assassination of Egyptian president Anwar Sadat in 1981, Hezbollah's terror campaign and the hostage crisis in Lebanon between 1983 and 1985, and the civil war in Algeria in 1992—eventually reached the West with the New York and Buenos Aires bombings.

The squalor found throughout much of the Middle East and the Persian Gulf has surely helped make those areas breeding grounds for Islamic fundamentalism. "Cities like el-Menyia or Malhawi (in Upper Egypt) are seemingly unchanged in the past two thousand years," noted Robert Fabricio in the first in a series of articles he wrote that appeared in the *Fort Lauderdale Sun-Sentinel*. "Clouds of flies cover the el-Menyia central market, where animals of various species mingle in narrow alleys with people stumbling over dung in their search for their meager daily meal. Here, it is not just Western culture that is the enemy; it is a world economy that somehow has left much of the Islamic world behind."

In places like Israel's West Bank, Fabricio stressed, the message remains clear to those who have little else. "Islam will take you to paradise," Fabricio recalled hearing Imam Fadel Abdullah tell more than a thousand Moslems assembled in a mosque. "Those other groups in your midst, if you follow them, you will go to hell." The imam—which means "preacher" in Arabic—then raised his head and asked God: "Please deliver us victory against our enemies, and help the Muslims evict the infidel from Palestine." He added: "For any good Muslim the overthrow of the infidel is a religious duty."

And those who criticize the message of the radicals have often found themselves in great peril. As of February 1996—seven years after the Ayatollah Khomeini sentenced British author Salman Rushdie to death for allegedly insulting Islam in his novel, *The Satanic Verses*—Iranian leaders remained adamant that all Muslims still had a religious duty to kill him. While Rushdie for the most part remained in hiding, in 1991 his Italian translator was knifed and his Japanese translator was stabbed to death.

It was also open season in Algeria as Muslim fundamentalists there began assassinating local celebrities—deemed enemies of Islam—to ensure that their killings received the maximum exposure. Reuters reported in February 1995 that Azzedine Medjoubi, the director of Algeria's National Theater, was also shot and killed outside a theater in central Algiers.

Yet the dangers radical Islamic fundamentalism presents to those who do not strictly adhere to its tenets might have been greatly diminished if only President Jimmy Carter had heeded National Security Advisor Zbigniew Brzezinski's advice. Brzezinski had wanted the shah of Iran to use force to quell the street rebellions in Tehran. The Iranian intelligence service—SAVAK—was brutal enough to effectively do the job. But Secretary of State Cyrus Vance opposed the use of force—this would have not gone down well at the time with the American media—and the president wavered. Since the shah would not act unless his American benefactors gave him the green light to do so, Carter's hesitation (he was informed that the "Peacock throne" was in no real danger) allowed the fundamentalist revolution the time it needed to succeed.

Consequently, the eventual secret U.S. arming of Iraq—that became a necessity to many Reagan and Bush advisors, in no small part because of Carter's indecisiveness on Iran— perhaps could have been avoided. If the shah had remained in power and kept the fundamentalists under the thumb of the dreaded SAVAK, it is altogether possible that the Ayatollah Khomeini would have remained a mere footnote in history. As for Saddam Hussein, while he might have been a regional bully, it is highly doubtful that he would have emerged as the world's most dangerous tyrant—a man who used biological and chemical weapons against American troops during the Gulf War and a demon who nearly caused the Persian Gulf to go up in nuclear flames.

The Khomeini revolution, meanwhile, continued to spread like a fire out of control. In 1992, Algeria had to come to terms with its own civil war launched by the Islamic Salvation Front (FIS). In the subsequent three years nearly fifty thousand people died in the fighting. Saudi Arabia, Morocco, Bahrain, Jordan, and, of course, Lebanon were all besieged by fundamentalists attempting to destabilize their governments. In Egypt—

the first Arab country to sign a peace treaty with Israel—ninety-four police officers were killed in 1994 alone by fundamentalists (in Egypt, most opposing Mubarak's rule are called "fundamentalists") bent on overthrowing the Mubarak regime.

On June 26, 1995, Mubarak himself escaped an assassination attempt during an ambush of his motorcade in Ethiopia. It was the third time Islamic radicals had tried to kill him. "Whatever happens, Egypt will not be shaken and we will not give up fighting terrorism," Mubarek said when he arrived back in Cairo. "I am a believer and I have always thought that God is protecting me."

In an interview that appeared a week earlier in *Newsweek*, Mubarak had warned his American readers that terrorist groups are an international phenomenon. "They are not a problem for Egypt alone; terrorism is spreading everywhere," Mubarak said. When the interviewer asked Mubarek whether Washington was pushing him in the direction of having a dialogue with the radical Islamic groups in his country, the Egyptian leader replied: "Look, we understand this area very well. And whoever says to me, 'dialogue,' I tell him, 'No. Go have a dialogue in your own country. 'We know our people, and how to deal with them.' "

Yet in spite of what revolutionary Iran represented, and in spite of the possibility that Iran had become the main focal point of world terrorism, the United States secretly sold billions of dollars of military equipment to the mullahs and their anti-American regime during that country's costly eight-year war with Iraq that lasted through most of the 1980s and resulted in the loss of tens of thousands of lives. There are, of course, many different theories as to why the United States did this, but one reason this policy was set in motion was actually quite simple: Arms sales play an important role in funding covert operations, especially when those operations involve "black money," meaning they are not funded through official budgets that have to be accounted for.

During the middle 1980s, some of this "black money" that came from Iran went to the funding of the Contras in Nicaragua. In addition, the

Americans, like the Israelis, also wanted to keep the war between Iran and Iraq from having a clear-cut winner.

There was no doubt a high-minded third factor for dealing with Iran as well: the desire to free any American hostages, including CIA agent William Buckley, being held by Iranian-backed Hezbollah terrorists.

The Israelis, as has been well documented, were also dealing with Iran. They, too, had their own agendas, not the least of which was a desire to weaken Saddam Hussein and to free their own Hezbollah-held hostages such as Israeli air force navigator Ron Arad.

Of course both the Americans and the Israelis were smart enough—at least when dealing with Iran—to hedge their bets. On January 12, 1987, an article in the *New York Times* quoted from intelligence sources that Iran was actually given "distorted or inaccurate" intelligence data obtained from U.S. spy satellites.[2]

William Northrop, then with Israeli intelligence, revealed that the Israelis played a similar game with Iran. At the time, Israel was moving so much material to the Iranians that there was always the off chance that, somewhere down the line, the Iranians would turn Israel's own material against them. After all, Iran's order of battle was the same as Israel's in that it was American-based.

"Now there are parts—an example is a radar system made by Westinghouse, the APQ-120 radar—that are installed in a wonderful airplane called the Phantom," Northrop said in a personal interview with me. "The Phantom, without modification, has two engines that pull in tandem. So you can't pull one Phantom engine out and make it work on one airplane. Meanwhile the computers hooked into the APQ-120 radar do everything for the pilot except make him coffee. The range-finding of the continuous wave lock on systems for the mid-range Sparrow missiles. Fire direction, everything, goes through this system. In that radar system they have a particular little box— let's call it a continuous wave multiplier—that burns out. What this does is it jacks an electric impulse up and holds the radar beam on the enemy target while the Sparrow missile rides the beam to the target."

When the Phantom was first designed in the late 1950s, Northrop continued, engineers could not "culture" 45-megahertz crystals, but they could culture 15-megahertz crystals. They therefore had to make a box big enough to hold three 15-megahertz crystals.

These days, Northrop went on, one 45-megahertz crystal is adequate to do the entire job. "So you had empty space in this box. And the box never reduced in size because the whole APQ-120 radar system was built around having a box this size.

"So what we would do is inside the box we would put a little pyrotechnic device that had a small UHF receiver. And if the Iranian Phantoms were ever to come toward Israel, one of the first things that would happen was the leader of an interceptor wing would switch to a particular megahertz, give it a pulse, the pulse would go out to these little receivers, the receiver would react by igniting the pyrotechnic charge, and the APQ-120 would shut down. Now, after your APQ-120 shuts down, if you're a Phantom driver you can do one of two things. If it's a clear day you can land. Or, you can crash. You can't do anything else. You can't shoot your guns; you can't shoot your missiles; you can't call home. This was known as a 'Shanghai Surprise.' This device was put in a great number of the spare parts—especially the aircraft spare parts, since the Iranian air force was deemed the primary threat against Israel.

"And in the unlikely event that the Iranian air force ever attacks Israel, there are many, many thousands of these Shanghai Surprises sitting right there waiting for them."

NOTES

1. The relationship between "Arturito" Cruz and Fawn Hall was also alluded to by Lt. Colonel Oliver North in his book, *Under Fire*. North wrote that Cruz began showing up in his office "fairly often, as he would always stop in the outer office to chat with Fawn. I didn't realize how close they had become until I received a report from the CIA that Fawn had been seen with Arturito in Miami."

2. The *New York Times* article stated that Iraq was also getting distorted satellite information, although my own intelligence sources are not so sure.

THE
COVER-UP
CONTINUES

C IA director William Casey flew to Paris during February of 1982 to meet the head of the Iraqi secret service. By late spring of 1982— as part of a covert program to save Iraq from military defeat at the hands of Iran—Casey was sending Saddam Hussein AWACS intelligence obtained by the planes recently sold to the Saudis, in spite of Israel's objections. A year later, by the spring of 1983, Casey had a secret CIA station in Baghdad and was giving Saddam Hussein everything from satellite photos to the Iranian order of battle. Well-connected sources insist that Lt. Col. Oliver North was one of those becoming unwelcome in the White House's inner circle during that time because the policy of those closest to the president had become decidedly anti-Israel and pro-Iraq.

Bob Woodward's sources confirmed that Iraq received U.S. satellite photos, even though the United States was also covertly sending arms to Iran in an effort to get Iranian-held U.S. hostages released while at the same time ensuring that there was no clear-cut winner in the Iraq-Iran War.

257

In *Veil: The Secret Wars of the CIA*, Woodward notes that John McMahon, who replaced Adm. Bobby Inman as Casey's deputy director of Central Intelligence, was "deeply concerned" about the agency's "elaborate, top-secret intelligence-sharing agreement with the Iraqis that provided them with data from satellite photos."

The existence of a sturdy chain linking Saudi Arabia to Iraq—a chain that was only temporarily broken during the Gulf War—was further exposed by Mohammed al-Khilewi, a Saudi diplomat applying for asylum in the United States, who had worked on nuclear proliferation issues at the Saudi mission to the United Nations. On July 7, 1994, Steve Coll and John Mints of the *Washington Post* reported al-Khilewi's allegations, first published the day before in the *London Sunday Times*, that, between 1985 and 1990, Saudi Arabia provided advanced technology and up to $5 billion for Iraq's nuclear weapons program. The Saudis did this, al-Khilewi alleged, in exchange for continued access to Iraqi nuclear-weapons technology. Al-Khilewi added that, during the 1980s, Saudi Arabia also sent billions of dollars to Iraq to help the Iraqis wage war against their mutual enemy Iran.

According to al-Khilewi, teams of Saudi scientists secretly received training in nuclear technology in Iraq during the 1980s. The *London Times* noted that the Saudis had established their own nuclear research center at a military complex sixty miles southeast of Riyadh.

Before al-Khilewi "came out of the closet," however, the Saudis had adamantly denied their involvement in any nuclear-weapons program. When asked a month earlier during an interview on ABC-TV's *20/20* whether Saudi Arabia was seeking a nuclear bomb, Saudi Arabia's ambassador to the United States, Prince Bandar bin Sultan, said that not only was Riyadh not seeking to produce its own nuclear weaponry, "but we will not support people who create it. This is a very vital point in our national security policy."

Bandar, when shown one of al-Khilewi's documents that would seem to back up al-Khilewi's charges, called the documents "forgeries."

But al-Khilewi said he had a stack of secret Saudi documents, some fourteen thousand pages thick, gathered over several years. The documents, Lawrence Cohler noted in *Jewish Week*, told a "sordid tale of Saudi involvement in terrorism, assassination attempts on U.S. soil, corruption, and criminal mischief."

Not surprisingly, U.S. officials said they had seen no evidence that Saudi Arabia deliberately funded Iraq's nuclear efforts during the 1980s. The State Department declined comment on the Saudi diplomat's charges. The FBI—contacted by al-Khilewi's attorneys who feared for their client's life—also declined comment on the case.

In late February of 1993, by a vote of 162–147 (with forty-one abstentions) the leadership of the National Jewish Community Relations Advisory Council rejected sending a letter to President Clinton asking for a commutation of Jonathan Pollard's life sentence. The rationale for NJCRAC's stand remained the same as it had always been. According to its leadership, NJCRAC had been carefully monitoring the Pollard case since 1987 with respect to any and all allegations of anti-Semitism and discrimination—but found no proof that this existed. Critics, as usual, disagreed, adding that NJCRAC's policy of neutrality continued to have the implied effect of acquiescence.

Soon after learning of NJCRAC's most recent decision, Rabbi Avi Weiss, national president of the Coalition for Jewish Concerns (AMCHA), again visited his friend Pollard in prison. It was the twenty-eighth time Weiss had gone to Marion Penitentiary's K-Unit to see him.

"This most recent visit with Jonathan Pollard was the most difficult since I began visiting him in 1988," Weiss wrote in an AMCHA press release. "I knew Jonathan would be disappointed, deeply disappointed, and I didn't want him to suffer alone.

"We embraced and sat opposite each other. I reached out to hold his hand as I always do throughout my visits, in order to provide the simple human connection that Jonathan's solitary confinement denies him, as it is intended to do. Within minutes I told him: 'Jonathan, we were turned down by NJCRAC.'

"His head dropped. His eyes glistened. We sat in silence. Gradually, Jonathan began to share his pain. . . ."

Weiss said Pollard felt "punch-drunk" after hearing the news.

"I've been in a battle for eight years and every day is a battle," Weiss recalled Pollard telling him. "Every day I rise is a victory. Sometimes the depression is so deep I can't get up; I don't feel like going on. I make it only because of determination.

"I know the consequences of surrender."

On June 21, 1993, Jonathan Pollard was transferred from Marion Penitentiary to the Butner Federal Correctional Institution—a medium-security prison in Butner, North Carolina. Both his father and sister called the move an important "first step" toward securing Pollard's freedom.

There were still many, however, who wanted to make sure there would be no second steps. Pollard—whose early release from prison was hardly a fait accompli—nevertheless heard some good news one week after his transfer to Butner when Benjamin L. Hooks, former executive director of the National Association for the Advancement of Colored People (NAACP), wrote a letter to President Clinton stating: "I have recently reviewed the facts in the case of Jonathan Pollard and have concluded that the term of his sentence is unduly harsh and unjust. I am therefore respectfully urging you to grant Mr. Pollard executive clemency."

The black leader added: "As a lawyer and minister, as well as a judge and CEO of the NAACP, I have rarely encountered a case in which government arbitrariness was so clear-cut and inexcusable."

With momentum seeming to build in Pollard's favor, Carol Pollard—aided by new congressional allies such as Representatives Charles Schumer (D-N.Y.), Ileana Ros-Lehtinen (R-Fla.), Gary Ackerman (D-N.Y.), and Peter King (R-N.Y.)—was invited to speak before Congress. During her testimony to members of the House of Representatives, on August 3, 1993, Carol Pollard hammered away at some old points.

"Jonathan was never accused of, or charged with, intending to harm the United States, or even having reason to believe that his actions would do so," Carol Pollard said, as she had said a thousand times before. She stressed that her brother felt sorry for what he had done, arguing that he "has repeatedly shown remorse for his actions and has demonstrated the potential to be a productive, law-abiding citizen upon release from prison. He has a wide circle of family and friends to support him in making the transition to life outside prison, and he has the educational background and intelligence to make lasting and positive contributions to society."

The Pollard family has often referred to a letter Pollard wrote to his parents from Marion Prison, dated June 6, 1991, as proof of his remorse. Noted Pollard in that letter: "I have always accepted the fact that I am not above the law, and deserve to be punished for my actions, however well motivated I may have believed them to be. At the time, I was faced with a cruel dilemma in which I thought I had to choose between the law and my conscience. The danger that I perceived to Israel's existence was so acute that I instinctively chose action over reflection. I now know that I was wrong. I should have made the effort to discover a legal solution to the predicament. For this error in judgment I am profoundly sorry.

"Also, I regret the adverse effect which my actions had on the United States and the Jewish community. I am now and always have been proud to be a citizen of this country. Moreover, the loyalty of American Jews to their nation and its laws has been unwavering and intense. In fact, American Jews have been particular champions of our legal system, in good part because they know that our American law is the major bulwark against bigotry toward minority groups. In taking the action I did, I failed to understand the critical nature of this stance, and the ammunition my actions provided to anyone who might want to accuse American Jews of having dual loyalties.

"During the past six years in prison I have also reflected on how and why, despite my idealism in the world and Israel's place in it, I was capable of taking the actions I did. My problem stemmed not from dual loyalties, but from my anxiety that the past would repeat itself unless I intervened.

Unfortunately, I failed to appreciate the fact that such concerns did not justify my indifference to the law. In my mind, though, assisting an ally did not involve or require betraying the United States. I never thought that enhancing Israel's security would in any way jeopardize America's strategic interests. But that judgment was not mine to make."

Ten days after Carol Pollard spoke before the House of Representatives, the *Forward* reported that the Justice Department was "quietly undertaking a new internal review of the Jonathan Pollard case" and reassigning it to a new investigator. *Forward* correspondent Judith Bolton-Fasman noted that while a spokesman for the Justice Department refused to confirm or deny whether a new review was being undertaken, "word that steps were being taken followed an unusually well-attended briefing about the case on Capitol Hill last week that featured Carol Pollard, Jonathan's sister, and was a bipartisan initiative."

"If such a review produces findings favorable to Pollard," Bolton-Fasman continued, "it would put enormous pressure on President Clinton to commute Pollard's sentence. If the findings are not favorable, however, they would deal a blow to those who have argued on his behalf for years. In any case, such a move by the Justice Department would help give President Clinton a chance to fulfill a campaign pledge to review the controversial case."

Abraham Foxman added fuel to the pro-Pollard fire when, on September 15, 1993, he wrote a letter to Clinton asking the president to consider clemency.

"Although I have written to you before in my capacity as national director of the Anti-Defamation League, in this letter I speak not for the ADL but only for myself," Foxman wrote. "I believe the time has come for you to grant clemency to Jonathan Pollard and commute his sentence to time already served, and I urge you to do so.

"There is no question that what Pollard did was wrong and cannot be justified. However, he has acknowledged his transgressions, and he has paid a steep price for them. Pollard deserves forgiveness and a chance to turn the page and begin a new chapter in his life. I hope you will give him that chance."

Numerous other pleas on Pollard's behalf began to reach Bill Clinton's desk. The president's response usually came back in the following form letter:

"As you may be aware, Mr. Pollard's original petition filed with the Pardon Attorney at the Department of Justice, in December 1992, was disapproved. Mr. Pollard then renewed his petition after January 20, 1993. I am currently awaiting the Justice Department's recommendation in this matter. Once I receive their recommendation, I will give consideration to all the relevant facts in order to make a fair and just determination.

"I appreciate your concern for this serious matter.

"Sincerely, Bill Clinton."

On November 10, 1993, two days before Clinton was to meet with Israeli prime minister Yitzhak Rabin in the White House—and two months after Rabin's historic handshake on the White House lawn with PLO leader Yasser Arafat—the president admitted to reporters that Rabin had also asked him to shorten Pollard's prison sentence.

"Mr. Clinton said he had asked the Justice Department for a recommendation on the request after which he will make a decision," wrote *New York Times* reporter Thomas L. Friedman on November 11. Friedman added, however, that Justice Department officials "have long been hostile to such a request, arguing that it would create a very bad precedent."

Friedman's words would soon prove to be prophetic. As a date neared when Clinton would make a decision on Pollard's commutation, articles and opinion pieces arguing strenuously against clemency began appearing with increased regularity, while certain Clinton administration officials—like Reagan and Bush administration officials before them—appeared to be closing ranks in an effort to keep the onetime spy behind bars.

An editorial in the December 2, 1993, edition of the *Washington Post* maintained that, contrary to what many Pollard supporters had been saying, there was never any injustice in his harsh sentence. "No innocent, Jonathan Pollard was a practiced intelligence analyst who knew the seriousness of his offense," the editorial declared. "He knew he could not control whether Israel would keep the information or how Israel might apply it, and that it could give Israel options that might or might not be in the American interest. That he was spying not for an enemy but a friend does not so much lighten his breach of trust as underline its grossness."

In an article appearing December 7, 1993, on the front page of the *New York Times*, writer David Johnston noted that Clinton's advisors were, indeed, now recommending that the president reject a petition for clemency. "Faced with solidifying opposition within the administration," Johnston wrote, "officials said it appeared unlikely that Mr. Clinton would shorten Mr. Pollard's sentence despite an intense lobbying campaign by American supporters and a personal plea to Mr. Clinton, last month, by Prime Minister Yitzhak Rabin of Israel."

A December 10, 1993, editorial in the *New York Times* also argued against a commutation of Pollard's sentence. "It is the responsibility of the U.S. government to put limits on intelligence sharing to protect the nation's wider interests," the editorial stated. "Individuals like Mr. Pollard, whatever their motivation, cannot be allowed to ignore the accountable government authorities and take matters into their own hands."

Only days earlier, *Time* magazine had reported that one document Pollard allegedly slipped to the Israelis was a huge National Security Agency compendium of frequencies, used by foreign intelligence services, that may have found its way into Soviet hands. In a December 10 letter to the magazine, Pollard's attorney, Theodore Olson, angrily retorted: "Five layers of innuendo, and no facts, equal a manifestly frivolous story. The 'officials' who are using you to sabotage the Pollard commutation effort obviously have no facts to back up their insinuations."

Nevertheless, the seeds of doubt about Jonathan Pollard were again being planted in the American psyche. More seeds began to sprout on December 27, 1993, when it was revealed in the *New York Times* that outgoing Secretary of Defense Les Aspin, in a December 23, 1993, memo, had written to Clinton that Pollard had tried to slip classified information into fourteen of his personal letters from prison. Michael R. Gordon noted in the newspaper that administration officials would not say to whom the letters were addressed.

In an effort to again stop the bleeding, Olson responded quickly to Aspin's statements. The attorney was quoted in the *New York Times* as saying that neither he, nor Pollard, had ever been told that Pollard's prison letters violated national security. Barton Gellman wrote in the *Washington Post* that Olson then accused the Pentagon of what he termed a "McCarthyesque" refusal to substantiate its damaging new charges.

On the day before he was gunned down by an assassin, Israeli prime minister Yitzhak Rabin wrote a note to Bill Clinton again asking the president to grant Pollard clemency. According to published reports, it wasn't the first time Rabin had made such a request. In November of 1993, and, again, during January of 1995, Rabin had also appealed directly to Clinton on behalf of Pollard. Presidential spokesman Mike McCurry acknowledged that Rabin once again raised the Pollard issue, although a well-connected Israeli source of mine insists that—behind the scenes at least—Rabin may have actually been a stumbling block for those who were fighting for Pollard's freedom. According to my source, Rabin, who had been Israel's defense minister during the time of Pollard's espionage activities, strongly opposed the granting of Israeli citizenship to Pollard—which would have sent an unmistakable signal to Washington—because this could be seen as an acknowledgment that Pollard had, in fact, been an Israeli agent and not just part of some rogue operation as many Israeli leaders had long insisted. "Rabin viewed the granting of Israeli citizenship to Pollard as a plot brewed by the 'Young Turks' in Israel's intelligence community," my source told me. "He was probably right."

In an interview allowed by Naval Intelligence censors that appeared in the September 24, 1995, edition of the Israeli newspaper *MA'ARIV*, Pollard was asked how the granting of Israeli citizenship would contribute to his fight for freedom. "The granting of citizenship would confer upon me legitimacy as an Israeli agent," Pollard said. "It would, at the same time, signal the government of Israel's willingness to accept responsibility for me, for my actions, and for my fate. Such a message would remove all doubt and would put the government of Israel in a position where it could enter into serious negotiations—and I do mean serious—for my release."

Soon after Rabin's death, Knesset member Gen. Ariel Sharon (the same Ariel Sharon who once went into private business with Rafi Eitan, the old spymaster who ran Pollard's operation for LAKAM) seemed to confirm what my source had implied: that some of the old guard in Jerusalem were speaking out of both sides of their mouths when it came to Pollard. According to a January 1996 report in *MA'ARIV* (and reprinted in English by Ben Caspit), Sharon shouted out, during a Knesset Foreign and Intelligence Committee meeting, that "it was the National Unity Government that put Pollard in prison!"

The coalition government Sharon was referring to was the one headed by Shimon Peres in the mid-1980s, and in which Peres's political rival, Yitzhak Shamir, held the post of foreign minister while Rabin was minister of defense. Sharon, who said he had told Peres and Shamir not to submit documents to the Americans in 1985 that could incriminate Pollard, was not finished with his tirade. Bellowed the portly general: "Yitzhak Shamir said, at the time when the Americans were asking for the material Pollard had passed, that the state 'has to know how to sacrifice a man.' Never has any serious effort been made to free Pollard. So the ultimate responsibility for his plight rests squarely upon Prime Minister Peres, and the one who was then foreign minister, Yitzhak Shamir."

While Rabin may or may not have been among those who were willing to make Pollard a sacrificial lamb, leaked media reports during Rabin's watch as Israeli prime minister linked Pollard's release to the release of Palestinian prisoners. The *Jerusalem Post* quoted Rabin as saying, in January of 1995: "I hope that if there is no delay in the release of prisoners, we will see the release of Pollard."

Ten months later, on November 5, 1995, Malcolm Hoenlein, executive vice president of the Conference of Presidents of Major American Jewish

Organizations, added his voice to those imploring Clinton to free Pollard as a way of honoring Rabin's memory. "I was deeply moved by your comments about Prime Minister Rabin and your eulogy at his funeral," Hoenlein wrote in a letter to the president. "While still numbed by this overwhelming tragedy, I thought of my last conversation with [Rabin] last week. Then, as on another occasion, he asked that we approach you on behalf of Jonathan Pollard. I truly believe that a meaningful last gesture to this courageous and great leader would be to grant his request to release Jonathan Pollard. The prime minister well understood the conflicting pressures on you, but asked that we intercede as well to help bring a positive decision."

What had surely begun as a bright ray of hope for Pollard's supporters was the arrest, on February 22, 1994, of Aldrich Hazen Ames, the onetime CIA Soviet Counterintelligence expert, who, as a double-agent, passed on reams of TOP SECRET data to his benefactors in Moscow. He and his Columbian-born wife, Maria, were accused of raking in more than $1.5 million for feeding classified information to Russian agents during the nine years Ames was on the Kremlin's payroll. Two weeks after his arrest, *Newsweek* revealed that sources told the magazine that the KGB used information supplied by Ames to "roll up" more than twenty CIA operations, and that at least ten agents—working for the CIA within the Soviet Union—died as a result.

Suddenly, new questions were being asked. In 1985, the year Pollard was arrested, Valery Martynov and Sergei Mortorin, two KGB officers recruited by U.S. intelligence, were reportedly executed. Was Jonathan Pollard believed to be indirectly responsible for the deaths of those CIA assets while, in truth, those agents had been exposed by the traitorous Ames? Was Pollard, in essence, paying the price for Ames's crimes?

As Ames himself told the *New York Times*: "In 1985 and 1986, as a result of the information I sold the Soviets, it was as if neon lights and search lights lit up all the way to the Kremlin saying: 'There is penetration.' No reasonable counterintelligence officer, FBI or the CIA, was under any doubt by the spring of 1986 that a penetration of S/E (the CIA's

Soviet/Eastern Europe Operations Division, headed by Ames) was the single, most logical reason for the disaster that had occurred."

In this type of atmosphere, and with the intelligence community in a literal panic over their inability to locate the source of the penetration, Pollard may have been the perfect foil. Note attorneys Arnold Forster and David Kirshenbaum in an article that appeared in the *B'nai B'rith Messenger*: "With Ames clearly quite interested in deflecting attention away from himself and focused elsewhere, the arrest of Jonathan Pollard must have been for Ames and others in the CIA like manna from heaven. Somebody made sure to capitalize on this opportunity."

John Loftus, who says he interviewed hundreds of present and former intelligence operatives for his book, *The Secret War Against the Jews*, also saw Pollard as a convenient scapegoat. In an article he wrote that appeared in the April 23, 1995, edition of the *Miami Herald*, Loftus said he believed Ames may hold the very key that could open Pollard's cell. Explained Loftus, who at the time told me he was also working on his own book about the Pollard case: "It was well known that there once had been KGB moles inside Israeli intelligence. If Pollard gave U.S. secrets to the Mossad it was quite plausible that an as-yet-undiscovered Soviet mole could have leaked them to the KGB. As it turns out, though, American secrets were safer in the Mossad than they were in the CIA while Ames was around."

Ames admitted as much in an interview that appeared in the *Washington Post*. "In the summer of 1984 [the time Pollard admits to have begun working for Israel], the CIA bureau in Moscow seemed on the verge of collapse," Ames recalled. "Not only the Moscow agents, but recruited Soviet officials in a handful of posts around the world were lost."

The CIA was obviously desperate to find the leak, while Ames would have had every reason to blame someone else for what was happening in the Moscow bureau. When Pollard was arrested in November of 1985, then sentenced to life in prison in March of 1987, Ames was the man in charge of Soviet and Eastern Bloc counterintelligence within the CIA. It's logical to assume that before then secretary of defense Weinberger sent his infamous "memo" to Judge Aubrey Robinson—recommending the harshest sentence allowable by law for Pollard—Weinberger likely conferred with Ames, or at least read his report. As Loftus succinctly puts it, "In order to hide his own espionage for the Russians, Ames successfully pointed the finger at Pollard."

Buoyed by Aldrich Ames's arrest, yet apparently still no closer to being set free, Pollard soon began turning for comfort to an ardent Canadian supporter of his named Esther Zeitz. Frustrated by his family's seeming inability to secure his release from prison by "playing ball" with the U.S. authorities, Pollard found himself being drawn to the dark-haired, attractive woman who had begun exchanging letters with him and felt that she could succeed where everyone else had so far failed. Before long, Pollard (who had since been divorced by Anne) and the strong-willed Zeitz were calling themselves "husband and wife," with Zeitz even being allowed to visit her new "husband" in prison. As for Pollard's family, they apparently saw Zeitz as an opportunist and described the marriage as a sham. They still believe Zeitz is hurting Pollard's cause rather than helping it. The resulting acrimony has especially driven a wedge between Pollard and his sister, Carol.

The growing family schism was quite obvious in a letter sent out to the media dated December 18, 1995, in which Pollard's new lawyer, Larry Dub, wrote: "As Jonathan Pollard's lead attorney, I wish to point out that Carol Pollard does not represent my client's interests, nor is she authorized to speak on his behalf. More than a year ago, Ms. Pollard was specifically asked by her brother, Jonathan, to cease any and all activities on his behalf. Since that time, she has neither seen nor spoken to her brother.

"Accordingly, she is not authorized to speak on his behalf and is not aware of the recent developments in his case. I therefore urge you to contact Mr. Pollard's wife, Esther, who is the only person authorized to speak on Jonathan's behalf, other than his attorneys."

Pollard was obviously in his wife's corner. In the September 24, 1995, *MA'ARIV* interview, he said there "is no end to the number of reasons for living that I have derived from my relationship with Esther. Our marriage helps me to define myself as a person in much the same way as my religion does." Asked how he felt about the strong attacks levied by "certain individuals" against Esther, Pollard replied: "There is nothing more contemptible than to attack the wife of a man who is in prison, who is unable to respond, and is in no position to defend her. It's an evil and cowardly thing to do. And it hurts me directly."

Pollard's bevy of lawyers even went so far as to file a lawsuit against Carol Pollard. Representing attorney Larry Dub, attorney Gidi Frishtik wrote to Pollard's sister, in a letter dated January 29, 1996: "On more than one occasion Jonathan Pollard has relayed the message to you that, in his opinion, your actions and your statements are damaging to his case. In spite of this, it is clear that you continue again and again to speak on his case while continuing to do damage to the effort to secure his release."

Frishtik said Pollard also wanted from his sister "a full accounting, in detail, of all the sums of money which have been paid to you since the start of his incarceration, monies which are intended for the campaign to secure his release."

The lawyer stated, further, that if Carol did not "cease and desist" from making statements about Pollard's case, his attorneys would be "compelled to pursue this matter through legal avenues."

No doubt, Esther Zeitz-Pollard gave her husband hope for a bright future where there had been little hope before. She also used her position as Pollard's wife to attract more media attention than had ever been the case in the past. The question is, did that publicity help or actually hurt?

It's difficult to know for sure. But when attorney Larry Dub stated that the family was "unaware of the recent developments in Pollard's case," it seemed to be self-serving, or just incredibly naive, to assume that the Pollard family—which almost from day one had dealt with high-ranking Israeli intelligence operatives and politicians on one end, and top Washington insiders (including President Reagan's own attorney) on the other—was suddenly out of the loop. Perhaps Mr. Dub was oversimplifying—and grossly underestimating—the political ramifications of what Jonathan Pollard must have stepped into the minute he crossed that line and became a double agent for his Jewish homeland.

When on October 16, 1995, it was reported that Lt. Cmdr. Michael Schwartz—accused of giving classified material to Saudi Arabia—was dismissed from Naval service rather than face a court-martial, it was seen by many as further evidence that the Pollard case was grounded in politics rather than law. The Navy had originally planned to court-martial Schwartz, a fifteen-year veteran who had been assigned to the U.S. Military Training Mission in Saudi Arabia and was accused of giving the Saudis daily intelligence summaries as well as other secret material.

According to a Navy spokesman, the charges were dropped because "the damage to national security, if any, was minimal." Pollard disagreed. "We're supposed to believe this?" he later wrote to me.

In an opinion piece that appeared in a December 1995 issue of *MA'ARIV*, Esther Zeitz-Pollard compared Schwartz's case to that of her husband's when she asked: "Why were there no public expressions of U.S. government outrage at the 'arrogance' and 'ingratitude' of Saudi Arabia for running a spy in the U.S. Navy, just one year after the United States saved the Saudis from destruction in the Persian Gulf War? Why wasn't the story of the Saudi spy front-page news? Why didn't the FBI start leaking information regarding the case and the character of the spy? And why didn't the Pentagon and the [U.S.] intelligence community question the continued viability of the American special relationship with Saudi Arabia?"

On December 6, 1995, Member of the Knesset (M.K.) Limor Livnat also had some questions regarding Schwartz, who is not Jewish, and she brought them up in front of Israeli Speaker of the House Shevach Weiss.

"Honored Speaker," Livnat said, "It is known that recently an American spy, Lt Cmdr. Michael Schwartz, was exposed and that he passed classified information to the Saudis. It is also known that the Americans have decided not to have him stand trial. I should like to ask: Do we know if this news is true, and whether the information that was passed is linked to

Israel's national security? And, given the similarity between the cases, will the government of Israel demand the immediate release of Jonathan Pollard who was given a life sentence?"

It was Deputy Defense Minister Ori Orr who responded to Livnat's questions.

"This will be a short answer," Orr said. "We have no information on any such case."

"No information, whatsoever?" Livnatt asked.

"I don't know from where this news appeared in the press," Orr said. "We have no information on any such spy caught by the Saudis. Therefore, the rest of the questions—"

"By the Americans, not the Saudis!" Livnatt snapped.

"I'm saying in Saudi Arabia, by the Americans," Orr corrected himself. "We have no such information. I assure you that if there will be any information, I will send it to you."

Two weeks later, Pollard sent me another letter that was short, but to the point. "Dear Elliot," the letter began. "In light of our government's decision not to prosecute Lt. Cmdr. Michael Schwartz for spying on behalf of Saudi Arabia, could you please tell me why I'm still in prison? Sincerely, Jonathan."

On November 21, 1995, only days after the assassination of Prime Minister Rabin, Jonathan Pollard finally became a citizen of Israel. The timing was hardly coincidental. News of Israel's decision, which came ten years to the day after Pollard was arrested, was greeted with joy, but also with guarded optimism.

Esther Zeitz-Pollard, allegedly speaking for her husband, said Jonathan told her it was his "happiest day in ten years." Rabbi Avi Weiss, Pollard's long-time personal rabbi, said he was ecstatic for his friend. "In speaking with Jonathan, and looking into his eyes over many years, I know of his deep sense of abandonment," Weiss said. "This no doubt will lift him tremendously."

Another good day for Pollard came during the second week of February 1996, when he was visited in prison by U.S. Rep. Benjamin Gilman, the influential chairman of the House International Relations Committee.

It was Pollard's first visit by a member of Congress. Still, the Clinton White House hardly seemed to be softening its tough posture.

"Our position on Pollard has not changed," White House Chief of Staff Leon Panetta told CNN on March 24, 1996. Asked if there was any chance of the president pardoning Pollard, Panetta replied. "No, not at this time. This is someone who was caught spying against the United States. In terms of law and order in this country, it's not easy to simply back away from that and say that someone ought to be released or pardoned when that kind of offense has been committed."

Panetta's blunt comments hardly came as a surprise to *Moment* magazine editor Hershel Shanks. "This is an election year," Shanks noted in an April 7, 1996, editorial. "There's no chance that President Clinton will alienate a substantial segment of the electorate over this insignificant issue. And, for Clinton, what's to be gained? Jewish votes hardly hinge on the Pollard case."

Nevertheless, in published reports the White House began to take umbrage at the "outspoken and noisy style of Pollard and those close to him." Whereas Pollard's sister, Carol, and father, Morris, had in the past led the charge by making plenty of noise themselves, they were also willing to work quietly behind the scenes to help secure Pollard's release. When Esther Zeitz-Pollard came into the picture, however, the tone of Pollard's new allies seemed to become more belligerent and confrontational—and the White House noticed.

So did Likud Party Chairman Benjamin Netanyahu. "The Israeli press has reported that you considered pardoning Mr. Pollard in recent years, but that you have reservations concerning the conduct of some of his relatives and supporters," Netanyahu wrote to Clinton in a letter dated May 5, 1996. "If these reports are true, I urge you to put aside such considerations. Undoubtedly, Mr. President, you share the humanitarian desire to alleviate the suffering of Mr. Pollard, who has paid dearly for his past mistakes, a desire that is shared by many in the United States and by all the people of Israel, regardless of their political affiliation."

Soon after his election as prime minister, Netanyahu again made his

273

point. On June 16, 1996, I received a fax from the Israeli consulate in Miami. In it were outlined certain areas that the Netanyahu administration was anxious to address. Mainly, those areas dealt with safeguarding security in Israel, the question of settlements, and maintaining the strong growth in Israel's economy. But point number 5, under the heading of "Peace, Security and Foreign Relations," left little room for misinterpretation. It read: "The Government of Israel will use all means at its disposal to bring home the prisoners of war and missing in action and all those who worked for the security of the state, and will insist on this point during negotiations with all relevant parties."

The "Young Turks," as my intelligence source called them, had apparently won. It appeared that, during the Netanyahu administration at least, the freeing of Jonathan Pollard would clearly be a priority.

As for Pollard, he could only keep hoping that his long nightmare was finally over.

"The only thing that sustains me now is my dream of leading a quiet life as a free man," he wrote as part of an open letter to the American media. "I long to be a productive member of Israeli society. To enjoy the companionship of good friends. To be a good husband and a loving father. These are my dreams and aspirations. I don't ask for much.

"I just want to go home."

In late May 1998, a high-level Israeli intelligence source, who spoke to me on condition of anonymity, told me that Pollard's release from prison could be "imminent." There was reason for his optimism. On May 11, 1998, after more than a decade of denials, the Israeli government acknowledged that convicted spy Jonathan Pollard was working as an Israeli agent when he spied on the United States. Despite worldwide pleas on his behalf, the Israelis, in the past, had always insisted that Pollard acted as part of a "rogue operation" and not under Israel's direction. Why, I asked my source, were the Israelis finally changing their tune?

"It's a moral obligation that the State of Israel felt it had," my source said. "Even though this is happening now [when the Likud government is in power], it was Shimon Peres who granted Pollard's Israeli citizenship [in November 1995, only days after Prime Minister Yitzhak Rabin's assassination]. That was the first step. So this has never been a political issue; but it has always been an Israeli issue."

Interestingly, just days before the Israeli government admitted that Pollard had been a de-facto agent, I received a letter from Pollard himself implying that Israeli attorney general Elyakim Rubinstein should be kept off an Israeli government panel trying to formulate a game plan to secure Pollard's release. In another letter, addressed to Prime Minister Benjamin Netanyahu, Pollard wrote: "Elyakim Rubinstein is not a disinterested party. He bears direct responsibility for the events that led to my bitter fate." .

True, Rubinstein was the most senior diplomat present when the FBI arrested Pollard outside the Israeli embassy in Washington on November 21, 1985. Rubinstein was in charge of the embassy that day because Meir Rosenne, then Israel's ambassador to the United States, was in Paris. If Rosenne had been at the embassy, my source told me, Pollard may not have been turned away—and history might have been quite different. As my source put it: "He [Rubinstein] just panicked, and blew the effort." Unbeknownst to Pollard, though, it was Rubinstein, my source insisted, who had also played one of the most important roles in getting the Israelis to admit that Pollard's operation was fully sanctioned, in the mid-1980s, by Israel's leaders.

As for the misery Pollard had been forced to endure in the years since, perhaps if he had been better at "playing the game" the U.S. government might not have come down on him quite so hard. Pollard's detractors in Washington had long argued that the Jewish spy hardly seemed penitent after he was caught. Said my source: "Pollard began to dissemble—which a trained agent is supposed to do—but he was never remorseful."

Notwithstanding, Pollard reportedly told an Israeli cabinet minister who visited him in prison that he felt "profound sorrow and remorse" for what he had done. Whether those feelings were genuine or not, they may have had little to do with the change in the political climate. "Pollard's imminent release, if it takes place, is not a question of atonement or anything else," my source told me. "It's just time for him to go home."

Still, Pollard was apparently no closer to being set free. Then, on Friday, October 23, 1998, he received an unexpected boost. The *Washington Post* reported that Pollard's fate had been made into a bargaining chip during the ongoing talks at Maryland's Wye River Conference Center. *Washington Post* reporter Walter Pincus noted that President Clinton promised Prime Minister Netanyahu to review Pollard's sentence since the issue of Pollard's continued incarceration was being seen by the Israeli government as an impediment to having the peace process move forward.

The response from U.S. intelligence quarters was immediate and understandably harsh. Former CIA director R. James Woolsey told a National Press Club audience that he had recommended against a pardon for Pollard in 1994 because, even though Pollard stole secrets for a friendly government, "what he stole was so massive and so highly classified that I thought a lengthy penalty was entirely justified." It was also widely reported that the chairman of the Senate Intelligence Committee, Sen. Richard Shelby (R-Ala.), wrote a letter to Clinton stating how "deeply disturbed" he was that the release of Pollard was even being considered by the president. Shelby said in the letter that he had "the strongest objections, now or in the future," concerning the pardoning of Pollard.

Irrespective of some of the comments made by Woolsey, Shelby, and others, my belief was that while Pollard's detractors had won most of the previous battles, they were finally about to lose the war. No longer would the Caspar Weinbergers, Edwin Meeses, and Joseph diGenovas of the world be able to completely bury the Pollard issue as they had done so successfully for the past thirteen years. At long last, as more bits and pieces would seep out, as the media would respond to the sudden feeding frenzy for information which would take on a life of its own, what really happened, and why Pollard felt compelled to do what he did, would increasingly be revealed.

Or so I thought.

For one thing, Pollard's enemies were not about to go down quietly. Not surprisingly, it was Joe diGenova who seemed to be kicking and screaming the loudest. DiGenova, the U.S. attorney who prosecuted Pollard—insisting on a life sentence after coercing Pollard into accepting what many believed to be a bogus plea-bargain agreement—seemed to be on every Washington talk show. On *This Week*, while being grilled by Sam Donaldson, diGenova stated emphatically that Pollard should stay in prison for the rest of his life. "If Clinton releases him, it will be one of the most disgraceful acts ever by an American president," diGenova fumed. DiGenova also insisted on *This Week* that Judge Aubrey Robinson, who handed Pollard his life sentence, did so because "Judge Robinson was a military man."

But, as I have already stated, Robinson, an African American, was also handed a "memo" from then Secretary of Defense Weinberger, the contents of which have remained secret but which purportedly linked Pollard to the passing of certain U.S. secrets to the then apartheid government of South Africa—charges that Pollard categorically denied.

Regardless, just as the government had done with Panamanian leader Manuel Noriega—a sleazy individual, but a person who nevertheless operated as a CIA asset when his country served as a clearing house for illegal drug shipments during the Iran-Contra years—Pollard, the spy who knew too much, had to be either "eliminated" or imprisoned to ensure his silence.

So silenced he was—and all but forgotten by most.

Just weeks earlier, when Rabbis Philip and Shoni Labowitz had me speak on the subject of Pollard at Fort Lauderdale's Temple Adath Or, after its Yom Kippur services, I asked the audience there how many of them had ever even heard of Pollard. Out of perhaps 150 people, only a dozen or so raised their hands. I then asked them, "Who has heard of Wolf Blitzer?" Just about every hand went up. I was struck by the irony. Wolf Blitzer was a print journalist with the *Jerusalem Post* when he wrote his book on the Pollard case, *Territory of Lies*, an extremely well-written book, but not a runaway best-seller. I wondered: Was there some kind of quid pro quo involved here (without Wolf's knowledge) that assured his mete-oric rise to the top of the TV journalism world? Or was it just a matter of timing, luck, and Mr. Blitzer's undeniable journalistic skills?

As for the expected counterattack against Pollard, meanwhile, it con-tinued almost unabated. On November 12, 1998, the government fired another salvo when the *New York Times* reported that CIA Director George Tenet told the president it would "be impossible" for him to continue as DCI (Director of Central Intelligence) if Pollard was released. Tenet allegedly told Clinton how strongly the U.S. intelligence community felt about Pollard's "betrayal," and that any appearance that Tenet had acqui-esced in Pollard's release from prison would force him to resign. As for the *Times* report, the CIA would neither confirm nor deny it.

According to other sources, however, Tenet denied ever saying any such thing at that time. Surely, if Tenet did speak to the president on the Pollard issue he would have done so in private. So was the story of Tenet's threat to resign even true? And if it was true, then who leaked it to the media? Common sense would dictate that it probably was the White House, protecting a beleaguered president looking to pass the buck while dodging the Pollard issue once again.

Clinton, for his part, continued to play the game. He promised he "would request advice" by mid-January 1999 from top government and national security officials before making his decision regarding Pollard. Attorney General Janet Reno, who previously opposed granting Pollard clemency, told reporters she would listen to her advisors in the Justice Department and would make a recommendation to Clinton by January 11. According to National Security Council spokesman David Leavy, White House counsel Charles Ruff also wrote to Defense Secretary William Cohen, Secretary of State Madeleine Albright, and CIA Director Tenet, seeking information and comments. Said Leavy: "The president has agreed to take a fresh look at this without any preconditions or time lines."

While the White House circled the wagons, Pollard's allies drew some media attention of their own. Pollard's old advocate Alan Dershowitz, an expert on the legalities of the case, began debating the issue, as he often had in the past, with any Pollard detractor who would have the nerve to take him on. Then, a month before the president was scheduled to receive recommendations on Pollard, an article appeared in the *Foreword* by reporter Seth Gitell stating that, according to former Senate Intelligence Committee staffer Angelo Codevilla, Pollard had been blamed all along for CIA turncoat Aldrich Ames's crimes. Codevilla, who was calling for Pollard's release, was being joined in that chorus by Dennis DeConcini, a former chairman of the Senate Intelligence Committee.

Codevilla, who had long been on record as especially critical of former Defense Secretary Weinberger, said, "I know as much as there is to know about the intelligence business. I've offered many times to talk to anybody who thinks Pollard has done great harm to U.S. intelligence." Addressing the accusations levied against Pollard that the information he gave Israel cost the lives of American operatives in the former Soviet Union, Codevilla said, "Those losses were later attributed to, and rightly so, to Aldrich Ames. It's significant that the man who wrote the damage report on Jonathan Pollard was none other than Aldrich Ames himself."

Gitell called me before his article ran asking whether I agreed with Codevilla. I told him that, from what I knew from my own intelligence sources at least, Codevilla was right on the money.

CIA spokeswoman Anya Guilsher disputed Codevilla's assertion, however. "Ames played no role in the damage assessment that was done on Pollard," Gitell quoted Guilsher as having said. Former CIA director Woolsey took issue with Codevilla's accusations as well. "I know the individual who did [the damage report] and it was not Aldrich Ames," Woolsey added, not elaborating on who that person was.

Told of the assertions by Guilsher and Woolsey, Codevilla said they struck him as "a bold-faced lie."

"If the assertion is made that Pollard had something to do with the compromise of agents in the Soviet Union and Eastern Europe, why would the chief of counterintelligence in Eastern Europe and the Soviet Union not have a role?" Codevilla rhetorically asked.

Guilsher responded: "In theory, you would think Ames had a role, but at the time the assessment was done, he didn't."

"[The CIA] is engaged in the Clintonization of language," Codevilla shot back. "The CIA is hiding the fact that Ames played a major role in convincing it that Pollard was responsible for agent compromises."

On January 11, 1999—the date the Justice Department was scheduled to make its recommendation to Clinton on the Pollard matter—several of the president's top aides once again advised him not to consider clemency for Pollard. What the American public had "learned," thanks in part to the trial balloons being floated the previous day, was that Pollard actually did far more harm to American security than had previously been revealed. In addition, the Pentagon, the White House, and the CIA, just like in an old "western," were aided when a top-flight (hired?) gunslinger—Seymour M. Hersh—rode into town.

A brilliant and respected Pulitzer Prize–winning writer (for his 1970 exposé of the My Lai massacre), and a winner of the National Book Critic's Circle Award (for *The Price of Power: Kissinger in the White House*), Hersh was not one to shy away from getting his hands dirty in his search for the ever-elusive "smoking gun." To his critics, though, and there are more than a few, Hersh, who also authored the controversial John F. Kennedy book, *The Dark Side of Camelot*, was hardly reticent about following the advice of journalist and wit Ben Hecht, a man given credit for the tongue-in-cheek utterance: "Never let the facts get in the way of a good story."

In an article that appeared in the January 18, 1999, issue of the *New Yorker* magazine entitled "The Traitor," Hersh took aim at his target and pulled the trigger. He ripped Pollard, "revealing" for the first time "information" about the case that, in the past, had been highly classified. Noted Hersh in the piece: "The president's willingness to consider clemency for Pollard so upset the intelligence community that its leaders took an unusual step—they began to go public. In early December [1998], four retired admirals who had served as directors of Naval Intelligence circulated an article, eventually published in the *Washington Post,* in which they argued that Pollard's release would be 'irresponsible' and a victory for what they depicted as a 'clever public relations campaign.' Since then, sensitive details about the secrets Pollard gave away have been made public by CBS and NBC."

It was interesting that this "information" had never been made public before—such as at the time of Pollard's original sentencing. It was also ironic that Seymour Hersh, a journalist, had been given access to alleged highly classified data that, over the previous thirteen years of his incarceration, even Pollard's attorneys—including Ted Olson, President Reagan's personal lawyer—had not been allowed to see. Why were the doors that had been closed on a Washington insider and presidential confidant like Ted Olson suddenly be opened to a reporter?

Hersh once again brought "into the open" the old (but unproven) allegations of cocaine use by Pollard (cocaine addiction, after all, can offer a reason for a spy "doing it for the money"), the main source of which was none other than "journalist" Kurt Lohbeck, who was interviewed by Hersh. Had Pollard's case gone to trial, one of the government's major witnesses against Pollard "would have been Lohbeck, who had a checkered past," Hersh wrote. "Lohbeck acknowledged that he was prepared to testify, if necessary, about his involvement in Pollard's unsuccessful efforts in 1985 to broker arms sales for the rebels in the Afghan war."

As detailed earlier in this book, though, Pollard insisted that the government would never have wanted his connection to Lohbeck revealed in a courtroom since, according to Pollard, Lohbeck was being "run" directly out of the National Security Council by then National Security Advisor Robert McFarlane—the same Robert McFarlane who, some sources allege, was the so-called "Mr. X" in the Pollard affair.

As the tangled web in the Pollard case kept spinning, and as the events around America's most controversial spy kept swirling, his friends, as well as his enemies, could only wonder whether Jonathan Jay Pollard, this person who so many admired and so many others feared, would ever be set free. Would he finally, at long last, be allowed to "come home"?

GENIE
IN THE
BOTTLE

O n December 21, 1998, three days after the United States stopped bombarding Iraq with Cruise missiles as part of Operation Desert Fox, and two days after President Bill Clinton was impeached by the U.S. House of Representatives, numerous stories had appeared in the media honoring the memories of those killed, exactly ten years earlier, during the terrorist bombing of Pan Am Flight 103.

What few knew, however, was that the case of Jonathan Pollard, who remained in prison despite renewed efforts by the Israeli government to secure his freedom, may have been inextricably linked to the tragedy that occurred over Lockerbie, Scotland, a decade before. It was Jonathan Pollard who first exposed Dr. Ihsan Barbouti. And Barbouti, the Iraqi-born engineer who designed a biological and chemical weapons plant for Libyan strongman Muammar el-Qaddafi—and was apparently allowed by his friends in the United States to construct and operate a plant in Boca Raton, Florida, that produced deadly cyanide to be exported to Iraq—was also connected by my intelligence sources to the tragic plane crash in which 270 people died. Was this yet another of the reasons why the CIA was so strongly opposed to Pollard being set free?

After the ill-fated jetliner exploded on December 21, 1988, the result of a terrorist bomb, American and Scottish forensic experts were actually able to trace the clothing which was in the suitcase containing the bomb to a clothing shop in the resort town of Selima, Malta: a clothing shop that was located directly across the street from the Malta offices of Ishan Barbouti International (IBI). Although two Libyan intelligence officers were indicted in the Pan Am 103 bombing, Dr. Ishan Barbouti—who was apparently being protected by U.S. authorities—was never arrested.

It's hardly a surprise that the work of Barbouti was first disclosed to Israeli intelligence by Jonathan Pollard, specifically when Pollard turned over a classified study to Israel that included, as an attachment, a contract between Barbouti's company, IBI, and Jurgen Hippennstiel-Imhausen of the German company Imhausen Chemie. The contract, dated October 1, 1984, called for the design and construction of a "multipurpose chemical plant" at Rabta, Libya.

The Rabta plant became the focus of international attention on January 4, 1989—five years after Pollard first uncovered its existence—when portions of the same document Pollard handed over to Israel were leaked by U.S. intelligence to the media.

In May of 1989, Hippennstiel-Imhausen was finally arrested by the German authorities after intense pressure was exerted by the United States. Barbouti "disappeared" from West Germany, however, and resurfaced in England. After German authorities searched IBI's offices in Frankfurt, Barbouti—facing extradition from England to West Germany—moved to the United States where he lived as a free man until his death in July of 1990.

Nevertheless, both Imhausen-Chemie and IBI had been named as the prime contractors for the Rabta plant which U.S. intelligence sources identified as a production facility for the deadly nerve gases Taubun and Sarin. The ABC *Nightline* segment "Saddam's Chemical Connection" (covered in great detail in chapter 3) also exposed Barbouti's connection to the Boca Raton plant, which began operating in 1988.

The investigation that followed the Pan-Am 103 disaster—that scattered bodies over a forty-four-square-mile area of the Scottish countryside—was aided, meanwhile, by the discovery of a small child's playsuit from the suitcase that contained the explosive device. Investigators traced the playsuit to the manufacturer, Yorkie Clothing. Through a manufacturer's batch number, investigators were further able to trace the playsuit to a little boutique called Mary's House located at 146 Tower Road in the tiny resort village of Sclima, Malta. At Mary's House, the store's owner identified the playsuit as one sold to "an Arab gentleman" on November 23, 1988. On a copy of a contract I've obtained, between Barbouti and Imhausen-Chemie, IBI's Selima, Malta, address is listed as 145 Tower Road.

But the "coincidences" do not end there. On October 27, 1990, almost four months after Barbouti's death and in a time frame during which the United States was bracing for a possible war with Iraq, Mr. Raja Hassan Ali wrote a letter from the Iraqi State Establishment for Textiles to IBI's offices in London. Raja Hassan Ali marked the letter—a copy of which I also received from my intelligence sources—to the attention of Mr. Haidar Barbouti, the late Ishan Barbouti's son, and Mr. Arie David, Haidar Barbouti's Israeli-born attorney.

The letter stated: "We expect the assistance that you promised to the Enterprise for Pesticide Production. Additional supplies of raw materials will insure future funding by the foreign minister. Abdul Senoussi knows our requirements."

According to my intelligence sources, the State Enterprise for Pesticide Production (SEPP) was the vehicle used by the Iraqi government to coordinate the acquisition, development, and production of such pesticides as Taubun and Sarin, in actuality deadly nerve gases which it is believed were used, only a few months later, against American troops stationed in Saudi Arabia during the Gulf War—although the Pentagon has continued to deny this.

Raja Hassan Ali, the author of the letter to Haidar Barbouti, would himself be indicted in Atlanta, Georgia, for his part in the Banca Nazionale Del Lavoro (BNL) affair. BNL was the Italian state-owned bank, with an office in Atlanta, that secretly financed the Iraqi military buildup, using American Department of Agriculture loan guarantees.

Abdul Senoussi, also mentioned in the letter, is Abdullah Senoussi, deputy director of Libyan intelligence, brother-in-law of Col. Muammar-el Qaddafi, and was identified by both American and French authorities as one of the planners of the Pan-Am 103 bombing.

To this day, Haidar Barbouti continues to run his father's various business enterprises. Jonathan Pollard, who first exposed to the Israelis Ishan Barbouti's relationship with Jurgen Hippennstiel-Imhausen of Imhausen Chemie, has already served more years behind bars than anyone in American history who spied for a U.S. ally.

In the great war movie *Patton*, there's a scene in North Africa's Allied headquarters in which Patton (George C. Scott) complains to a British commander that his (Patton's) American troops are being slaughtered on the ground because of a lack of British air cover. "I can assure you that we control the skies," the commander tells him.

Suddenly, there's a German bombing raid and explosions everywhere. When the smoke clears, Patton, knowing he'll now finally get the air cover he needs, brushes himself off, glances at his aide, and tells him, "If I could find those Nazi sons-of-bitches I'd give 'em all a medal."

The enormous publicity generated by Pollard's enemies in the days leading up to President Clinton's decision on Pollard, that at the time had been scheduled for January 11, 1999, is the main reason this book finally got published. Pollard's family and friends are no doubt grateful.

BIBLIOGRAPHY

Bainerman, Joel. *The Crimes of a President: New Revelations on the Conspiracy and Cover-up in the Bush and Reagan Administrations.* New York: S.P.I. Books, 1992.

Blitzer, Wolf. *Territory of Lies: The Rise, Fall, and Betrayal of Jonathan Jay Pollard.* New York: Harper & Row, 1989.

Bodansky, Yossef. *Target America: Terrorism in the U.S. Today.* New York: S.P.I. Books, 1993.

Brewton, Pete. *The Mafia, CIA and George Bush.* New York: S.P.I. Books, 1992.

Chafets, Ze'ev. *Double Vision: How the Press Distorts America's View of the Middle East.* New York: Morrow, 1985.

Dershowitz, Alan M. *Reversal of Fortune: Inside the von Bulow Case.* New York: Random House, 1986.

———. *Chutzpah.* Boston: Little, Brown, 1991.

Earley, Pete. *Family of Spies: Inside the John Walker Spy Ring.* New York: Bantam Books, 1988.

Friedman, Alan. *Spider's Web: The Secret History of How the White House Illegally Armed Iraq.* New York: Bantam Books, 1993.

Goldenberg, Elliot. *The Spy Who Knew Too Much: The Government Plot to Silence Jonathan Pollard.* New York: S.P.I. Books, 1993.

Haig, Alexander M., Jr., with Charles McCarry. *Inner Circle: How America Changed the World: A Memoir.* New York: Warner Books, 1992.

Hersh, Seymour M. *The Price of Power: Kissinger in the Nixon White House.* New York: Summit Books, 1983.

———. *"The Target Is Destroyed": What Really Happened to Flight 007 and What America Knew About It.* New York: Random House, 1986.

———. *The Samson Option: Israel's Nuclear Arsenal and American Foreign Policy.* New York: Random House, 1991.

———. *The Dark Side of Camelot.* Boston: Little, Brown, 1997.

Loftus, John, and Mark Aarons. *Secret War Against the Jews: How Western Espionage Betrayed the Jewish People.* New York: St. Martin's, 1994.

Lohbeck, Kurt. *Holy War, Unholy Victory: Eyewitness to the CIA's Secret War in Afghanistan.* Washington, D.C.: Regnery Gateway, 1993.

Meir, Golda. *My Life.* New York: Putnam, 1975.

North, Oliver, with William Novak. *Under Fire: An American Story.* New York: HarperCollins, 1991.

Ostrovsky, Victor, and Claire Hoy. *By Way of Deception: The Making and Unmaking of a Mossad Officer.* New York: St. Martin's, 1990.

Raviv, Daniel. *Every Spy a Prince: The Complete History of Israel's Intelligence Community.* Boston: Houghton Mifflin, 1990.

Raviv, Dan, and Yossi Melman. *Friends in Deed: Inside the U.S.-Israel Alliance.* New York: Hyperion, 1994.

Redfield, James. *The Celestine Prophecy: An Adventure.* New York: Warner Books, 1993.

Rushdie, Salman. *The Satanic Verses.* New York: Viking, 1988.

Sick, Gary. *October Surprise: America's Hostages in Iran and the Election of Ronald Reagan.* New York: Random House, Times Books, 1991.

Taheri, Amir. *Holy Terror: Inside the World of Islamic Terror.* Bethesda, Md.: Adler & Adler, 1987.

Teicher, Howard. *Twin Pillars to Desert Storm: America's Flawed Vision in the Middle East from Nixon to Bush.* New York: William Morrow, 1993.

Weinberger, Caspar W. *Fighting for Peace: Seven Critical Years in the Pentagon.* New York: Warner Books, 1990.

Woodward, Bob. *Veil: The Secret Wars of the CIA, 1981–1987.* New York: Simon and Schuster, 1987.

Woodward, Bob, and Scott Armstrong. *The Brethren: Inside the Supreme Court.* New York: Simon and Schuster, 1979.

INDEX